PRAISE FOR *PEOPLE ANALYTICS: USING DATA-DRIVEN HR AND GEN AI AS A BUSINESS ASSET*

'In this book Cole Napper offers a provocative and practical roadmap for the future of work and workforce decision-making. He challenges conventional people analytics to move beyond dashboards and data plumbing, to position people analytics as a strategic enabler of business value. This book will inspire leaders to reimagine HR from a cost center to a competitive asset, driven by evidence, experimentation and emerging technologies.'
John W. Boudreau, Professor Emeritus and Senior Research Scientist, Marshall School of Business, University of Southern California, Author of *Work Without Jobs* and *Beyond HR*

'This book is fabulously insightful and practical and will push the field of people analytics to new levels. With his years of experience in the field, Cole Napper has written a book that is easy to read and full of practical takeaways. By dedicating sections to business value and GenAI, then dovetailing those together with real world examples, Cole makes this book important for all leaders who want to use analytics to grow their business.'
Jonathan Ferrar, CEO of Insight222; Author of *Excellence in People Analytics* and *The Value of People Analytics*

'This book is a provocation. Cole Napper doesn't just want people analytics to feel smarter, he wants it to matter more. He challenges people analytics teams to move beyond interesting work and become existential to the business. He calls on the field to stop optimizing around the edges and start tackling bigger questions about how work shapes identity, growth and value. He argues that none of this happens without courage. The courage to take risks. The courage to lead transformation before you're invited. Because if people analytics doesn't define its value, someone else will decide it's not worth keeping. Cole is also one of the field's great community builders, always shining a light on the people behind the practice. If you care about bringing data, science and technology into the heart of the people function—and using them to reimagine what work can become—this is a guide worth reading.'
Prasad Setty, Former VP, Google, Founding Leader of Google People Analytics

'Cole Napper paints a compelling picture of how the next generation of CHROs will emerge from the ranks of people analytics leaders, who inform strategy, improve decisions, and optimize processes with data, and champion employee voice, employee experience and the ethical use of AI.'
Dr. Amit Mohindra, Founder and CEO of People Analytics Success, People Analytics Instructor at Stanford School of Continuing Studies, and Former People Analytics Leader at Apple, Wayfair, McKesson and Goldman Sachs

'Cole Napper has written the definitive guide for people analytics professionals ready to embrace the AI revolution. This book doesn't just describe the future—it provides the roadmap to get there.

Cole masterfully demonstrates how AI can transform people analytics from a cost center into a profit-driving powerhouse. His integration of talent intelligence principles with cutting-edge AI applications shows exactly how external labor market data combined with internal analytics can create unprecedented competitive advantage. This isn't theoretical—it's practical, actionable strategy that every HR leader needs to implement today.

The future of work is analytical, and this book ensures you'll be leading the charge rather than left behind.'
Toby Culshaw, Vice President Strategy - Talent Intelligence at Lightcast, Author of *Talent Intelligence*, Founder of the Talent Intelligence Collective, and former Global Head of Talent Pipeline Strategy and Intelligence Worldwide Amazon Stores

'Cole Napper has rapidly established himself as a pre-eminent voice in people analytics. Cole rightly asserts that people analytics stands at a crucial crossroads, urging a focus on delivering tangible business value. For any chief people officer seeking to build a truly impactful, future-fit people analytics function in the age of AI, this book offers invaluable guidance.'
David Green, Managing Partner at Insight222, co-author of *Excellence in People Analytics*, host of the Digital HR Leaders podcast

'This is the book the field has been waiting for. Cole Napper brings sharp clarity, urgency and vision to the future of the function—backed by years of frontline experience leading people analytics teams inside global companies,

startups and vendor organizations. His unfiltered take challenges practition-ers and HR leaders alike to rethink their purpose and step fully into a value-driving, AI-native future. If you're in or around the people analytics space, this isn't just a read—it's a wake-up call.'
Ross Sparkman, previous Head of Strategic Workforce Planning at Meta, Nike and LinkedIn, and author of *Strategic Workforce Planning*

'Cole Napper has translated his broad and deep expertise in People Analytics into the definitive book on the subject, with content and ideas that will elevate your practice whether you are a business leader, a newcomer to People Analytics or an experienced professional in the field. Written in an approachable style, this book will accelerate your journey into delivering undeniable value for your organizations. You'll come away inspired and equipped to build the future!'
Alexis Fink PhD., world-renowned people analytics leader, formerly of Meta, Intel and Microsoft, co-author of *Investing in People*

'Cole Napper has written the book that every people analytics professional needs right now—and frankly, should have read yesterday. *People Analytics* is a survival manual for a field standing at the edge of transformation. This book arrives at exactly the right moment. People analytics teams everywhere are grappling with how to prove their value while AI transforms their toolkit. Napper provides both the wake-up call and the roadmap we need to not just survive, but thrive in this new landscape. If you work in people analytics, organizational psychology, or HR strategy, this book isn't optional reading—it's essential preparation for the future that's already here.'
Shonna Waters, PhD, CEO and Co-founder, Fractional Insights, author of *The Practical Guide to HR Analytics*

'In an era where workforce intelligence defines competitive advantage, *People Analytics* by Cole Napper provides a timely, practical, and actionable guide for transforming how organizations understand and manage their talent. This essential book presents a clear roadmap for integrating people analytics, predictive modelling, and generative AI into core HR practices—not as future aspirations, but as tools for immediate, measurable business impact.'
Mark Huselid, PhD, Distinguished Professor of Workforce Analytics and Director, Center for Workforce Analytics, D'Amore-McKim School of Business, Northeastern University

'The book is a timely challenge and exploration of the ways people analytics can improve decision making; and a roadmap for navigating the turbulent seas of AI integration with the work of HR.'
Dr. Alec Levenson, Director at the Center for Effective Organizations, and author of *Strategic Analytics* and *Workforce Analytics: A Global Perspective*

People Analytics

*Using Data-driven HR
and Gen AI as a Business Asset*

Cole Napper

KoganPage

First published in Great Britain and the United States in 2025 by Kogan Page Limited

Kogan Page
Kogan Page Ltd, 2nd Floor, 45 Gee Street, London EC1V 3RS, United Kingdom
Kogan Page Inc, 8 W 38th Street, Suite 90, New York, NY 10018, USA
www.koganpage.com

EU Representative (GPSR)
Authorised Rep Compliance Ltd, Ground Floor, 71 Baggot Street Lower, Dublin D02 P593, Ireland
www.arccompliance.com

Kogan Page books are printed on paper from sustainable forests.

© Cole Napper 2025

ISBNs
Hardback   978 1 3986 2218 0
Paperback   978 1 3986 2216 6
Ebook   978 1 3986 2217 3

British Library Cataloguing-in-Publication Data
A CIP record for this book is available from the British Library.

Library of Congress Control Number
2025940724

Typeset by Integra Software Services, Pondicherry
Print production managed by Jellyfish
Printed and bound by CPI Group (UK) Ltd, Croydon CR0 4YY

CONTENTS

PART TWO
Gen AI

4 Introduction to People Analytics and Generative AI Use Cases 95

5 Building a Foundation: Data Infrastructure for AI 126

6 Leveraging AI for Taking Predictive Action 153

PREFACE

We are at a crossroads in the field of people analytics. For years, we have grappled with our identity—are we a strategic function driving business outcomes, or are we merely a data and reporting team, responding to requests and providing insights that often go unused? This question has lingered, but it can no longer remain unanswered. The rise of generative AI has accelerated the urgency of this decision. Much of what we have traditionally called "people analytics" is rapidly becoming automated. The transactional, repeatable tasks that once defined our work—data cleaning, report generation, simple insights—are being taken over by algorithms. Vendors are racing to automate these functions, and many already have. This leaves us with an existential choice: Retreat into irrelevance as a reporting function or embrace a new identity as a value-driving force in the business.

The motivation behind this book is to address this inflection point head-on. I want to issue a call to action. If we want to exist five or ten years from now in a meaningful way, we must make a fundamental shift. We must quantify the value of everything we do. This is no longer optional—it is the key to our survival. The businesses we serve are becoming more data-driven, more automated, and more focused on efficiency. If people analytics fails to align with this shift, if we cannot prove our worth in terms that business leaders understand, we will become obsolete. The work we do must directly contribute to business value, and we must be able to articulate that contribution in a way that is undeniable.

But here's the paradox: If we embrace this transformation, if we step fully into our potential, something incredible will happen. We will not only continue to exist, but we will ascend to a new level of influence. We will become the strategic leaders of the HR function of the future. For years, HR Business Partners (HRBPs) have been at the forefront of driving HR strategy, often relying on intuition, relationships, and experience. But in a world where data is king, where organizations demand measurable impact, the role of people analytics is poised to become the centerpiece of HR decision-making. This is our time. This is our opportunity. And it cannot be squandered.

I have spent my career immersed in this field. I have worked in large, multinational corporations with established people analytics functions, where scale and complexity are constant challenges. I have experienced the urgency and innovation of hyper-growth startups, where agility and rapid experimentation define success, and been part of a small, venture capital (VC)-backed people analytics and employee listening vendor, where we pushed the boundaries of what technology could do for organizations. And now I work at the leading people analytics, workforce planning, and talent intelligence platform, Lightcast, seeing firsthand how the future of this field is being shaped. I have had the privilege of viewing people analytics from every angle—practitioner, vendor, strategist, innovator.

Beyond my own work experiences, I have engaged deeply with this community. I have spoken to thousands of professionals in our field, sharing ideas, debating strategies, and exploring the future together, and hosted over a hundred episodes of a podcast dedicated to people analytics, bringing together thought leaders, pioneers, and practitioners to discuss where we are and where we need to go. I have spent countless hours learning, refining my own thinking, and educating myself on what makes this field successful. Through it all, one thing has remained constant: My love for this work and my belief in its potential.

People analytics is not just about numbers. It is about people. It is about business impact. It is about driving organizations forward with intelligence, insight, and strategic clarity. But we are at a moment of truth. If we do not evolve, we risk fading into the background, our voices drowned out by automation and competing priorities. If we do evolve—if we take ownership of our value, if we assert our role as the stewards of data-driven decision-making in HR—we will not only remain relevant; we will thrive.

The Next 10 Years

If you ask anyone reasonable to look ten years into the future, they will tell you that the entire model of HR will be unrecognizable. The shifts brought about by generative AI will not be incremental; they will be transformative. The Ulrich model of HR—centers of excellence, shared services, and strategic HR business partners—will not survive. Change will not happen in a linear fashion, with one-tenth of the transformation occurring each year.

Instead, it will be cumulative and exponential. The moment one fundamental shift becomes possible, others will cascade in rapid succession.

For years, HR business partners have been in the driver's seat of the function, ever since HR secured its seat at the metaphorical strategic "table." But I have long argued that the biggest roadblock to the widespread adoption of people analytics—and the broader development of analytical and numerical capability within HR—was generational. The leaders who took over HR before the analytics revolution were never going to be the ones to drive that revolution forward. Instead, progress would come when a new generation of HR leaders, those who had come of age during the rise of people analytics, took their place at the helm. That shift is now inevitable. In the next decade, there will be no HR leaders left whose formative years predate the emergence of people analytics.

Yet, analytics is not the only force rewriting the function. Generative AI is poised to automate vast portions of HR. Anything that is repeatable will be eliminated. Shared services will be fully automated, much of HR technology will be redundant, and centers of excellence—especially in learning and development and talent acquisition—will be transformed beyond recognition due to advancements in technology. Even the HR business partners will not be spared. Already, we are witnessing the rise of AI-driven chat interfaces capable of coaching, providing strategic input, and playing the "organizational therapist" role that HRBPs have traditionally occupied.

So what remains? True business-led decision-making. True strategic management and deployment of talent resources. True data-driven insights built on analytics capabilities at a scale that HR has never before possessed. And who will be positioned to lead this transformation? AI-native HR professionals.

For years, we have discussed the need for HR to become more digitally literate, to embrace the digital transformation. But in reality it was the same legacy HR leaders—those who came of age before analytics and were passively or sometimes actively resistant—who slowed that shift. People analytics, however, has always been a digitally native function. That is why it stands alone in its ability to transition into the AI-native era. It will no longer be enough for HR leaders to understand technology or data; they will need to be fully AI-native, integrating AI capabilities into every aspect of strategic decision-making. People analytics is positioned to be the only AI-native HR profession.

HR technology could join us as being AI-native, and while critical, has shown little interest in leading the HR function forward. It remains focused on infrastructure rather than shaping talent strategy. That leaves people analytics as the only discipline within HR capable of taking the reins. The opportunity is clear: If we push our leadership forward, if we make the case for being AI-driven, analytically powered HR to our core, if we embrace our role as early adopters, we will shape the conversations of the future. And as our influence compounds, we may look back ten years from now to see that the only part of the "old" HR that remains is the legacy of people analytics—the function that led HR into the promised land. That is an exciting future.

This book is my contribution to that future. It is a roadmap for making this shift, for stepping into the role that people analytics must play in the years ahead. It is my way of saying: We can do this. We can build something extraordinary. But we must act now.

I want nothing more than for readers to come back in the 2030s and say that this book was the catalyst and the roadmap for showing the people analytics, workforce planning, and talent intelligence fields how to build a thriving future. I love this field. I believe in its potential. And I want, more than anything, for us to be successful beyond our wildest dreams. Let's make it happen—together.

BIOGRAPHY

Cole Napper is the Vice President of Research, Innovation, and Talent Insights at Lightcast, a leading labor market intelligence and insights firm. In this role, he leads the publication of major research and thought leadership pieces that have been cited by The Wall Street Journal, Forbes, Fortune, Morning Brew, and other influential outlets. His work at Lightcast focuses on bridging the power of labor market data with people analytics, talent intelligence, and workforce planning, helping organizations navigate the evolving world of work. He extends these insights to C-suite leadership, policymakers at all levels of government, and higher education institutions, ensuring that workforce strategies align with broader economic and business trends.

With a career spanning both Fortune 500 enterprises and high-growth startups, Cole has led large-scale people analytics, workforce planning, and talent intelligence functions. He most recently led a 50-person people analytics team at FedEx dedicated to these areas and has led similar functions at Texas Instruments, Grainger, and Toyota North America. Additionally, he has held multi-functional HR leadership roles at venture-backed, hypergrowth companies such as Motive and Booster Fuels. As a trailblazer in the HR tech space, he played a key role in the development and exit of Orgnostic, a cutting-edge people analytics startup later acquired by CultureAmp, who was first to market with a generative AI application in people analytics. Throughout his career, he has continuously pushed the boundaries of behavioral science, people analytics strategy, and generative AI applications in HR.

Beyond his corporate roles, Cole is deeply committed to advancing the people analytics profession. As the founder and owner of Directionally Correct LLC, he hosts Directionally Correct the #1 global people analytics podcast and Substack newsletter, providing industry insights to a broad audience of HR and business leaders. He serves on the Leadership Council of the Society of People Analytics (SPA) and is a leader in the Society for Industrial-Organizational Psychologists (SIOP). In 2018, he launched the Dallas-Fort Worth People Analytics Meetup, and has since helped inspire the creation of similar communities in Houston, Chicago, Atlanta, and

Denver. Passionate about education, he has taught people analytics courses at SMU, TCU, and Louisiana Tech and has been a guest lecturer at over 20 universities. He is also an HR tech advisor, partnering with multiple startups to drive innovation in people analytics and workforce solutions.

Cole holds a PhD. in Industrial-Organizational Psychology from Louisiana Tech University. Originally from Monroe, Louisiana, he now resides in the Dallas, Texas area with his wife and two children. Outside of work, he enjoys golf, reading, family time, and exploring new podcasts and streaming content.

PART ONE

Business Value

1

The Resurgence of People Analytics for Business Dominance

Through the introduction of the foundational concept of using people analytics as a powerful tool for business domination, this chapter explores the strategic significance of analytics in achieving superior performance, innovation and competitive advantage across industries.

"If you always do what you've always done, you'll always get what you've always got"—Henry Ford

What if the future was not predetermined? What if you had the ability to influence the outcome? What if you knew that the choices you made today would have a lasting impact on the real world? You would act differently, right? You would make better, more informed decisions. As Henry Ford once said, *"If you always do what you've always done, you'll always get what you've always got."* This sentiment applies perfectly to the field of people analytics. For too long, people analytics has been content with "cool" research projects, workplace pop-psychology, and a sense of prestige from being one of the "hot new fields" of HR (Napper, 2023). While these efforts have built credibility and curiosity, they have not consistently translated into business impact.

The future of people analytics is not guaranteed to be bright. It is incumbent upon us to change our trajectory. What is the one thing we have rarely done as a field? Generate tangible business value in financial terms—whether that be in dollars, quid, yen, pesos, euros, dinars, or yuan. That is the purpose of this book: To transform people analytics from a cost center into a profit center. This transformation will not come at the expense of employees, but rather because of employee well-being. Helping the business thrive and supporting employees are not competing priorities; they are interdependent.

We are in a time of disruptive change. The rise of generative AI (Gen AI) is reshaping every discipline—including people analytics. The way we collect, analyze, and act on workforce data is evolving at an unprecedented pace. This book will provide the insights needed to navigate the transformation Gen AI is bringing to our field, and more importantly, to leverage it to elevate people analytics into a function that drives real business value. There is no time like the present to make the right investments and embrace the creative destruction necessary for people analytics to emerge as the true strategic leader of HR. The future is here. Let's build it together.

Why Now?

If you have followed the evolution of people analytics, you will recognize a pattern that mirrors the Gartner Hype Cycle (Hanna and Wigmore, 2023). Our field has already climbed the **Peak of Inflated Expectations**, where thought leadership, promising case studies, and enthusiastic HR conferences made it seem as if people analytics was poised to revolutionize business overnight. Then came the **Trough of Disillusionment**. Organizations that had invested in people analytics soon realized that extracting business value was harder than expected. Many teams spent years producing insightful reports and dashboards that executives appreciated in theory—but which failed to drive meaningful change. Enthusiasm waned. Funding was cut. Some early adopters questioned whether people analytics had overpromised and underdelivered.

But just as we were beginning to emerge onto the **Slope of Enlightenment**—where true impact and repeatable value propositions were taking shape—Gen AI arrived.

Disruption or Acceleration?

Now, people analytics faces an existential question: Will Gen AI replace what we do, or will it augment and improve our function? The answer is not predetermined. Gen AI is not merely another tool—it is a fundamental shift in how we work. It is capable of automating insights, synthesizing vast amounts of data, and generating real-time recommendations at a scale we have never seen before. This could either render traditional people analytics teams obsolete—or empower them to operate at a level of strategic impact previously unimaginable.

This book is written to answer that question. Before we explore how Gen AI will transform people analytics, we must first diagnose the ills of our current state. Have we lost our way? People analytics was meant to be a game-changer for HR, yet it has struggled to prove its business impact. Why?

1 **Misaligned priorities**—Too much focus on engagement surveys, headcount dashboards, and "interesting" insights, rather than solving actual business problems.

2 **Failure to speak the language of business**—Many HR analytics teams produce compelling workforce reports but fail to tie them directly to revenue, cost savings, or profitability.

3 **Data without action**—Analytics that do not lead to clear, measurable action are just academic exercises.

4 **Lack of integration with business strategy**—People analytics must be embedded into decision-making processes, not operating in a silo.

How We Return to the Path of Value Creation

To regain momentum, people analytics must undergo a paradigm shift. We must recenter ourselves around what matters most. The way forward lies in:

- **Focusing on business impact.** Every analytics initiative should answer the question: *How does this drive financial value?*

- **Harnessing Gen AI as an accelerator, not a replacement.** AI will not eliminate people analytics—it will remove the inefficiencies that have held it back.

- **Making people analytics the decision-making engine for HR.** Data should no longer be an afterthought; it should drive strategy in real time.

- **Solving problems that matter.** Instead of creating more reports, we should be answering critical business questions.

We are at a turning point. People analytics has the opportunity to become the most valuable function within HR. It will no longer be enough to simply analyze employee trends—the field must evolve to drive business decisions with the precision and urgency of a CFO managing financial data. This book is a roadmap for making that transformation. In the chapters ahead, we will explore:

- How to use Gen AI as a force multiplier rather than a disruptor.

- The new skill sets people analytics leaders need to thrive in an AI-powered world.
- How to build a people analytics function that directly drives business profitability.

This is not about keeping up with trends. This is about ensuring that people analytics is the most valuable investment a company can make, and that it adds business value. Now is the time. Let's rebuild people analytics the right way.

Business Value

So, what is business value? **Business value** is the overall worth a company creates, including financial gains (like profits and growth) and non-financial factors such as customer satisfaction, operational efficiency, employee engagement, innovation, and brand strength. It represents both immediate and long-term benefits to the business (Indeed, 2025).

In Ferrar and Green's (2021) book *Excellence in People Analytics* they advocate that we are moving into the "Age of Value" for people analytics functions. In many People Analytics practitioners' minds, "value" equates to "important work" or "the business found it valuable/helpful." That is not what this book's definition of "business value" means. When this book refers to "business value" we are talking about money and/or ROI. That's it. Are you producing dollars for the business? If the answer is yes, you are producing "value." Value is not a synonym for important. There is confusion about what constitutes value in people analytics because of what I term the "Four Phases of Impact."

Four Phases of Impact

What are the four phases of impact? They are:

1 Interesting
2 Helpful
3 Needed
4 Existential

FIGURE 1.1 Four Phases of Impact

Interesting	Helpful	Needed	Existential
"That's so interesting!"	"This is helpful, thank you!"	"I needed this yesterday."	"I can't do this without your data."

Phase 1: Interesting—The Illusion of Impact

As Levenson, Stevenson, and Fink (2021) and other leaders in the field have pointed out, people analytics and Org Development are two sides to the same coin, and therefore doing "*interesting*" work is the enemy of impact. The scenario typically unfolds like this:

A people analytics team presents their findings to a key stakeholder, who responds enthusiastically: "*Wow, this is really great work. Super interesting!*"

While the work is appreciated, it does not drive any meaningful action. If it doesn't inform a decision or influence behavior, then it lacks ROI. In the eyes of business leaders focused on measurable value, "interesting" is a polite way of saying *this was a nice-to-have, but ultimately unnecessary.*

Phase 2: Helpful—The Potential for Influence

At times, "helpful" and "interesting" overlap. The distinction is that *helpful* insights have the potential to influence decision-making. In an ideal scenario, the response might be:

"*Wow, this is really interesting and helpful. Now that I see this data, I realize where I've been making mistakes and can correct them. Thank you!*"

However, *helpful* insights don't always drive value. Just like "interesting," "helpful" can sometimes be a diplomatic way of acknowledging the work without committing to action. The real test of impact is whether behavior changes as a result.

Phase 3: Needed—Moving Toward Business Integration

The *needed* phase is a step up. It typically occurs when stakeholders actively *pull* insights from the people analytics team, rather than having those insights *pushed* to them. The conversation sounds like this:

"*Thanks for getting me the analysis I asked for. We've really been needing this data—we were flying blind on this topic.*"

While this is a significant improvement, there's still no guarantee of action. The stakeholder acknowledges the data is necessary but hasn't explicitly stated that it will drive a decision. The work is valued, but it has not yet become indispensable.

Phase 4: Existential—The Ultimate Goal

The term *existential* may seem dramatic, but this is where people analytics shifts from a cost center to a profit center. In this phase of impact, stakeholders *cannot operate* without the insights provided. The ideal, yet often unexpected, response sounds like this:

> *"I really wish you had gotten this analysis to me sooner. I've been waiting over a week to make this decision, and I couldn't move forward without this data. Next time, I need it faster."*

At first glance, this might seem like a complaint. But in reality, it's a sign of success—the work is so critical that delays cause real business friction. This is where people analytics becomes a *business necessity* rather than an optional resource.

Why This Progression Matters

People analytics, as a function, often struggles with *accountability*. Many teams seek safe, low-risk projects where there's little upside but also little downside. Producing "interesting" work fits this mold—stakeholders praise the effort, but there's no pressure to ensure that insights drive action. However, true business impact requires embracing accountability. That means:

- Delivering insights that directly inform decision-making
- Accepting that not all findings will be well-received
- Moving at the speed of the business, or risk being left behind
- Competing with other functions to remain relevant
- Taking risks, even if it means being proven wrong

Leaning into accountability may feel uncomfortable, but it's the path to making people analytics indispensable. The more existential our insights become, the more we cement our role as a profit-driving function—one that business leaders cannot afford to ignore.

REAL-WORLD EXAMPLE

"How Do We Produce Value in the Future with People Analytics?" with Prasad Setty, former leader of People Analytics at Google

(Paraphrased for length from Ep. 102 of "Directionally Correct, A People Analytics Podcast")

Reimagining People Analytics for the Next Decade

Dr. Prasad Setty, the former leader and creator of People Analytics at Google, emphasizes the transformative potential of generative AI and long-term, high-impact research in shaping the future of work. He challenges organizations to move beyond incremental improvements and instead focus on tackling big-picture, systemic questions about work, identity, and value creation.

Generative AI: The Game-Changer in Work

Setty predicts that generative AI will dramatically reshape how work is done and how organizations create value. With compute capacity and algorithmic power projected to grow exponentially over the next decade, new opportunities will emerge to leverage AI agents and tools. This evolution calls for a reassessment of how we define work, engage with it, and measure its outcomes.

Exploring Work Identity and Longitudinal Impact

Dr. Setty highlights the importance of understanding how societal shifts in work will impact individuals' identities and career satisfaction. He draws attention to a Google initiative called gDNA, inspired by the Framingham Heart Study, which followed Googlers over their lifetimes to examine the relationship between work and life satisfaction.

This type of longitudinal research offers opportunities to:

1 Track Career Progression: Follow entry-level employees throughout their careers to identify factors contributing to executive-level success.

2 Combat Survivorship Bias: Study entire populations to understand career trajectories, not just the experiences of those who succeed.

3 Define High Potential: Investigate what truly accelerates career growth and organizational impact.

The Call to Swing for the Fences

Prasad critiques the current state of people analytics for failing to take on ambitious, high-stakes challenges. He argues that many organizations focus on short-term, incremental improvements that limit the potential impact of people analytics. Instead, he calls for bold, strategic investments in solving foundational problems that have broad implications for both organizations and society.

Key Takeaways for the Future of People Analytics

1   Leverage generative AI: Organizations must explore how emerging technologies can transform work processes and redefine value creation.

2   Invest in Longitudinal Studies: Research that follows individuals over time can provide deep insights into life and career fulfillment, offering actionable intelligence for organizations.

3   Address Systemic Questions: Move beyond operational metrics to tackle questions about the future of work, identity, and career progression.

4   Take Big Risks for Big Impact: People analytics teams should aim to solve transformative problems, rather than settling for incremental gains.

5   Balance Short-Term and Long-Term Goals: While addressing immediate organizational needs, leaders must also focus on initiatives that will shape the future of work.

The Role of Vision in People Analytics

Setty's insights challenge organizations to think expansively about the role of people analytics. By embracing generative AI and committing to ambitious, long-term research, companies can redefine how work is understood and create lasting value. This visionary approach positions people analytics as a critical driver of organizational and societal progress.

The Evolution of People Analytics Over the Last 15 Years

To understand the challenges facing people analytics today, it's crucial to examine its trajectory over the past 15 years. The field has experienced significant growth, but recent trends indicate that its future is at a crossroads. The momentum that fueled people analytics' rise is now facing headwinds, raising fundamental questions about our long-term viability and strategic value.

The research shown in this section paints a two-part story: A period of substantial expansion spanning 13 years, followed by a more recent phase of decline and plateauing. Understanding this shift is essential to grasp why making an impact is now more critical than ever—and why an aversion to accountability could threaten the future of the discipline.

Trends in People Analytics Employment Over the Last 15 Years

The rapid expansion of people analytics over the last 15 years led many to assume that employment in the field would continue growing at an accelerated pace; perhaps forever. However, before this research there was little concrete data on exactly how many professionals practiced people analytics, partly due to the ongoing debate over its definition. Despite this ambiguity, a clear trend emerged: Since 2022, people analytics headcount began to decline, primarily due to layoffs, then plateaued leading into early 2025.

Using Lightcast's data, Figure 1.2 represents the count of people analytics-related job profiles in the U.S. based on the presence of the skill "People Analytics" within the "Human Resources" branch of Lightcast's open skills taxonomy, which is considered the industry standard for job and skills classification. Figure 1.2 presents one key data point:

- The total line represents the total count of positions that include people analytics responsibilities, either in title, skill, or description.

Between 2009 and 2022, the number of professionals practicing people analytics in the U.S. nearly quadrupled, growing from approximately 7,500 to a peak of 24,000. The highest annual growth rate occurred in 2012, with a year-over-year increase exceeding 20 percent. However, this trend reversed in 2022, and the number of people analytics practitioners has since declined by nearly 2,000, bringing the total down to around 22,000 in early 2025.

One striking discovery is that a significant number of people analytics responsibilities exist within traditional HR roles rather than in dedicated people analytics positions. Figure 1.3 highlights that HR specialists—such as HR tech analysts, Total Rewards leaders, and People and Culture leaders—often have people analytics as a secondary function within their broader HR responsibilities.

The Role of HR in People Analytics

One of the most unexpected findings is the extent to which traditional HR professionals and centers of excellence (COE) talent are responsible for people analytics work—despite not holding dedicated people analytics roles. The highest concentration of these responsibilities outside of specialized roles falls on some other COEs including total rewards and culture but also including HR Business Partners as well, reinforcing the idea that people analytics is not just a niche discipline confined to large corporations with dedicated analytics teams. Instead, it has become a widely distributed function across companies of various sizes and industries.

FIGURE 1.2

People analytics positions have been decreasing recently

Number of people analytics positions in the U.S.

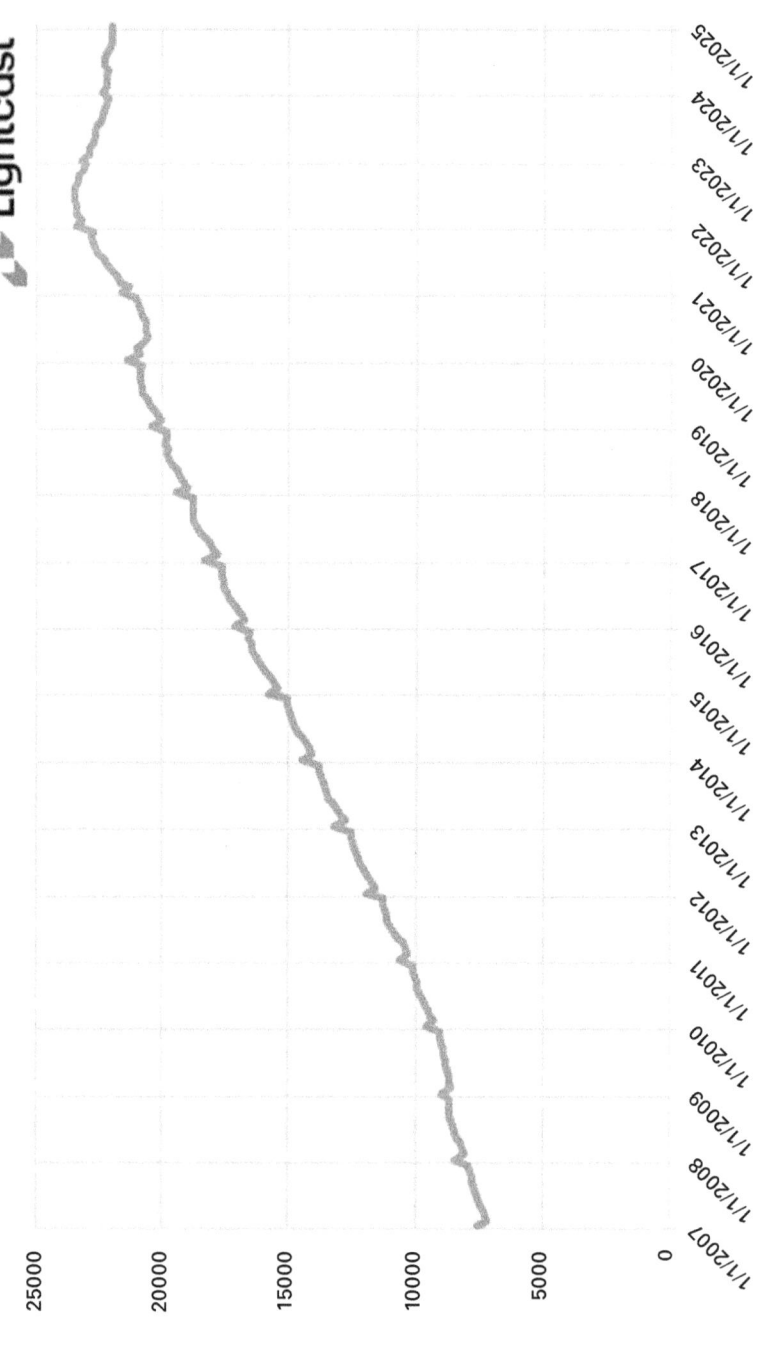

FIGURE 1.3

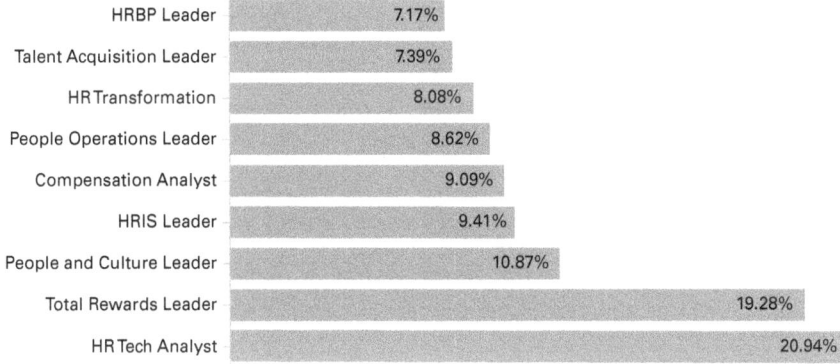

Many HR specialists also support people analytics in their job functions

Top roles among people analytics adjacent positions (share of positions that mention people analytics keywords in the description only)

Role	Percentage
HRBP Leader	7.17%
Talent Acquisition Leader	7.39%
HR Transformation	8.08%
People Operations Leader	8.62%
Compensation Analyst	9.09%
HRIS Leader	9.41%
People and Culture Leader	10.87%
Total Rewards Leader	19.28%
HR Tech Analyst	20.94%

Lightcast

SOURCE Lightcast

According to this research, only about 50 percent of professionals performing people analytics work hold roles dedicated exclusively to the field. The other half are embedded within HR functions, balancing analytics alongside other responsibilities. This challenges the conventional wisdom that people analytics is a specialized, standalone function—it appears to be far more integrated into broader HR roles than previously assumed.

The Decline of People Analytics: Where Are Practitioners Going?

Perhaps the most concerning trend is the exit of over 2,000 people analytics professionals from the field in just the past 2–3 years. Although people analytics job growth stalled in late 2022, the decline appears to have stabilized more recently. The question remains: Where are these professionals going?

This research shows that the majority of those leaving people analytics are not returning to the field. Instead, they are transitioning into regular HR roles, such as HR generalist, HR associates, or HR consultants.

Using Lightcast's profile data, Figure 1.4 tracks the career transitions of people analytics professionals who have exited their roles. The data shows that:

- 82 percent of individuals leaving people analytics move into broader HR roles.

FIGURE 1.4

People analytics practitioners are transitioning into other roles
Share of external outflows of people analytics practitioners since 2021

SOURCE Lightcast

- The most common new positions are HR Generalists and HR Associates (see Figure 1.5).

This shift is particularly striking because people analytics has long been considered one of the most in-demand and "hot" areas of HR. The fact that professionals are leaving the field in significant numbers suggests deeper structural issues. We must fix these issues if we want to continue to grow and move into the decision-making realm for which this book advocates.

From a push vs. pull perspective, we identified two main drivers behind this trend of people analytics practitioners leaving the field:

1 **Market Pressures ("Push")** – The wave of layoffs that began in 2022, starting in tech startups and FAANG companies before spreading across industries, disproportionately affected people analytics roles. Many professionals were forced to pivot into adjacent HR functions where opportunities were more stable.

2 **Salary Incentives ("Pull")** – Professionals who left people analytics for broader HR roles received, on average, a salary *decrease*, whereas those who remained in people analytics saw their salaries stay roughly the same, but the people analytics roles were tougher to come by than in the past. Even after accounting for promotions (which accounted for only 17 percent of transitions), the incentives to stay in people analytics were weak.

FIGURE 1.5

People analytics practitioners are more likely to transition into other HR roles
Share of external outflows of people analytics practitioners since 2021

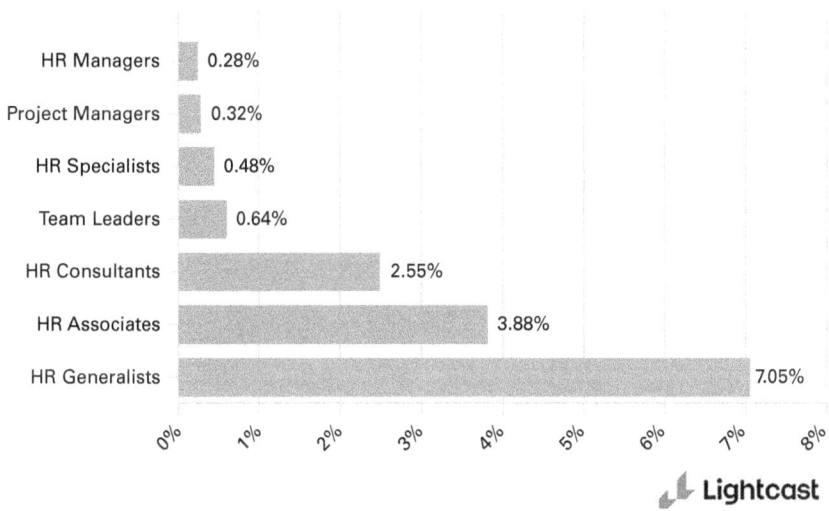

SOURCE Lightcast

In essence, staying loyal to people analytics post-2022 carried some career risk. Those who transitioned out of the field tended to have lower salaries but perhaps in hope of greater job security. This is a problem. People analytics needs to not only provide job security, but career growth and financial incentives to stay within the discipline.

The Future of People Analytics: A Field at a Crossroads

The past 15 years tell a compelling story: People analytics experienced unprecedented growth, reaching a peak in 2022, only to enter a period of contraction and uncertainty. This recent stagnation is not just a temporary setback—it raises serious questions about the discipline's long-term sustainability. If people analytics continues to be absorbed into broader HR functions rather than existing as a standalone practice, what does that mean for its future? Can the field sustain itself if high-caliber talent continues to exit in favor of more stable HR roles?

The data suggests that the people analytics function, as we currently know it, is at an inflection point. Organizations must decide whether to fully integrate analytics into HR generalist functions or double down on specialized, high-impact people analytics roles. Without meaningful change—whether through clearer career paths, greater job security, or a shift in organizational priorities—the risk is that people analytics could cease to exist as an independent function and instead become just another skill set within traditional HR roles.

The next few years will determine whether people analytics remains a distinct and valuable practice or gets absorbed into the broader HR ecosystem. The choices that organizations and practitioners make now will shape the future of the field for years to come. This book is here to help navigate the next few years, and put people analytics back on track to dominate through evidence-based practice to help bring about business value.

REAL-WORLD EXAMPLE

"How to be Evidence-Based with People Analytics?" with Nicholas Bremner, Head of Organizational Analytics at Uber

(Paraphrased for length from Ep. 50 of "Directionally Correct, A People Analytics Podcast")

Adopting Evidence-Based Management in People Analytics

Dr. Nicholas Bremner, Head of Organizational Analytics at Uber, emphasizes the importance of evidence-based management (EBM) in people analytics. Rooted in a framework originally developed in medicine, EBM advocates for using multiple sources of evidence to inform decision-making. Bremner has applied this model at Uber to enhance the organization's ability to make better, more informed decisions.

The Evidence-Based Management Framework

EBM involves integrating various forms of evidence to guide decisions, including:

1   Organizational Data: Internal data collected through reporting and analytics.
2   External Research: Insights from academic literature, industry benchmarks, and external sources.
3   Cultural Context: Understanding the cultural and situational factors that influence decision-making.
4   Professional Expertise: Leveraging the informed judgment of experienced professionals, which improves over time through repeated exposure and feedback.

This multi-pronged approach ensures that decisions are not made in isolation but are informed by a robust, holistic understanding of the factors at play.

The Hierarchy of Evidence

Dr. Bremner highlights a key aspect of EBM: the hierarchy of evidence. At the bottom are opinions, which, while subjective and prone to bias, often contain valuable kernels of truth. As one moves up the hierarchy, the quality of evidence improves, culminating in randomized controlled trials (RCTs) and other rigorous methods.

While opinions are less reliable on their own, they play a role when combined with higher-quality evidence, especially when viewed through the lens of expertise. Professionals develop expertise through repeated exposure to similar situations, enabling them to anticipate outcomes with greater accuracy.

Practical Applications of EBM in People Analytics

1   Combining Internal and External Data: Bremner stresses that internal organizational data should be supplemented with external research to ensure a broader perspective. This might include leveraging academic studies, industry trends, and benchmarks.

2   Considering Cultural Context: Data must be interpreted within the cultural and situational context of the organization. Decisions that might work in one setting may not translate directly to another without adjustment for cultural nuances.

3   Developing Expertise: Over time, analytics professionals build expertise by repeatedly encountering and solving similar problems, refining their intuition and decision-making capabilities.

Key Takeaways for People Analytics Teams

1   Adopt a Multi-Layered Approach: Use organizational data, external research, cultural understanding, and professional expertise to inform decisions.

2   Value Opinions as Starting Points: While opinions are not definitive evidence, they provide valuable context and can guide further inquiry.

3   Aim for Rigor: Use higher levels of evidence, such as controlled experiments or robust statistical analysis, wherever feasible.

4   Integrate Cultural Context: Decisions should account for the unique cultural and environmental factors of the organization.

5   Develop Expertise Over Time: Encourage learning through feedback and experience to enhance professional judgment and decision-making accuracy.

Building Better Decisions with EBM

Dr. Bremner's approach underscores the value of combining multiple evidence sources to guide decisions in people analytics. By integrating data, research, cultural insights, and expertise, organizations can make more informed and impactful decisions. This evidence-based approach enhances the credibility and effectiveness of people analytics, ensuring it contributes meaningfully to organizational success.

Is People Analytics a "Luxury" HR Function?

The employment trends in people analytics raise a fundamental question: Is people analytics a strategic necessity, or merely a luxury that organizations can afford only in times of economic prosperity? This concern is not hypothetical. In a 2022 conversation, I had a CEO and Chief People Officer bluntly state to me, *"People analytics is a luxury we cannot afford right now"* when they were discussing why they were letting some of their people analytics talent go. This sentiment is not unique, and it reflects the precarious positioning of people analytics in many organizations today.

The rise of people analytics as a discipline over the past 15 years may not have been purely due to its strategic value, but rather an artifact of historically low interest rates. When borrowing money was cheap, companies were more willing to invest in new functions with uncertain but promising returns—people analytics being one of them.

We all know the landmark moments that helped define the people analytics movement:

- Google's Project Oxygen (Garvin, 2013) and Aristotle (Duhigg, 2016), which linked managerial behaviors and team effectiveness to business outcomes.
- The Harvard Business Review article "Competing on Talent Analytics" which framed data-driven HR as a competitive advantage (Davenport, Harris, and Shapiro, 2010).
- The cultural phenomenon of *Moneyball* (2011) the film, which demonstrated the power of analytics in sports and inspired organizations to take a data-driven approach to workforce management.

During the era of low interest rates, it was nearly risk-free for companies to follow these examples and establish people analytics functions. HR leaders, eager to emulate prestigious organizations and avoid the fear of missing out (FOMO), rushed to build people analytics teams. The movement gained momentum, and people analytics became the *en vogue* HR discipline.

THE CHANGING ECONOMIC REALITY: ARE LOW INTEREST RATES OVER?
Economic conditions have shifted dramatically since 2022. Interest rates have risen sharply, making capital more expensive and forcing organizations to scrutinize every investment more closely. As a result, the speculative period of people analytics growth appears to be ending.

This shift is reflected in employment trends. Figure 1.6 highlights a clear negative correlation between the number of people analytics roles and the Federal Funds Effective Rate. As interest rates increased in 2022, the number of people analytics positions declined. A similar pattern emerges when comparing the number of people analytics positions to the M2 monetary supply (Figure 1.7)—as the money supply shrank, so did the number of people analytics jobs.

These findings support the hypothesis that the rapid rise of people analytics was largely fueled by low interest rates. A correlation of well over 0.90 between the M2 money supply and people analytics employment reinforces the idea that easy money enabled people analytics growth—but now, that era is over, at least for now, as interest rates are slowing decreasing and the money supply is slowly starting to swing upwards again.

Breaking the Link: How to Avoid Becoming a Casualty of Economic Cycles

If people analytics is to survive and thrive, it must break its correlation with interest rates, money supply, and other economic variables unrelated to its actual value to organizations. The field must evolve beyond being seen as a discretionary expense and establish itself as a critical driver of business success. No one can predict future economic conditions with certainty. Interest rates, inflation, and global financial trends will continue to fluctuate. But the organizations that future-proof their people analytics functions—by focusing on measurable business impact rather than economic cycles—will be the ones that succeed in maintaining and expanding their teams. This brings us to the most important question:

- **Does people analytics impact the bottom line?**

The strongest argument for sustaining people analytics through economic downturns is proof of its impact on business performance. While many studies (Wall and Wood, 2005) suggest a link between HR performance and business success, measuring the specific contribution of people analytics remains challenging at scale. That said, there is compelling evidence that companies with strong people analytics functions are perceived as more valuable.

FIGURE 1.6

People analytics positions
Number of people analytics positions in the U.S. vs. Federal Funds Effective Rate

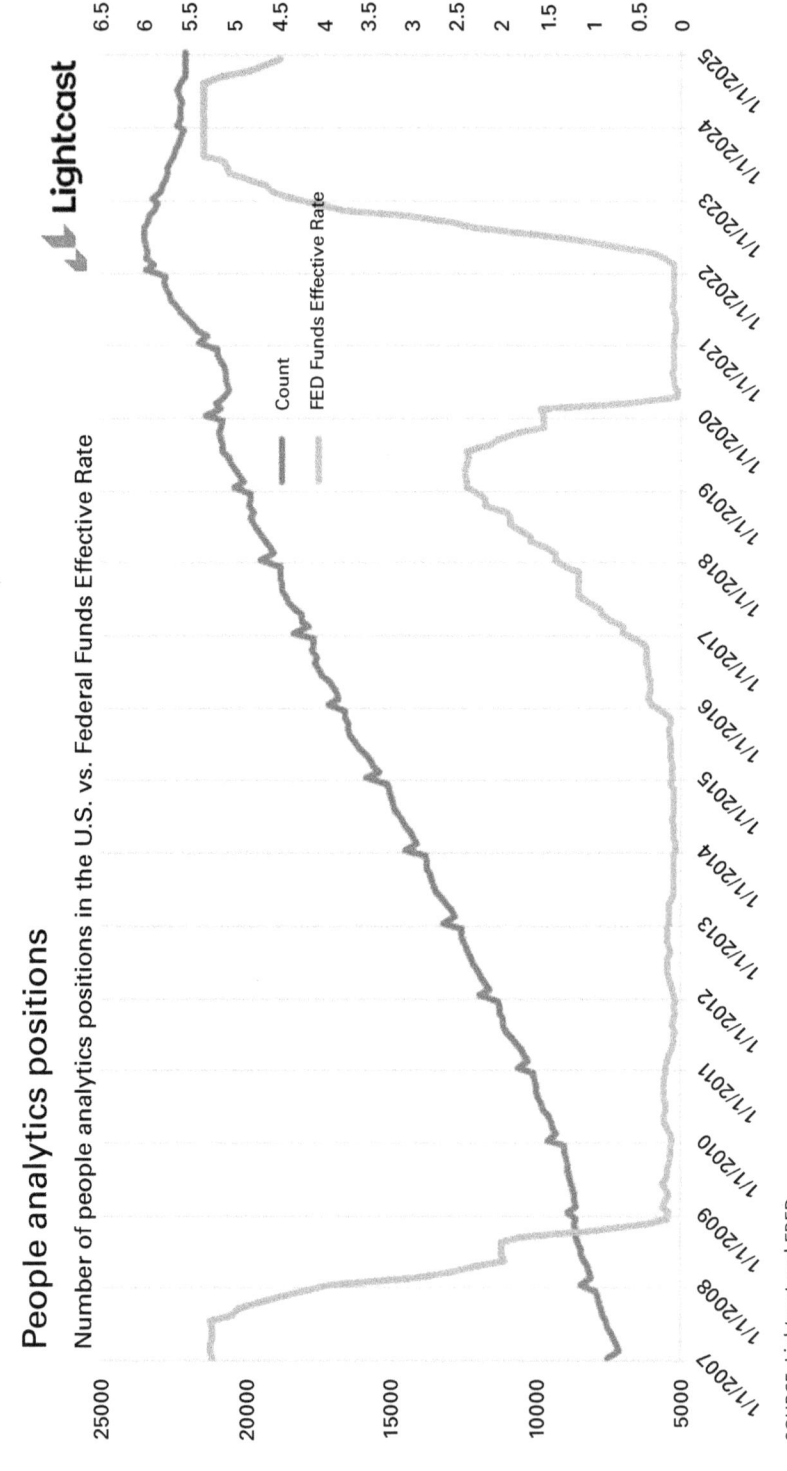

SOURCE Lightcast and FRED

FIGURE 1.7

People analytics positions
Number of people analytics positions in the U.S. vs. M2 Monetary Supply

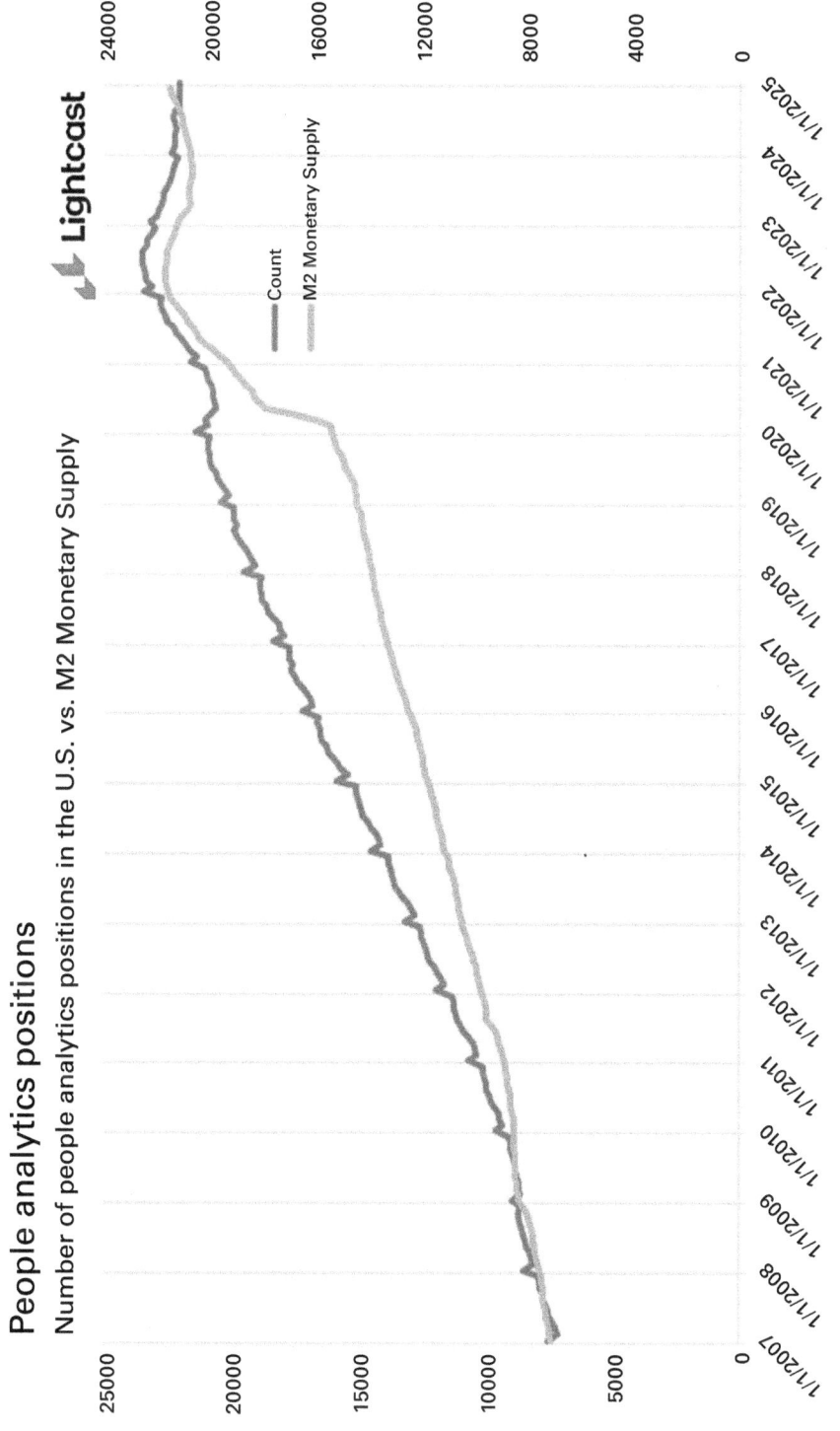

SOURCE Lightcast and FRED

Prestigious People Analytics Teams Correlate with Performance

My research examined 1,824 companies with a "prestigious" people analytics team and compared them to 2,125 companies with a "less prestigious" team. Figure 1.8 presents a fascinating trend:

- Companies with a prestigious people analytics team scored the highest in employee sentiment ratings across all categories.
- Companies with a less prestigious team still outperformed those without any people analytics function, except in CEO and senior leadership ratings.

This pattern is exactly what we would expect:

- *No people analytics team = lowest ratings.*
- *Less prestigious team = middle-tier ratings.*
- *Prestigious team = highest ratings across the board.*

The data suggests that organizations with mature and respected people analytics functions tend to be better-run companies overall—whether due to better workforce insights, stronger leadership, or an overall culture of data-driven decision-making, causality cannot be inferred. Moreover, only 46 percent of people analytics teams (1,824) are considered prestigious, while 54 percent fall into the "less prestigious" category, which means that opportunities abound for people analytics to mature more broadly at a majority of organizations. Now is the time to fix that.

People analytics must prove its worth.

The resurgence of people analytics depends on its ability to demonstrate clear business value. The field can no longer rely on the assumption that every forward-thinking company will invest in people analytics simply because it is the *trendy* thing to do. People analytics is here to stay. The next phase of people analytics will be defined not by hype, but by impact. If the field continues to deliver measurable value to organizations, it will thrive—regardless of economic conditions. However, if people analytics is perceived as a cost center rather than a value driver, it risks being sidelined during periods of financial tightening.

The challenge for people analytics leaders is clear: Prove that the function is indispensable, or risk being seen as a luxury that businesses cannot afford in difficult times.

FIGURE 1.8

Companies with a prestigious PA team are rated higher among employees

Employee ratings (on a scale of 1–5) among companies with a prestigious PA team, a less prestigious PA team, and without a PA team

| | Prestigious PA Team | Less Prestigious PA Team | Without a PA Team |

Diversity and Inclusion: 3.9 / 3.83 / 3.68
Overall: 3.73 / 3.57 / 3.52
Business Outlook: 3.71 / 3.55 / 3.46
CEO: 3.68 / 3.52 / 3.55
Recommend to Friend: 3.68 / 3.48 / 3.39
Compensation and Benefits: 3.65 / 3.48 / 3.32
Culture and Values: 3.63 / 3.46 / 3.43
Work-Life Balance: 3.58 / 3.43 / 3.45
Career Opportunities: 3.54 / 3.44 / 3.31
Senior Leadership: 3.29 / 3.17 / 3.19

SOURCE Directionally Correct

How People Analytics Can Get Back on Track

Step One: Add Real Value & Break the Cycle

Do you want your career prospects in people analytics to be dictated by factors beyond your control—like interest rates or budget cuts? Of course not. It's time to reclaim control by delivering undeniable business value.

People analytics must focus on driving measurable impact for the business— on both the top and bottom lines. If we want to secure the future of the field, we must prove our worth in ways that are impossible to ignore. As I have often said, "It's very hard to lay off a team that's paying for itself 10× every year" (DC News, 2023). That should be the gold standard for every people analytics function. This isn't just a mindset shift; it should be a concrete commitment to HR leadership, the C-Suite, and even the board of directors if necessary. People analytics should have clear, quantifiable business objectives that are integrated into corporate goals, whether through MBOs, OKRs, or other performance frameworks. Everyone in the function should be able to articulate their impact in a way that resonates with executives. Make a dollar figure ROI target to the C-Suite and then keep your commitment—and make dollar value commitment worth ten times the costs of your team. Meaning, it will likely be in the millions of dollars.

KEY RECOMMENDATIONS

1 **Move beyond economic dependence**—The era of low interest rates fueled people analytics growth, but the field must now establish its value independently of economic cycles.

2 **Demonstrate measurable impact**—Organizations must track and communicate how people analytics directly contributes to revenue growth, cost savings, and workforce productivity.

3 **Invest at the right level**—Underinvestment in people analytics teams leads to underwhelming results. Organizations must ensure that teams are large enough and well-resourced to deliver meaningful insights.

4 **Build prestige through impact**—Companies with mature, well-regarded people analytics teams score better across employee sentiment metrics. Investing in high-quality people analytics functions contributes to overall company success.

Step Two: Advance People Analytics with Gen AI

The most valuable teams in any organization don't just report on what's happening—they shape the future. People analytics must evolve beyond static dashboards and reports to deliver strategic, predictive, and prescriptive insights. Gen AI presents an opportunity to accelerate this transformation. However, technology alone isn't the solution—teams must actively build the skills, infrastructure, and operational frameworks to use it effectively. That means:

- Identifying high-impact AI use cases
- Strengthening data infrastructure to support advanced analytics
- Moving beyond reporting to prediction and optimization
- Ensure rapid but responsible AI adoption

Regardless of how much an organization is currently investing in Gen AI, people analytics **professionals** must take ownership of their growth. Learning new skills—whether in developing our own apps, creating new startups, embracing machine learning, or AI implementation—is essential to keeping the field at the forefront of HR innovation. At one point, people analytics was the *bleeding edge* of HR. It's time to reclaim that role.

For **vendors**, the message is clear: Invest in the community first. If the field shrinks, so does the market opportunity for everyone. Extracting value without reinvesting will only accelerate decline. A rising tide lifts all boats, and it's in everyone's best interest to grow the pie, not just take from it. Be innovators first.

For **educators**, the focus must shift from teaching research to teaching *impact*. People analytics must deliver real business value, not just interesting insights. That means quantifiable ROI—not theoretical improvements, but actual dollars saved or generated. Those educating the next generation of people analytics professionals must emphasize this reality.

People analytics must have a tangible ROI. Yes, that means real dollars, not just theoretical impact. Whether you're a vendor, educator or practitioner and you're looking to get up to speed on some of the basics of quantifying impact, John Boudreau, Wayne Cascio, and Alexis Fink wrote an excellent book called *Investing in People* (Cascio, Boudreau, and Fink 2019), which is a great place to start to learn how. See the additional reading section at the end of Chapter 2 for more details.

Step Three: Focus on Growth & the Future

Yes, the current trajectory of people analytics has been challenging. But that does not define its future. To move forward, we must first commit to change. The way forward is clear:

- Prioritize work that directly influences business decisions

- Embed people analytics deeper into the strategic fabric of the organization
- Move beyond reporting and into true business transformation
- Innovate relentlessly to stay ahead of the curve

This is how people analytics reclaims its place as an indispensable function—one that doesn't just support the business but actively drives its success. It's time to refocus, rebuild, and move forward together. Let's get back to growth, together.

What is Ahead?

It's clear that people analytics is not just an HR function but a critical business strategy for achieving success as an organization. As we move forward, this book will explore three key areas: *Business Value, generative AI*, and *How to Win*.

The first section, *Business Value*, establishes the foundation for leveraging people analytics as a competitive advantage. In Chapter 2, we will explore how organizations can move from simply using analytics for HR efficiency to deploying it as a driver of business dominance, and builds on this by showing how HR can transition from a cost center to a profit center. Chapter 3 reframes analytics as an investment with measurable returns and provides a structured, step-by-step guide for companies to implement people analytics successfully, ensuring that organizations can integrate these insights into everyday business operations for sustained competitive advantage.

In the second section, *Gen AI*, Chapter 4 introduces the revolutionary impact of artificial intelligence on HR and workforce management, and the potential of generative AI, demonstrating how it enhances people analytics and reshapes business decision-making. Chapter 5 highlights the critical role of high-quality data infrastructure, showing that without a strong foundation, AI-driven analytics can falter. Chapter 6 takes AI to the next level, illustrating how businesses can move from passive insights to predictive actions that optimize workforce strategy in real-time. Chapter 7 tackles the ethical considerations of AI in people analytics, ensuring that while businesses leverage these tools for competitive advantage, they do so with integrity and fairness.

In the final section, *How to Win*, Chapter 8 brings these concepts together with real-world applications, and showcases real world examples from innovative companies, demonstrating how people analytics has been successfully deployed to drive business success. Chapter 9 explores emerging HR technologies and trends, emphasizing how businesses must continually adapt to stay ahead. Finally, Chapter 10 reinforces that the future of HR and business leadership will be deeply analytical, requiring organizations to embrace data-driven strategies to sustain long-term success.

By the end of this journey, it will be clear that mastering people analytics and generative AI isn't just an option—it's the blueprint for sustainable success in the evolving business landscape.

Summary

This chapter explores the renewed strategic importance of people analytics in driving business success. Historically, people analytics has struggled to demonstrate clear financial value, often being viewed as a cost center rather than a profit driver. However, with the rise of generative AI and increasing business pressure to justify investments, people analytics must shift from producing "interesting" insights to generating tangible business impact. This chapter outlines why now is the time for this transformation, what challenges have held the field back, and how organizations can leverage people analytics as a tool for competitive advantage.

Key Takeaways

1 **People Analytics Must Evolve Beyond "Cool" Insights**
   While people analytics has gained credibility through research and workplace psychology, it has often failed to drive meaningful business outcomes. The next phase of evolution must focus on financial ROI.

2 **The Hype Cycle: From Inflated Expectations to Business Necessity**
   The field has gone through phases of excitement, disillusionment, and slow progress. Now, with Gen AI, people analytics can either be disrupted or become an indispensable decision-making function.

3 **A Misalignment Between HR and Business Needs Has Stalled Progress**
   Traditional HR analytics has focused on engagement surveys, dashboards, and reporting rather than solving real business problems like profitability, workforce productivity, and operational efficiency.

4 **The "Four Phases of Impact" Framework**
   o **Interesting:** Data that fascinates but doesn't drive decisions.
   o **Helpful:** Insights that inform, but aren't essential.

- o **Needed:** Data actively sought out for decision-making.

- o **Existential:** Analytics so crucial that business leaders cannot operate without them. Moving to Existential is key for people analytics to secure its role in business strategy.

5 **Generative AI is a Game-Changer, Not a Replacement**
Gen AI automates insights, enhances prediction models, and scales analytics capabilities, allowing people analytics teams to provide real-time, strategic input rather than just reports.

6 **People Analytics Needs to Speak the Language of Business**
HR teams must quantify their impact in dollars and business KPIs, rather than relying on engagement scores and survey results that executives struggle to translate into value.

7 **People Analytics Faces an Existential Threat if It Doesn't Prove Value**
The field contracted after 2021, with layoffs and role reductions signaling that organizations don't yet see people analytics as a necessity. To reverse this trend, analytics must become a function that drives profit and reduces risk.

8 **Lessons from Google: Think Long-Term, Not Just Incrementally**
Dr. Prasad Setty, former People Analytics leader at Google, emphasizes that organizations should use analytics to address systemic workforce challenges rather than just optimize for short-term HR decisions.

9 **People Analytics Must Break Free from Economic Dependence**
The rapid expansion of people analytics was fueled by low interest rates and easy funding. As companies now scrutinize spending, analytics teams must justify their ROI or risk elimination.

10 **The Path Forward: Making People Analytics a Profit-Driving Function**

- o Align analytics with critical business decisions (e.g., revenue growth, cost savings).

- o Integrate AI-powered analytics to move from reporting to real-time decision-making.

- o Ensure accountability by setting clear, measurable ROI targets.

- o Secure C-suite buy-in by demonstrating financial impact.

The resurgence of people analytics hinges on proving business value. The future of the function depends on its ability to evolve from an HR support role to a business-critical, profit-driving entity. The coming chapters will provide a blueprint for making this transformation a reality, ensuring that people analytics is not just relevant—but indispensable.

References

Cascio, W. F., Boudreau, J. W. and Fink, A. A. (2019). Investing in People: Financial Impact of Human Resource Initiatives. Society For Human Resource Management.

Davenport, T. H., Harris, J. and Shapiro, J. (2017). Competing on Talent Analytics. Harvard Business Review. https://hbr.org/2010/10/competing-on-talent-analytics. (archived at https://perma.cc/2P63-A5GL)

DC News. (2023). How Do You Measure Peak Performance? Substack. directionally correctnews.substack.com/p/how-do-you-measure-peak-performance?r=ybtwi& utm_campaign=post&utm_medium=web&triedRedirect=true (archived at https://perma.cc/57C2-KVHN).

Duhigg, C. (2016). What Google Learned from its Quest to Build the Perfect Team. *The New York Times*, February 25. www.nytimes.com/2016/02/28/magazine/what-google-learned-from-its-quest-to-build-the-perfect-team.html (archived at https://perma.cc/QDC5-VQWU).

Ferrar, J. and Green, D. (2021). *Excellence in People Analytics: How to Use Workforce Data to Create Business Value*. KoganPage.

Garvin, D. (2013). How Google Sold Its Engineers on Management. Harvard Business Review. hbr.org/2013/12/how-google-sold-its-engineers-on-management (archived at https://perma.cc/5ASP-N52U).

Hanna, K. T. and Wigmore, I. (2023). What is Gartner Hype Cycle? – Definition from WhatIs.com. WhatIs.com. www.techtarget.com/whatis/definition/Gartner-hype-cycle (archived at https://perma.cc/LMC4-F73D).

Indeed Career Guide. (n.d.). Business Value in IT: Definition, Components and Strategies. www.indeed.com/career-advice/career-development/business-value (archived at https://perma.cc/QUR7-HUSY).

Levenson, A., Stevenson, M. and Fink, A. (2021), Are OD and Analytics Twins Separated at Birth? Toward an Integrated Framework. In *Research in Organizational Change and Development* (Research in Organizational Change and Development, Vol. 29), edited by A. B. (Rami) Shani and D. A. Noumair. Emerald Publishing Limited. https://doi.org/10.1108/S0897-301620210000029002 (archived at https://perma.cc/8S6B-WK6M)

Napper, C. (2023). Should People Analytics Take Over Human Resources? | HR Exchange Network. www.hrexchangenetwork.com/people-analytics/articles/should-people-analytics-take-over-human-resources (archived at https://perma.cc/44RC-Q6P8).

Napper, C., Scott, H. and Nicholas, B. (2023). How to be Evidence-Based with People Analytics? Directionally Correct. www.podbean.com/eas/pb-qqayf-151f6db (archived at https://perma.cc/T5VA-P6QG) Ep. 50.

Napper, C., Scott, H. and Prasad, S. (2024). How Do We Produce Value in the Future with People Analytics? Directionally Correct. www.podbean.com/eas/pb-i8ra8-16ce919 (archived at https://perma.cc/6GTW-B2PK) Ep 102.

Wall, T. D. and Wood, S. J. (2005). The Romance of Human Resource Management and Business Performance, and the Case for Big Science. *Human Relations*, 58 (4): 429–462. doi.org/10.1177/0018726705055032 (archived at https://perma.cc/S3ZH-T3PP).

Zaillian, S., Sorkin, A., Chervin, S. and Lewis, M. (2011). *Moneyball*. IMDb. www.imdb.com/title/tt1210166/ (archived at https://perma.cc/7W2R-YD32).

2

Transforming People Analytics: From Cost Center to Profit Center

This chapter discusses the transformation of HR from traditional to strategic roles powered by analytics, showcasing how this shift from people analytics being a cost center to a profit center creates competitive advantage.

"Genius is the fire that lights itself"—Unknown

We can be the catalyst of our own change. We are not beholden to external factors forcing us to change or improve. We can make the changes we need ourselves. We can be the fire that lights itself. To truly transform people analytics from a cost center to a profit center, organizations must embrace a proactive mindset—one that sees data not just as a tool for reporting but as a driver of strategic action. This shift requires HR leaders to move beyond reactive insights and actively shape business outcomes, proving the tangible value of analytics. When we take ownership of this transformation, we move from simply measuring change to leading it, ensuring that people analytics becomes a core driver of profitability and competitive advantage.

The Scorekeeper Fallacy

Have you ever stopped to consider the origins of analytics in business? Before *Moneyball* revolutionized sports, analytics began with a simple yet critical role: Scorekeeping. A scorekeeper's job was straightforward—record the truth of the game, capture the raw numbers, and ensure accuracy. But when analytics professionals entered the picture, they transformed this function. No longer just passive recorders of data, they uncovered deeper insights, developed new metrics, and gave forward-thinking teams a competitive edge.

Yet, therein lies a limitation. Much like traditional scorekeepers, modern people analytics teams—and adjacent functions like workforce planning and talent intelligence—often find themselves stuck in a "decision support" role. They influence decisions, but they don't make them. They report, analyze, and advise, yet they lack true power. The uncomfortable truth? Analytics professionals, like scorekeepers, only gain power when they depart from objectivity—when they bias their findings. And that is a dangerous path.

Stepping Beyond the Scorekeeper's Role

But what if there's another way? What if we could sidestep the Scorekeeper Fallacy altogether? The key is not to remain in the stands, passively observing the action, but to step into the arena. As Theodore Roosevelt famously said, true influence belongs to the *"man in the arena."* For analytics professionals, this means evolving beyond decision support into decision-making roles.

In sports, the coach and general manager decide; the statistician observes. In business, CHROs and executives decide; analytics teams sit in the back office. If our collective fields—people analytics, workforce planning, talent intelligence—want to move beyond being a support function, we must take a more active role in shaping outcomes. We must aspire to become players in the game, not just recorders of it. So here's the challenge: Are we content being scorekeepers, or are we ready to move from the back office to the front lines? Because those who aspire to lead must step beyond the Scorekeeper Fallacy—and become true decision-makers.

Profit Center is Greater than Cost Center

Most of what is written about how to do people analytics effectively is based on case studies of the top 50 (or less) people analytics organizations. These are the people analytics teams that are flush with resources, talent, technology, travel, global dispersion, and [insert positive characteristic] here. If you were to follow the advice of how to be effective at people analytics, it would go something like this:

> *"First, get a 50 person team and a $15M dollar budget. Purchase expensive enterprise software and hire the team to support it. Spend 3–4 years curating your own cloud-based data infrastructure, and sprinkle in a few PhDs to 'science' up the place."*

Is this realistic for most organizations? It is wishful thinking at best, and detrimental at worst to set the narrative that this is what it takes to be effective at people analytics. If you have fewer resources than the top 50 most well-resourced people analytics teams, here are some steps you can take to gain credibility while delivering value.

Effective Maturity Steps

1 Take whatever resources you have, and prove value
2 After proving value and demonstrating credibility, tackle bigger problems and ask for more resources to do so
3 Deliver value on the bigger problems
4 Repeat

This book is written from the vantage point that any people analytics team or leader should be able to take away value. Building a people analytics team that is seen as an asset to a business is something that every team should strive for and is available to any size team or organization. It all starts with the mindset of: **Profit Center > Cost Center.**

It's nothing magical. It's how you run an effective people analytics team.

Five Simple Commitments:

1 Get commitment to take action before starting any project
2 Embed measurement of ROI into all workstreams before starting them
3 Quantify the value of all workstreams
4 Tally up the value of workstreams on (*at least*) an annual basis
5 Pay for your team 10 times over every year

At the beginning of the year, or at the onset of the team's creation, tabulate the fully loaded cost of the team. This includes the cost of salaries and fringe benefits, technology, licenses, contractors, travel, and any cost directly borne by the team. Multiply that number by 10. That is the value your team needs to bring in that year.

It's a mentality shift and capability building exercise as much as it is a change in technical expertise of a people analytics team. Publicly commit to the 10× figure to the HR and business leadership. Put it into your goals and OKRs. Be held accountable to this goal.

Everything the team does must be quantified and the measurement has to be baked into the work before it begins. This is a secret weapon. Most teams wait until work is complete to try to quantify its value, and then end up moving on to other competing priorities before the value is derived. Then, nothing ever changes. If you can't quantify the value, don't do the work. Get creative/directional on quantifying the value of workstreams. Be conservative. Everything that is built must be supported by an ROI.

On the same token, don't commit to a project until the stakeholders commit to taking action based on the result. How can you possibly quantify the value of your work if no one is willing to take action based on the results? When speaking to people analytics teams on this subject, I get asked *"Can I do that? Can I say no to work if the requestor isn't willing to take action based on the results?"* and the answer is yes. Most of these recommendations are just textbook behavior change and level-setting expectations of a people analytics team.

Why Does People Analytics Avoid Accountability?

As far as I can tell, virtually no people analytics teams are operating in the way described above today. Considering the skillset to do so exists within many teams, this is more likely a *will* issue than a *skill* issue. There are surely a variety of reasons why teams may not be quantifying their ROI, but the one that sticks out the most is people analytics teams and often more broadly HR teams lack a will for accountability. We don't own profits and losses, we usually aren't the sole decision-makers or implementers of major initiatives, and we aren't a money-oriented function, like Finance. Accountability doesn't come naturally to us.

Here's an alternative viewpoint: What if you knew that if you followed the "five simple commitment" steps that not only was it achievable to pay for yourself ten times over every year, but it may even be, in fact, *easy*. To use the example for Figure 2.1, you would be surprised how easy it is to hit a

FIGURE 2.1

Example: Team of 5 people

Salaries and Fringe - $1.5M
Technology - $500K
Travel/Miscellaneous - $500K
_____

Total = $2.5M Dollars

$2.5M X 10 = $25M

The team needs to bring in this much value annually

$25M target, even with a team of five people. The reason why this is the case is the simple concept of *scale*. Relatively few decisions impact huge numbers of people within large organizations. It stands to reason, then, that if people analytics is influencing those small numbers of decisions, it can influence large sums of money relatively easily with a large impact.

A report or dashboard on its own has no intrinsic value. The only value in those tools is to influence decision-making, and to influence it at scale. At one previous organization in which I worked we made a $50M ROI commitment to the business for that year. We *easily* passed over $200M in ROI that same year because of the scale of impact. People analytics teams are leaving money and influence on the table by not making these commitments and holding ourselves accountable. That changes today.

REAL-WORLD EXAMPLE

"The CHRO Guide to What is Needed in the C-Suite" with Dan George, former people analytics leader and former CHRO at JumpCrew

(Paraphrased for length from Ep. 61 of "Directionally Correct, A People Analytics Podcast")

From People Analytics to CHRO: The Value of Analytics in Leadership

Dan George, a former people analytics leader turned Chief Human Resources Officer (CHRO), highlights how his background in analytics equipped him to thrive in the C-Suite. While traditional HR knowledge is valuable, George emphasizes that a strong understanding of analytics, technology, and business operations is increasingly critical for future CHROs. This expertise enables HR leaders to speak the language of other executives, build data-driven business cases, and compete effectively for resources.

Bridging the Gap Between HR and the C-Suite

Dan identifies two key challenges for HR leaders entering the C-Suite:

1   Competing for Budget: To secure resources for HR initiatives, CHROs must understand the priorities of peers in finance, operations, and other functions. Speaking their language—whether it's operational metrics or financial strategies—is essential to advocating for HR's role in driving business success.

2   Overcoming Stigma: HR often faces skepticism in the boardroom, where its initiatives may be dismissed as less critical than those in IT, supply chain, or other business areas. CHROs must overcome this bias by aligning HR strategies with broader business goals and demonstrating measurable impact.

Building Influence in the C-Suite

George recounts his experience building a people analytics team at Bridgestone Americas, where he started with limited resources and had to navigate the political and business aspects of securing funding. He highlights the importance of understanding three elements of budget allocation:

1   Business Need: Articulating how HR initiatives address critical operational or strategic challenges.

2   Politics: Building alliances, understanding the priorities of peers, and aligning goals to gain support.

3   Inertia: Leveraging existing budgets while strategically pushing for incremental funding when opportunities arise.

Lessons Learned from the Boardroom

One of George's key insights is the importance of tailoring business cases to the audience. Early in his career, he presented a 100 percent ROI on an HR analytics system, only to be met with skepticism. Over time, he learned that more conservative estimates, such as break-even points, were more credible and persuasive. He also realized that success often depends on bartering and aligning incentives with other leaders, fostering a coalition of support for HR initiatives.

Key Skills for CHROs

Dan identifies critical skills and strategies for CHROs navigating the C-Suite:

1   Business Acumen: Understanding finance, operations, and strategy is essential to building credibility and securing resources.

2   Analytics Expertise: Leveraging data to build compelling business cases and demonstrate ROI strengthens HR's position in decision-making.

3   Political Savvy: Recognizing and navigating the political dynamics of budget allocation is crucial for success.

4   Collaborative Influence: Aligning HR goals with the priorities of other leaders fosters buy-in and support.

5   Iterative Learning: Adapting messaging and strategy based on feedback ensures continued progress and influence.

The Future of CHROs: Data-Driven Leadership

George believes the future of CHROs lies in integrating analytics into HR strategy. As organizations become more data-driven, CHROs must leverage analytics to demonstrate the strategic value of HR initiatives and align them with overall business goals. Leaders who master this balance of technical expertise, business understanding, and political acumen will thrive in the evolving role of HR leadership.

George's journey from people analytics leader to CHRO offers a blueprint for aspiring HR leaders, emphasizing the importance of adaptability, influence, and data-driven decision-making in achieving success at the highest levels of an organization.

Role of Faith, Science, and Utility in People Analytics

It may not seem obvious, but if you follow the real world example with Dan George, you'll see that faith, science, and utility all play critical roles in the success of a people analytics function. If you want your people analytics function to be a profit center rather than a cost center, it would be wise to understand why.

Faith

Almost anyone with a scientific background would recoil at the suggestion that faith has any bearing in people analytics. Faith is frequently used interchangeably with the disdain of intuition-based judgment, an absence of reason and facts, and even religiosity. But what if you were told that every people analytics project is successful because of faith? Is your organization establishing its first people analytics team? Faith. Are you tackling a project that's never been completed before? Faith. Are leaders willing to take action based off a people analytics team's results, who they don't know? Huge leap of faith.

The reason why faith plays such a large role has little to do with religion and a lot to do with the word *influence*. The godfather of influence research is Robert Cialdini and his most famous book, *Influence* (2007), is littered with appeals to faith, such as faith in authority (*leaders and experts know better*), social proof (*if others have tried it, it probably works*), and scarcity (*if there is less of something, it must be more valuable*). Notice, none of these characteristics are scientifically quantified; rather, they are gut-reactions made by human judgment. If you go deep enough into influence, it's an infinite regress or "turtles all the way down" until you get to pure faith (Chris, 2022).

There are three ways that faith concretely plays a role in people analytics:

1 People analytics teams, first, have to believe in what we do and say

2 Customers, second, have to believe in what people analytics recommends and be willing to take action

3   Third, the employees we support have to have faith in us to do the right thing

You could even make an argument that faith is the most important component of people analytics success. Many times members of our community, present company included, complain that they are doing amazing work, but none of our customers are listening and no one is taking action based on the results. The reason? **They don't have faith in us.** That's why. The first step in changing something is recognizing the problem. We have to do better.

Science

The fact that science plays a role in people analytics may seem self-evident to most people analytics practitioners. And yet, it is not self-evident that science plays a central role in people analytics as we are currently constituted. Many people analytics practitioners are *not* classically trained in science and research methods and—with the rise of data science and "black box" models (Kenton, 2020)—increasingly common applications in people analytics have no grounding in science or theory whatsoever.

Science and reason—although not synonymous—both play a role in the success of people analytics. Reason is the precursor to science. Reason is important because of the relationship between critical and analytical thinking in breaking down a problem and succeeding in a feat of problem solving. My bifurcation of science vs. reason is as follows: *"Science is related to the scientific method. Reason, however, is related to critical and analytical thinking."*

In regard to reason, there is value in both inductive and deductive reasoning. Both kinds of reasoning play a role in effective people analytics. Someone has to generate the hypotheses (*inductive*) and then test the hypotheses with data (*deductive*). First principles thinking, a subset of reason and logic, also plays a role in people analytics. Breaking problems down to their most base elements and assumptions and working your way back up from there. A simpler version of first principles thinking, root cause analysis, can be a very helpful framework to diagnose and fix problems using science and data. All of that to say, **science plays a role in people analytics.**

REAL-WORLD EXAMPLE

"Competitive Advantage and The Value of Human Capital" with Max Blumberg, Principal at Blumberg Partnership Ltd. and Affiliated Research Scientist at Center for Effective Organizations, University of Southern California.

(Paraphrased for length from Ep. 12 of "Directionally Correct, A People Analytics Podcast")

Linking HR to Business Strategy Through Systems Thinking

Dr. Max Blumberg, Principal at Blumberg Partnership Ltd. and an affiliated research scientist at CEO, emphasizes the importance of aligning HR processes with business strategy to create competitive advantage. At the core of his work is the *Human Capital Value Profiler*, a framework designed to link HR activities to organizational outcomes, such as revenue, innovation, and customer acquisition. This tool provides a systematic approach to demonstrate how human capital initiatives contribute directly to business success.

Overcoming Common Challenges in HR

Dr. Blumberg identifies two key challenges in HR:

1   Understanding Business Strategy: Many HR professionals lack a deep understanding of how the business generates revenue or achieves strategic goals. This disconnect limits their ability to design processes that align with organizational needs.

2   Creativity Deficit: HR functions often struggle to envision how their initiatives can support and enhance business strategy. The *Human Capital Value Profiler* helps bridge this gap by providing a clear framework to link HR activities, such as recruitment or leadership development, to measurable business outcomes.

The Importance of Standardized Processes

Max advocates for process standardization in HR, arguing that inconsistent, ad hoc practices lead to inefficiencies and variability. By establishing clear links between HR processes and outcomes—such as recruitment processes driving leadership capabilities, which in turn enhance productivity and revenue—organizations can focus their creativity on refining processes rather than reinventing them repeatedly.

Shifting Beyond Descriptive Analytics

He critiques the overreliance on dashboards and descriptive statistics in HR. While these tools are useful for reporting, they do not drive strategic decision-making. He emphasizes the need to move toward predictive analytics and qualitative approaches that are "directionally correct" and aligned with business strategy.

For example, eliciting workforce capabilities from business leaders does not always require deep statistical analysis; much of this work can be done qualitatively by translating business plans into actionable people processes.

Key Takeaways from the Human Capital Value Profiler

1   Align HR with Strategy: HR processes must directly support the capabilities needed to execute the organization's business strategy.

2   Standardization Before Creativity: Establishing consistent processes enables HR to focus creativity on designing effective solutions rather than managing variability.

3   Focus on Outcomes: HR's ultimate goal is to deliver workforce capabilities that drive productivity, innovation, and revenue.

4   Go Beyond Descriptive Analytics: Move from dashboards and visualizations to predictive and qualitative approaches that inform strategic decisions.

5   Directionally Correct, Not Perfect: Business decisions often require timely, good-enough insights rather than perfect statistical precision.

Reframing People Analytics

Max defines people analytics as the function that ensures organizations have the workforce capabilities needed to execute their business strategy. This simple yet powerful definition reorients HR's focus from reporting metrics to delivering strategic value.

Blumberg's insights underscore the power of systems thinking in HR. By linking HR processes to business outcomes through frameworks like the *Human Capital Value Profiler*, organizations can enhance their competitive advantage. HR professionals who embrace this approach can move beyond operational metrics, positioning themselves as strategic partners in achieving organizational success.

Utility

Why does "utility" play a role in people analytics? The reason utility plays a role in people analytics is that people analytics only has value to a firm if it positively influences business outcomes—usually in the form of increased data-driven and data-influenced decision-making by organizational leaders in regard to their human capital. The school of people analytics thought related to "business outcomes" and being "strategy-first" —subscribed to by this author, Center for Effective Organizations-affiliated researchers such as Alec Levenson and Max Blumberg, and other key leaders in our field (i.e., Alexis Fink, Mark Huselid, John Boudreau, Wayne Casico, etc.)—regretfully appears to be a minority view in the field. Focus on utility will be the future of people analytics, if people analytics is to have a future.

The word utility often has a positive connotation. It's about being useful and usable. Disciplines, such as user experience (UX), have cropped up in the softer sciences as ways of attempting to increase the utility, and therefore value, of modern software applications. People analytics has often missed the memo in regard to utility. Research for no one, not moving at the speed of decision-making in the business, seeing humanism and the success of the business as adversarial, and making tools that are inaccessible or inaccurate all hinder people analytics utility. People analytics can do better.

One hears many phrases in the common business lexicon related to "utility," such as maximizing shareholder value, minimum viable products, "agile" innovation, and "disruption" or creative destruction. Common business wisdom dictates to reduce overhead and expand profitable sectors. People analytics only survives if it adds value and serves as a profit center. Some examples of being a profit center include improving retention at a cost lower than the cost of turnover, increasing the quality of hires without increasing recruiting costs, driving increased innovation with existing talent, building efficiency into HR and into the business, etc.

Synthesizing All Three: Faith, Science and Utility in People Analytics

Science, faith, and utility appear to be acting like the "metaphorical balloon" in the present world. When you squeeze on one side, air pops out on the other side. We must ensure people analytics combines science, faith, and utility of our applications. We must not neglect any of the three pillars. It is much easier as a people analytics team to neglect the "legs of the stool" for which you have less interest or skill.

FIGURE 2.2 Building a Business Case

Building a Business Case – Some Advice

Whatever you do, remember KISS. Keep it simple stupid. Here are some simple questions that need to be answered in any business case:

- What is the problem we're facing?
- What are we proposing to do to fix it?
- How much will it cost us to do something?
- How much will it cost us if we do nothing?
- Why now?
- What is the *expected* ROI?
- When will we report back with the *actual* ROI?

SOURCE Directionally Correct

But what happens when you neglect a leg of the stool?

- If you neglect faith, your work will fall on deaf ears
- If you neglect science, your work will be a sham
- If you neglect utility, your work will have no impact

Business Acumen

For most people analytics practitioners' schooling and training, one of the key areas that is neglected is business acumen. Knowing the business. Knowing how businesses operate. The language, the jargon, the form and function. Here's a quick test to know if you have business acumen:

- *Can you explain how your company makes money in a way that if the CEO heard you, you wouldn't be embarrassed?*

Make sure you can pass this test. To have business acumen, you must know the problems the business is facing. In people analytics, this should be our primary concern. We continue to struggle, however, with building the business case to justify our work, or even our existence. Here are some steps to start with for improving our business acumen:

1 **Identify the business problem:** Start by identifying the business problem that you want to solve with people analytics. This could be anything from improving employee retention to increasing productivity.

2 **Define the scope:** Once you have identified the business problem, define the scope of your project. This includes identifying the data sources you will use, the metrics you will track, and the stakeholders who will be involved.

3 **Gather the data:** Collect the data you need to support your business case. This could include data on employee performance, engagement, and satisfaction.

4 **Analyze the data:** Analyze the data to identify patterns and trends. This will help you to understand the root causes of the business problem you are trying to solve.

5 **Develop a solution:** Based on your analysis, develop a solution that addresses the business problem. This could involve changes to HR policies, training programs, or other initiatives.

6 Create a business case: Create a business case that outlines the problem, the proposed solution, and the expected benefits. This should include a cost-benefit analysis that demonstrates the return on investment (ROI) of your project.

7 Present your business case: Present your business case to key stakeholders, including senior management and HR leaders. Be prepared to answer questions and provide additional information as needed.

This is a pretty good starting point. However, let's go a step deeper and focus more on Step 6. **Create a business case:** This is where you will outline the problem, the proposed solution, and the expected benefits. Your business case should include the following sections:

1 Executive summary: This should be a brief overview of the business problem, the proposed solution, and the expected benefits.

2 Problem statement: This should provide more detail on the business problem you are trying to solve. It should include data and metrics that demonstrate the scope and impact of the problem.

3 Proposed solution: This should describe the solution you have developed to address the business problem. It should include details on the changes you plan to make to HR policies, training programs, or other initiatives.

4 Expected benefits: This should describe the benefits of your proposed solution. It should include a cost-benefit analysis that demonstrates the return on investment (ROI) of your project.

5 Implementation plan: This should outline the steps you will take to implement your proposed solution. It should include timelines, milestones, and details on the resources you will need.

6 Risks and challenges: This should identify any risks or challenges that could impact the success of your project. It should also include a plan for mitigating these risks.

7 Conclusion: This should summarize your business case and emphasize the importance of your proposed solution.

REAL-WORLD EXAMPLE

"Strategic Analytics to Help People Analytics" with Alec Levenson, Economist and Senior Research Scientist at Center for Effective Organizations, University of Southern California.

(Paraphrased for length from Ep. 20 of "Directionally Correct, A People Analytics Podcast")

The Value of Systems Thinking in Analytics

Dr. Alec Levenson, economist and senior research scientist at the Center for Effective Organizations, advocates for a systems-thinking approach to analytics. In his book *Strategic Analytics* (2015), Levenson emphasizes the importance of working backward from competitive advantage to enterprise analytics and finally to human capital analytics. This framework enables organizations to understand how their workforce directly contributes to business success and aligns with their overarching goals.

Analytics at Different Levels: From Enterprise to Individual

Dr. Levenson outlines a hierarchical model of analysis:

1 Competitive Advantage Analytics: Identify what sets the organization apart in the market and what drives its success.

2 Business Model Analytics: Examine the processes and structures supporting the organization's operations.

3 Human Capital Analytics: Drill down to understand the contributions of teams and individual roles within the organization.

This layered approach ensures that people analytics is tied directly to organizational outcomes, rather than being siloed or disconnected from strategic goals.

Qualitative Analysis: The Role of Structured Interviews

Alec highlights the importance of qualitative methods, such as structured interviews with stakeholders, in diagnosing organizational challenges. He offers a simple yet powerful guideline: "Do interviews until you stop hearing something new."

- Quantitative Insight: Typically, around 30 interviews provide sufficient data to diagnose a problem. However, internal practitioners who already understand the organization's dynamics may require fewer interviews.

- Organizational Network Analysis (ONA): Using ONA to identify key influencers or "hidden connectors" within the organization can help target interviews more effectively, enabling practitioners to gather critical insights from a smaller number of stakeholders.

Limits of Quantitative Analytics in Organizations

Levenson points out a key limitation in people analytics: organizations often operate as "n=1," meaning there is only one organization with many driving factors. Traditional statistical models cannot fully explain organizational outcomes at this level. Instead, practitioners must rely on logic models, qualitative insights, and compelling narratives to interpret and address complex problems.

Practical Insights for People Analytics Professionals

1   Use Systems Thinking: Start with competitive advantage and work backward to align people analytics with strategic outcomes.

2   Balance Qualitative and Quantitative Methods: While data is important, qualitative tools like structured interviews provide context and depth to understand organizational dynamics.

3   Focus on Stories and Logic Models: Create compelling narratives that integrate data with qualitative findings to explain why things happen and recommend actionable solutions.

4   Adapt Based on Context: Internal practitioners can leverage their knowledge to conduct fewer interviews, while external consultants may need broader engagement to uncover insights.

Strategic Analytics in Action

Dr. Levenson's approach demonstrates how systems thinking and a blend of qualitative and quantitative methods can transform people analytics into a strategic tool. By aligning analytics with competitive advantage and leveraging deep organizational insights, HR leaders can drive meaningful change and deliver measurable value to their organizations. This real world example underscores the importance of integrating analytical rigor with practical, human-centered methodologies.

HR & People Analytics Strategy: Don't Be a Copy-cat

Childhood wisdom: *No one likes a copy-cat.*

We all remember being children once. Kids are known to tease each other from time to time. One common reason to be teased when you were a child was being called a "copy-cat." It didn't feel good, often because we knew that if we were labeled a copy-cat, it was likely true. **We were copying some-one else.** It felt bereft, unoriginal, and commonplace. We knew we were capable of being more, but we had settled for less. We were better than that. HR and people analytics strategy can be better than that too.

In the present moment in HR being a copy-cat is commonplace and frequently rewarded. A priestly caste of HR influencers, HR tech consultants,

FAANG companies, and sometimes even academics determine what is considered *en vogue* as an HR strategy. Then, early adopter HR departments fall in line; followed by the early majority and late majority of HR departments (Gainsight, 2024). Being a copy-cat all the sudden became cool. Why be original when you could be doing what everyone else is doing?

In the African savanna, large numbers of herd animals, such as wildebeest, zebra, and gazelles, travel in packs. Why do they do this? Because there is safety in numbers. A zebra with a single imperfection or mark is easily identified and is pulled from the pack by predators. Is the same true for HR? Are we safer in a pack? Is there wisdom in being a copy-cat? Would anything identifying and different make us stand out and therefore be put in danger? I think not. I think the opposite is true, in fact. *If you do all the same things as your competitors, how can you expect to get different results?*

What to Do, What to Do?

If your organization and team want to be radically better, you're going to have to try strategies that are radically different. Your people analytics strategy should have components to it that are as unique to your business as your business strategy is unique to your business. It's really as simple as that.

HR strategy is upstream from people analytics. **A vanilla, copy-cat HR strategy is going to lead to vanilla, copy-cat people analytics.** In my opinion, people analytics doesn't spend enough of its resources trying to familiarize itself, influence, and control HR strategy. People analytics should speak in the strategic currency of the organization. We should embed ourselves and influence key decision-making, and have a seat at the table by speaking in the language of the business. There is social capital to be had, and the more we learn, the more we realize the necessity of this alternative currency. People analytics should drive strategy. With generative AI disrupting the value that human capital brings, what organizations are going to be the innovators of tomorrow? Will your people analytics team get the message?

"Best Practices"

I am tired of the term "best practices." Research and benchmarking can be important, but best practices are a road to mediocrity. No one ever got fired for "going with IBM" (as the old saying goes), and no one ever got fired for using best practices… until the whole firm loses to its competition, and everyone gets fired. Read it again and think about that. It's a short-term thinking vs. long-term thinking dilemma. Obviously, balance the two, but one must also think with the end in mind when formulating a strategy.

Here are steps for how to differentiate your HR strategy:

- A/B test your HR strategy against those of other firms
- Use opposition research to understand your competitors' HR strategy better, so you can do something different (Sullivan, 2023)
- Implement evidence-based practices on commoditized work, but experiment with firm-specific practices in the most strategically relevant work (Change Effect, 2023)
- Focus on first principles thinking as to how firm value is derived by its talent (DC News, 2023)
- Choose function over fad, when it comes to HR strategy

Rebuild your HR strategy like the Oaklands As and the Houston Astros tore down and rebuilt their teams based on talent-derived insights and data. Embed data, measurement, accountability, and the improvement feedback loop into every single workstream that HR engages. As mentioned in Chapter 1, Henry Ford once said *"if you always do what you've always done, you always get what you've always got."* Average is over and differentiation is king. Strategic neglect (*i.e., neglecting to focus on things that don't add value*) is also a valuable tool (Braunuis, 2022). Where do we need to be world class? Where can we be average? Answer those questions, then execute.

Rebuilding HR Around Data & Measurement

In most HR functions, data is only used to validate, not to guide. There are very few independent thinkers who think for themselves. Mimicry abounds. People analytics is a competitive advantage for firms who use it properly. Firms who are not embedding data into the way they do business, evaluating what they do with data, and projecting the future with data are going to be irrelevant in the next few years due to AI.

Even with advances in generative AI, there is only one currency, and **that is truth**. Truth can only be derived as *data put into practice*. Classical test theory states that all measurement is "truth plus error" (Cappelleri et al., 2014), with error being any deviation between measurement and the truth. Some stakeholders take that to mean that truth can never be attained because error will always exist. Practically, this is a misinterpretation. Organizations that can manifest the best data with the least error will be the closest to truth, and therein lies the root of competitive advantage via data.

People analytics is not inherently useful. Data is not inherently useful. Only accurate data, followed by analysis and cogent results, derived into a form that facilitates timely and accurate decision-making, is useful. Then, that same process iterating across the aggregate of thousands, if not millions of small decisions made, leads one organization to prevailing over another.

Paying for Yourself

In Chapter One, I introduced the concept of paying for your team 10 times over each year. There are three ways to pay for yourself, as a people analytics function: 1) directly, 2) indirectly, and 3) people liking/valuing your work.

How to pay for yourself

1 **Directly**—This is the most linear route. Your team's work must clearly show a tangible benefit to the business. An easy example is sales. A people analytics project helps employees in sales sell more products. 1 + 1 = 2. Instant ROI.

2 **Indirectly**—This route takes more science and more time to prove but is likely more common. Your people analytics team's work improves some facet of work performance, which by extension proves to have a tangible benefit to the business. Another easy example is improving sales leadership. A people analytics project improves sales leadership; then the improved leadership improves sales performance. Analytics + Leadership = Improved Leadership. Improved Leadership + Sales = Improved Performance. Simple enough ROI.

3 **Stakeholders liking/valuing your work**—Honestly, this route sometimes keeps the lights on. It shouldn't, but it does. As much as it would be nice to be a pure empiricist, for the people who are footing the bill for your team's existence, liking and valuing your work—regardless of the direct or indirect impact—matters quite a lot.

It is important to know if your work in people analytics is having an impact. One observation that I have never heard anyone else say in relation to the impact people analytics has, but seems to be true is:

> *"There is no correlation between the effort and impact of people analytics projects."*

As a personal example, people analytics models I've literally completed on the "back of the napkin" have sometimes been more helpful and insightful to key stakeholders than projects that took months or years to complete. The aforementioned dictum necessitates a recommendation to ensure your team's effort is not wasted in gratuitous ways, and my prescription is minimum necessary force (MNF). The premise of MNF is this: *Bring the minimum amount of complexity of analysis to answer the research question/hypotheses of your work that is possible. Only add complexity if it is necessary, adds value and is considered important by stakeholders/customers; otherwise, stop* (Kiener, 2019).

Implementing this strategy will help keep wasted effort and resources to a minimum. One helpful way I've found to conceptualize minimal necessary force is the 2 × 2 chart shown in Figure 2.3. The vertical axis is the project's "value to the business" (high/low); the horizontal axis is "time/scientific rigor necessary to answer the question" (high/low). Check out the commentary in each quadrant to know what type of work is important.

Pressure on CEOs from BoD & Investors

Everyone has a boss. Even CEOs have a boss—namely, the board of directors and investors in the organization. Your CEO's bosses are asking for more. Profits are being squeezed by commodity prices, inflation, and spikes in cost of labor. CEOs are being presented with tough choices on what to do about it. No one signed up for this. However, someone has to make the changes necessary for the business to continue to thrive.

FIGURE 2.3 Time/Value 2 × 2 Chart

	High/Low:	High/High:
Value	This quadrant is nirvana. Live here. Stay here. Plant seeds and grow crops here.	This quadrant is good too, but you can only afford to have a minimal number of projects here at a time.
	Low/Low:	Low/High:
	This quadrant is OK. And, it is frankly more of our job than we would like to admit.	This is your *great* idea that will take two years and will sit on the shelf once completed. AVOID.

Time/Effort

SOURCE Directionally Correct

FIGURE 2.4 The Value of People Analytics to Leadership

The Value of People Analytics

Let's make this simple. The value of people analytics for each key stakeholder at the C-Suite is as follows:

- **To the CEO** – People analytics only has value to the CEO if it helps the organization execute its business goals and strategy more effectively.

- **To the CFO** – People analytics only has value to the CFO if it makes the company more money, reduces overhead and/or helps the company spend less money, while demonstrating a positive ROI coefficient in the process.

- **To the COO** – People analytics only has value to the COO if it makes the company's operations run more efficiently.

- **To the Board of Directors** – People analytics only has value to the BoD if it helps the organization do all the things the CEO, CFO, and COO desire, along with understanding the health of the organization's workforce to produce sustainable value into the future.

SOURCE Directionally Correct

C-Suite Top People Analytics Priorities

If you are leading people analytics, it is strongly recommended to have an established relationship with key C-Suite executives. This relationship is easier to build if you've made a commitment, such as paying for yourself ten times over every year, because the executives will know you share skin in the game with themselves for helping the business execute effectively. However, every organization is different, and every leader has different wants and needs. That said, here are some commonalities amongst the top care-abouts for C-Suite executives:

- **Succession Planning and Critical Roles**—These concepts are traditionally associated with talent management, not people analytics. Analytics on succession planning and critical roles (*Are they engaged? Are they leaving? etc.*) are very important to senior management. This is sometimes a blind spot for people analytics teams.

- **Workforce Planning**—Related to the last point, senior leaders are focused on unforeseen risks to the business. Is a wave of retirements coming? Do we have enough software engineers to meet business demand? How is the merger/acquisition affecting the makeup of the workforce? Analytics on the answers to these questions are table stakes for executives.

- **Labor Costs**—Does the business have a handle on the total cost of the workforce? Finance and compensation usually partner on determining the cost of employee compensation. People analytics can bring employee cost benchmarks to fruition, and executives are quite attuned to this information. How does the business's revenue per employee stack up to competitors? You should know the answer to these questions.

- **Hiring to Plan**—Definitionally, you must have a hiring plan to be able to track progress to the plan. People analytics should not only be providing analytics end-to-end on critical hiring metrics to executives but should also be providing data to make more informed hiring plans in the first place. People analytics usually is good on the former, less so on the latter.

- **Regrettable Turnover**—Now we get into the people analytics bread-and-butter. Executives care about turnover insofar as it affects the business negatively. Basic turnover statistics are fine. More refined metrics, like cost of turnover, turnover projections, and turnover's impact on operational effectiveness, are better. Sometimes the business may even want turnover to go up, but never regrettable turnover.

- **Engagement and Productivity**—Only humanist executives will likely care about engagement for engagement's sake. People analytics teams are better served to effectively demonstrate the linkage between engagement and productivity. Once done, leading and lagging indicators of increased or decreased engagement and productivity will be requested by executives. People analytics can help executives "see around the corner" if these types of metrics are reported effectively.

Transforming from Cost-Center to Profit-Center—The Conclusion

The future of people analytics hinges on one fundamental shift—moving from a cost center to a profit center. For too long, people analytics has been positioned as a support function, providing insights without direct accountability for business outcomes. But as pressures on CEOs intensify—from boards, investors, and economic realities—data-driven workforce decisions are no longer a luxury. They are a business imperative.

To secure a permanent seat at the executive table, people analytics leaders must speak the language of business—ROI, margin impact, cost containment, and revenue growth—not just headcount reports and engagement scores. The C-suite priorities are clear, and people analytics is uniquely positioned to provide intelligence, risk assessments, optimization, and insights.

But delivering on these priorities requires more than dashboards and reports—it requires a shift in mindset.

The organizations that win the future will be those that harness people data as a competitive advantage—not just to report what has happened but to shape what happens next. This is where people analytics must go. If you can demonstrate direct financial impact, you won't have to fight for resources—they will come to you. The opportunity is there. The question is: *Will you seize it?*

For more resources on how to build competitive advantage via people analytics and quantify the value, please check out the following references:

- *Investing in People* by Wayne Cascio, John Boudreau, and Alexis Fink (2019)
- *Strategic Analytics* by Alec Levenson (2015)
- *The Workforce Scorecard* by Mark Huselid, Brian Becker, and Richard Beatty (2005)

Summary

This chapter outlines the fundamental shift required to transform people analytics from a cost center into a profit center. Historically, people analytics has been seen as a support function—offering insights without accountability for financial impact. However, for HR to be seen as a strategic business driver, people analytics must quantify its value, secure executive buy-in, and actively influence decision-making. The chapter presents a clear framework for achieving this transformation and ensuring that people analytics becomes an indispensable, revenue-generating function within an organization.

Key Takeaways

1 **The Scorekeeper Fallacy: Why People Analytics Lacks Power**
  People analytics has traditionally operated in a "scorekeeper" role—recording and reporting workforce data without making decisions or driving strategy. To move beyond this, analytics teams must step into decision-making roles and influence business outcomes.

2 **Profit Centers Drive Business Strategy—Cost Centers Don't**
  HR functions have often been positioned as cost centers, meaning they consume resources without being seen as revenue generators. People

analytics must break this perception by demonstrating how it contributes directly to financial success.

3 Resource Constraints Shouldn't Limit Impact
Many organizations assume that only large companies with massive budgets can run successful people analytics functions. This chapter debunks that myth, showing that value creation, not budget size, determines effectiveness.

4 The Five Simple Commitments to Proving ROI

   a. **Commit to action before starting a project**—Ensure stakeholders will use the insights before investing resources.

   b. **Embed ROI measurement into every initiative**—Don't wait until the end to quantify impact.

   c. **Quantify the value of all workstreams**—Tie every project to a business outcome.

   d. **Report impact annually**—Demonstrate cumulative ROI to secure continued investment.

   e. **Pay for your team 10 times over**—A strong people analytics function should generate at least 10× its operating cost in business value annually.

5 People Analytics Avoids Accountability—That Must Change
Many analytics teams fear financial accountability because they aren't natural profit owners like Finance. However, holding people analytics accountable for measurable ROI is the only way to secure long-term investment and credibility.

6 Faith, Science, and Utility: The Three Pillars of People Analytics Success

   o **Faith:** Leaders and employees must believe in the value of people analytics.

   o **Science:** Data and analytics must be rigorous, evidence-based, and accurate.

   o **Utility:** Insights must be actionable and drive meaningful business decisions. If any of these elements are missing, people analytics will fail to create lasting impact.

7 Moving from Reporting to Decision-Making
Reports and dashboards have no inherent value. Their only value comes from influencing decisions at scale. If analytics doesn't shape business strategy, it's just an exercise in reporting.

8 The CHRO as a Business Leader, Not Just an HR Expert
Former people analytics leader Dan George emphasizes that future CHROs must master analytics, business acumen, and financial strategy to secure their place in the C-suite.

9 Why Copying Best Practices Leads to Mediocrity
Many HR and people analytics teams blindly adopt "best practices" without considering their unique business context. True competitive advantage comes from customized, data-driven strategies, not just following industry trends.

10 The Path Forward: Rebuilding HR as a Data-Driven Function

- Shift from validating decisions to guiding them with data.
- Embed financial accountability into every HR initiative.
- Use first principles thinking to design talent strategies that directly support business goals.
- Stop measuring for the sake of measurement—focus on outcomes that impact revenue, cost, and productivity.

Transforming people analytics from a cost center to a profit center is not just possible—it is necessary. The most successful organizations will be those that embed analytics into business strategy, tie insights to financial impact, and shift HR from a reporting function to a revenue-driving force. People analytics teams that embrace this mindset won't have to fight for resources—they'll attract investment because they generate measurable business value. The opportunity is clear. The question is: Will you seize it?

References

Braunius, B. (2022). Strategic Neglect. CLC. churchleadershipcenter.org/strategic-neglect/ (archived at https://perma.cc/2ULQ-PCGJ).

Cappelleri, J. C., Jason Lundy, J. and Hays, R. D. (2014). Overview of Classical Test Theory and Item Response Theory for the Quantitative Assessment of Items in Developing Patient-Reported Outcomes Measures. *Clinical Therapeutics*, 36 (5), 648–662. doi.org/10.1016/j.clinthera.2014.04.006 (archived at https://perma.cc/G9UD-WKFT).

Cascio, W. F., Boudreau, J. W. and Fink, A. A. (2019). *Investing in People: Financial Impact of Human Resource Initiatives*. Society for Human Resource Management.

Change-effect. (2023). People Strategies Are Unnecessary Noise. change-effect.com/2023/07/24/people-strategies-are-unnecessary-noise/ (archived at https://perma.cc/4VWG-UC53).

Chris (2022). 'Turtles All the Way Down': The Problem of Infinite Regress. Home For Fiction – Blog. blog.homeforfiction.com/2022/04/11/infinite-regress/ (archived at https://perma.cc/VAD2-PUW5).

Cialdini, R. B. (2007). *Influence: The New Psychology of Modern Persuasion.* Morrow.

DC News. (2023). You're Leading People Analytics, Now What: The First Principles of Talent. Substack. https://directionallycorrectnews.substack.com/p/youre-leading-people-analytics-now-what-the-first-principles-of-talent-5b29e 450f213?r=ybtwi&utm_campaign=post&utm_medium=web&tried Redirect=true (archived at https://perma.cc/9RDM-45LC).

Gainsight Software. (2024). Technology Adoption Lifecycle | Gainsight. www.gainsight.com/glossary/technology-adoption-lifecycle/ (archived at https://perma.cc/WY5Z-MP2Z).

Huselid, M. A., Becker, B.E. and Beatty, R.W. (2005). *The workforce scorecard: Managing human capital to execute strategy.* Boston, Mass.: Harvard Business School Press.

Kenton, W. (2020). Black Box Model. Investopedia. Available at: www.investopedia.com/terms/b/blackbox.asp (archived at https://perma.cc/5AHN-3Z2Y).

Kiener, K. (2019). Crime Prevention & Criminal Justice Module 4 Key Issues: 3- The General Principles of Use of Force in Law Enforcement. UNODC. www.unodc.org/e4j/zh/crime-prevention-criminal-justice/module-4/key-issues/3--the-general-principles-of-use-of-force-in-law-enforcement.html (archived at https://perma.cc/SXL7-BYQV).

Levenson, A. (2015). *Strategic Analytics.* Berrett-Koehler Publishers.

Napper, C., Hines, S. and Blumberg, M. (2023). Competitive Advantage and The Value of Human Capital. Directionally Correct. www.podbean.com/eas/pb-429bd-151f703 (archived at https://perma.cc/KR8F-5GW6) Ep. 12.

Napper, C., Hines, S. and George, D. (2023). The CHRO Guide to What is Needed in the C-Suite. Directionally Correct. www.podbean.com/eas/pb-r8mqq-151f6d0 (archived at https://perma.cc/S5K8-L4UL) Ep. 61.

Napper, C., Hines, S. and Levenson, A. (2022). Strategic Analytics to Help People Analytics. Directionally Correct. www.podbean.com/eas/pb-mgepz-151f6fa (archived at https://perma.cc/G65Y-86EG) Ep. 20.

Sullivan, D. J. (2023). Opposition Research Improves Employer Branding, Recruiting and Retention (So that you win more side-by-side employer comparisons). Dr John Sullivan. drjohnsullivan.com/articles/opposition-research-improves-employer-branding-recruiting-retention/ (archived at https://perma.cc/47EB-EJU5).

Zaillian, S., Sorkin, A., Chervin, S. and Lewis, M. (2011). *Moneyball.* IMDb. www.imdb.com/title/tt1210166/ (archived at https://perma.cc/2X8J-42GQ).

3

Implementing People Analytics to Succeed: A Step-by-Step Guide

This chapter provides a practical guide to implementing a people analytics strategy, detailing how such initiatives can be structured to maximize business outcomes and ensure ongoing dominance in the industry.

"The more you know, the less you use"—Aristotle

People analytics is a field that can easily lead practitioners down endless rabbit holes chasing the form, fashion, and fad of whatever is in the zeitgeist of the moment. Every year, new trends, tools, and frameworks emerge—each promising to be the next big thing. It's easy to get caught up in the noise, chasing every branch of the proverbial "decision tree" of analytics in an effort to stay ahead. Yet, despite the ever-changing landscape, I keep coming back to the same foundational branches that consistently deliver value: *People analytics, behavioral science, workforce planning, and talent intelligence.* These aren't just trends—they are the core pillars of human capital strategy to bring value with HR data.

I call the relationships between these concepts the **Tree of Value.** While innovation is critical, true impact in people analytics comes not from chasing fads but from mastering and implementing these four fundamental disciplines. They serve as the roots that anchor data-driven decision-making, ensuring organizations don't just collect data but use it effectively to drive meaningful outcomes. In this chapter, we'll explore the origins of these branches—how they developed, why they matter, and, most importantly, how to implement them to create value and competitive advantage for your firm.

Origin Stories

People analytics is not just here to help our organizations go into a "managed decline." We are here for growth, prosperity, and productivity. We are here

FIGURE 3.1 The Tree of Value

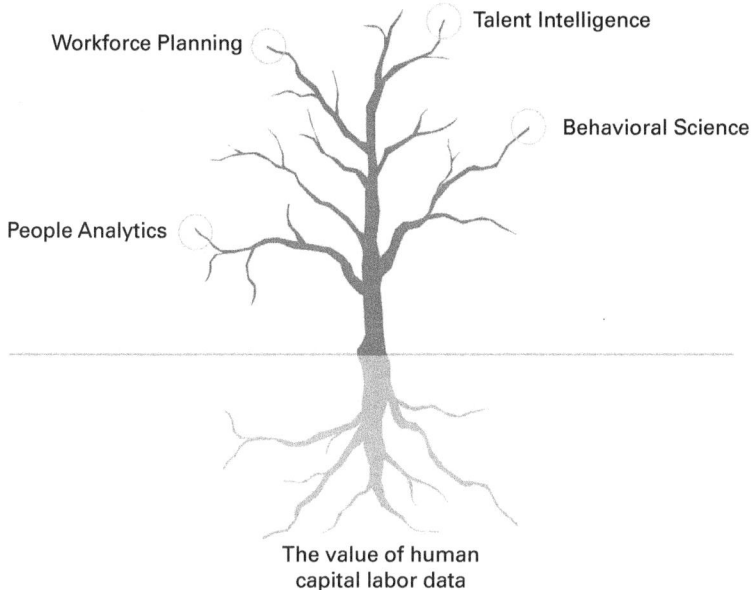

The value of human
capital labor data

to help businesses and the employees who work there thrive. If all we do is "count things" we are neither helping businesses succeed or fail. We are a thermometer not a thermostat in that instance. We cannot settle for this. To produce value, we must enact real change. The forebears of this profession knew that. Although a small minority in their organizations, the people who pioneered this profession knew that a mighty few could make a big difference in the competitive landscape of the businesses in which they resided. They called themselves a variety of titles and came from a diverse set of backgrounds. Some were called people analytics (or HR analytics, workforce analytics, talent analytics, etc.), but others were called workforce planning or talent intelligence.

Therefore, it might be helpful if we discussed: What are the roots of people analytics, talent intelligence, and workforce planning? And how did their origin stories impact the future of the field?

People Analytics

Many have attempted—and, in my opinion, failed—to define people analytics. In his dissertation research on people analytics leaders, Amit Mohindra (2021) uncovered over 200 different definitions of the field. Given this vast

FIGURE 3.2 The Tributaries of People Analytics, Talent Intelligence, and Workforce Planning

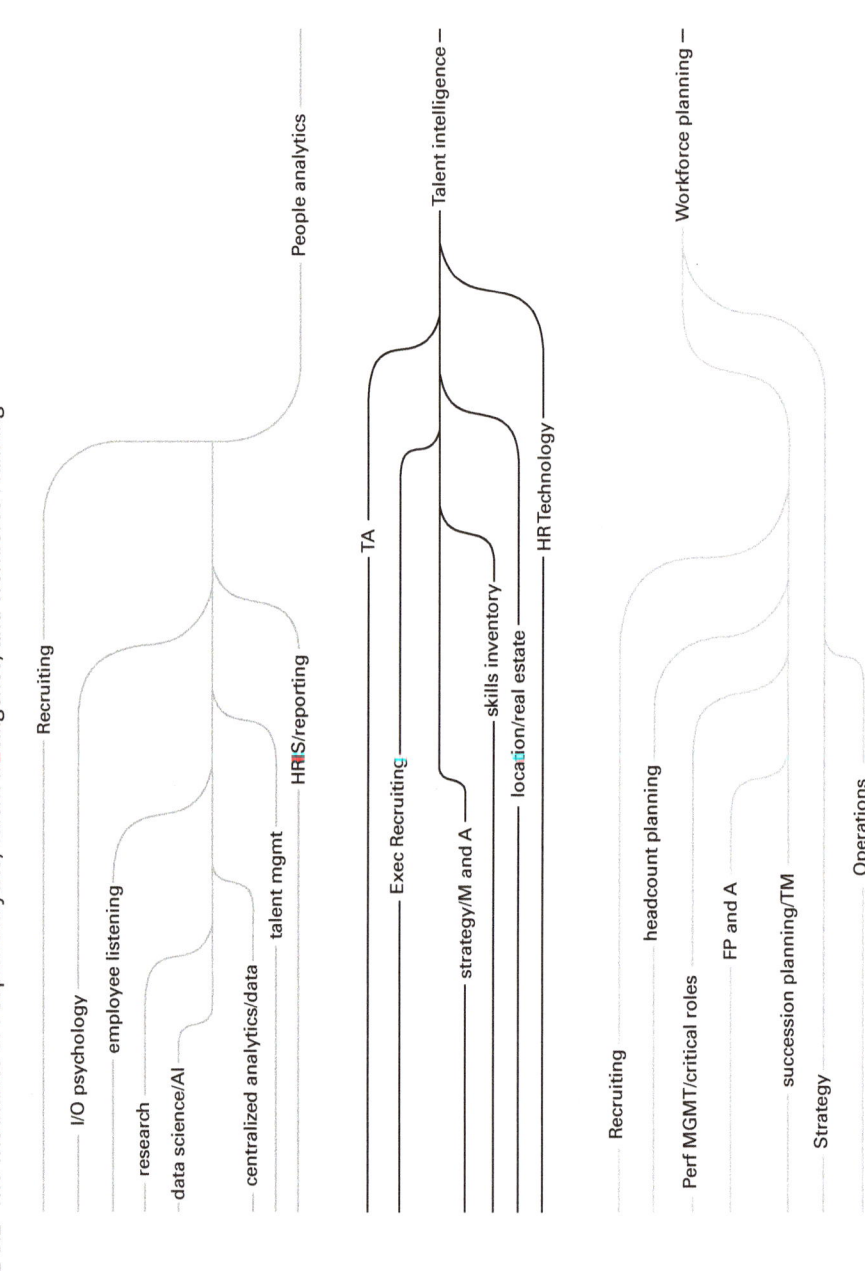

range of interpretations, for the sake of brevity, this book will define people analytics as "what is commonly referred to as people analytics by those who practice people analytics." A circular and arguably unsatisfying definition, but one that practitioners will intuitively understand. Perhaps a more useful approach than asking *"what is people analytics?"* is to explore *"where did it come from?"*—a question that provides far more insight into its meaning.

Much like the transistor, calculus, or other major discoveries, people analytics emerged from multiple origins, independently but around the same time. While no single moment defines its birth, through both formal research and informal conversations, a few key sources stand out as pivotal in shaping the field:

- **HR Technology**—As HR functions transitioned from paper to digital systems (e.g., HCMs, ATSs, and LMSs), the first wave of HR technology emerged. This digitization made vast amounts of employee data accessible, and with it came the need to justify the cost and effectiveness of these systems. The term *human capital* gained traction, signaling a shift toward leveraging data for strategic workforce decisions.

- **Recruiting**—Early people analytics efforts originated within recruiting teams seeking to optimize applicant funnels—tracking who applied, who was hired, and when. Simple counts evolved into sophisticated analytics on efficiency, quality, and hiring effectiveness, setting the stage for broader applications.

- **Reporting**—The rise of HR technology made employee data more accessible, but extracting insights required specialized expertise that many HR teams lacked. Organizations began hiring analysts to generate reports. Over time, some of these analysts sought to do more than just pull data— they wanted to leverage it for real organizational change.

- **Behavioral Science**—The expansion of fields like industrial-organizational (I/O) psychology and behavioral economics led many academically trained professionals to move beyond consulting and academia into corporate HR. Their expertise introduced scientific rigor, evidence-based practices, and advanced statistical methods into workforce decision-making. These professionals tackled topics such as predicting high-potential employees, analyzing workforce sentiment, and optimizing selection methods, all of which required access to HR data that was now more available than ever.

- **Data Science**—Early maturity models of people analytics often described prediction as the field's ultimate goal. As disciplines like data science, machine learning, and AI advanced, these methodologies began to permeate HR. The rise of "big data" enabled organizations to identify hidden patterns and extract novel insights from HR datasets. Tech companies were the first to heavily invest in these approaches, but the trend quickly spread to most large enterprises.

Ironically, even this long list of origin stories is not exhaustive. For instance, key military applications of workforce analytics are not covered in this text, though they played a crucial role in shaping the field. As Figure 3.3 indicates, the origin stories are complex due to different disciplines incorporating data to orient themselves to the past, present, or future, and the clear distinction between a preference for data internal to an organization or comparing internal data to external market conditions. What's clear, however, is that people analytics has always been an evolving discipline, shaped by diverse influences rather than a single defining moment. Yet, it was not the first attempt to derive value from human capital data—its precursor, workforce planning, laid much of the groundwork that people analytics would later build upon.

FIGURE 3.3 Mapping the Disciplines of the Tree of Value

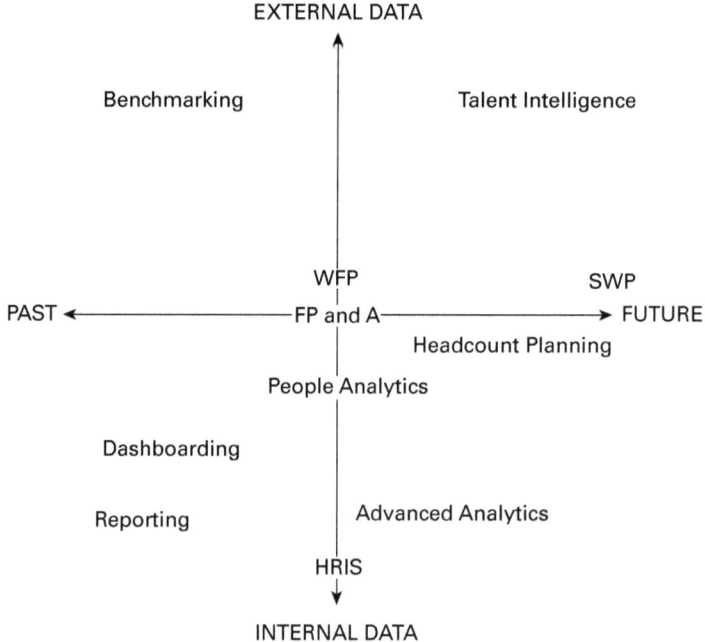

Workforce Planning

It's surprising how few people analytics practitioners have a strong under-standing of workforce planning, despite its deep interconnection with people analytics and its significantly longer history. As an example, I began my career in workforce planning, and over time, my title changed from work-force planning to workforce analytics, then HR analytics, and eventually people analytics (with "workforce intelligence" incorporated at one point as well). I often joke that while my title kept changing, my work remained the same.

So, what exactly is workforce planning? Unfortunately, the debate over its definition is just as contentious—if not more so—than the debate over people analytics. As the old joke goes: *"If you ask 50 different companies what workforce planning is, you'll get 50 different answers."* At its core, workforce planning is about matching the supply of workers with the demand for workers in a given company, organization, or industry. The field can be categorized into three key approaches:

- **Strategic Workforce Planning (SWP):** Focused on long-term planning, typically looking 3–5 years ahead to align workforce strategy with busi-ness objectives.

- **Operational Workforce Planning:** Near-term planning, usually covering a 90- to 180-day horizon, often used for high-volume hiring environments.

- **Headcount Planning:** The most tactical form of workforce planning, focused primarily on how many people need to be hired within the next fiscal year.

THE ORIGINS OF WORKFORCE PLANNING

Much like people analytics, workforce planning has evolved from multiple disciplines, often independently but in parallel. Below are some of its key origin stories:

- **Government**—The U.S. government has played an outsized role in devel-oping and formalizing workforce planning. Dating back to World War II, the armed forces pioneered workforce planning methodologies, which later expanded into the civil service, the Office of Personnel Management (OPM), and broader government workforce initiatives. These efforts laid the foundation for modern workforce planning through tools like O*NET, government labor surveys (e.g., Current Population Survey), the

Bureau of Labor Statistics, and Census workforce tracking. The government's emphasis on workforce readiness, job analysis, and forecasting labor supply and demand makes it the undisputed leader in workforce planning history.

- **Recruiting**—While the government was building structured workforce planning frameworks, corporate HR teams—particularly talent acquisition—were unintentionally developing their own version. As recruiting functions became more specialized, they took on headcount planning, analyzing turnover rates, external talent availability, competitor hiring trends, retirements, and business growth or contraction. Over time, recruiting leaders realized that effective hiring couldn't be done in isolation—it required workforce planning and people analytics integration.

- **Financial Planning and Analysis (FPandA)**—The Finance function has always been closely intertwined with workforce planning, though it has traditionally approached it from a budgeting perspective rather than a talent strategy perspective. FPandA teams often dictate how much headcount an organization can afford, making workforce planning a necessary component of annual financial forecasting. In many organizations, this leads to a sometimes tense relationship between workforce planning and FPandA, as finance holds the purse strings while HR attempts to forecast and plan talent needs.

- **Operations**—In high-volume hiring industries (e.g., call centers, distribution centers, fast food, retail), operational workforce planning emerged as a business necessity rather than an HR initiative. These industries quickly realized that if they couldn't forecast and optimize hiring throughput, their business would suffer from operational shortfalls. While HR functions eventually took notice, operations teams were the true pioneers of workforce planning in these environments. Interestingly, I/O psychologists played a major role in developing validated pre-hire assessments to optimize high-volume hiring, and their primary stakeholders were often business leaders, not HR.

- **Talent Management**—As HR Centers of Excellence (COEs) evolved in the 1980s and 1990s, talent management functions began overlapping with workforce planning. Concepts such as critical roles, succession planning, single points of failure, and skills inventories became common in boardroom discussions. While the government operationalized workforce planning, talent management elevated it to a C-suite priority.

FIGURE 3.4 Talent Intelligence Use Cases

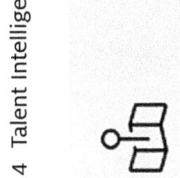

MARKET RESEARCH

How can we identify and recommend the best markets for talent?

TALENT SUPPLY

How can we determine the approximate supply of talent in an area?

MARKET COMPETITORS

How can we define the level of competition in a particular region?

COMPENSATION BENCHMARKS

How can we uncover salary insights to help inform pay decisions?

CURRICULUM EDUCATION

How can I determine what courses should be offered?

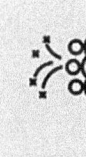

JOB and SKILL ARCHITECTURE

How can I normalize my roles and create skill profiles to analyze and compare my talent?

OPEN TAXONOMIES

How can I adopt a common language for skills and job titles to bring structure to my data?

STAFFING ANALYTICS

How do I sell a requisition to existing customers and what requisitions should I go after?

DEI BENCHMARKS

How do I compare to the market for diverse talent?

SCALABLE DELIVERY

How can I pipe external insights into my existing applications or dashboards?

SOURCE Lightcast (2024)

THE WORKFORCE PLANNING LANDSCAPE TODAY

This list of origin stories isn't exhaustive—for instance, performance management, promotions, and compensation structures also shape workforce planning. However, one key takeaway is clear: Workforce planning often evolved outside of HR rather than within it. Certain industries have consistently led the way in mature workforce planning practices:

- **Defense contractors, semiconductors, and consulting firms**—Their structured, pyramidal workforce models make long-term workforce planning easier and more predictable.

- **Oil and gas and technology companies**—These industries experience high volatility, requiring strong forecasting and scenario modeling to mitigate talent risks.

- **Healthcare, retail, and logistics**—These sectors struggle with supply–demand imbalances, making workforce planning essential for ensuring labor availability.

For organizations that don't fit neatly into one of these three categories, workforce planning can be more challenging to operationalize. This is where a different kind of intelligence is required—specifically, talent intelligence.

REAL-WORLD EXAMPLE

"Talent Intelligence as Competitive Intelligence" with Toby Culshaw, head of Talent Intelligence at Amazon and founder of the Talent Intelligence Collective

(Paraphrased for length from Ep. 63 of "Directionally Correct, A People Analytics Podcast")

The Role of Talent Intelligence in Strategic Decision-Making

Toby Culshaw, head of Talent Intelligence at Amazon and founder of the Talent Intelligence Collective, highlights the transformative potential of combining internal and external data to leverage talent intelligence as competitive intelligence. While much of talent intelligence today focuses on "location feasibility" (accounting for 60–70 percent of the work), Toby demonstrates how deeper applications—such as analyzing competitor structures, talent flows, and market pivots—can offer strategic advantages.

Competitive Intelligence Through Talent Data

Culshaw explains how talent intelligence can uncover critical insights about competitors. For example:

1 Organizational Structure Analysis: By examining external data, such as job postings and industry benchmarks, Culshaw's team identified a competitor with

an unusually large credit control function. This anomaly revealed a critical weakness: While the competitor's product was in high demand, they struggled to collect payments effectively, leading to cash flow issues. This insight, derived from talent data, informed strategic decisions during M and A due diligence.

2 Tracking Market Pivots: Monitoring job advertisements and talent movements enables organizations to anticipate competitors' strategic shifts. For example, Culshaw's team identified competitors launching new business lines or entering new markets before these moves were publicly announced, allowing leadership to proactively mitigate potential risks to market share or product lines.

The Value of Integrating Internal and External Data

By merging internal data (e.g., organizational benchmarks, workforce analytics) with external data (e.g., job ads, market benchmarks), talent intelligence teams provide a holistic view of industry trends and competitor strategies. This approach moves beyond traditional HR functions, positioning talent intelligence as a strategic asset for decision-making in areas like:

- Market Expansion: Determining the feasibility of entering new regions based on talent availability.

- R and D Investment Monitoring: Tracking where competitors are hiring for innovation-focused roles to infer future product developments.

- Organizational Health Assessments: Identifying inefficiencies or vulnerabilities in competitor structures that can inform competitive strategies.

Key Takeaways for Talent Intelligence as Competitive Intelligence

1 Beyond HR Functions: Talent intelligence is not just an HR tool—it's a strategic asset that informs business decisions like M and A, market entry, and competitive positioning.

2 Early Detection of Market Shifts: Analyzing external data, such as job postings and talent flows, can reveal competitors' strategic moves before public announcements, enabling proactive responses.

3 Organizational Insights: Examining competitors' organizational structures through talent data can uncover weaknesses, inefficiencies, or strategic vulnerabilities.

4 Integrating Internal and External Data: Combining internal workforce metrics with external market data provides a comprehensive view that supports strategic decision-making.

5 Moving Beyond Location Feasibility: While location analysis is a core function, talent intelligence teams must evolve to tackle broader competitive challenges.

Culshaw's insights illustrate how talent intelligence can extend far beyond traditional HR boundaries, providing organizations with actionable insights that enhance competitiveness and strategic foresight. By leveraging talent data creatively, businesses can make smarter decisions and stay ahead in a rapidly evolving market.

Talent Intelligence

If we were to play a game of *"which of these is not like the others,"* talent intelligence would stand out as distinct from workforce planning and people analytics. It is the newest discipline among the three, but its relevance in positioning HR as a truly strategic function cannot be overstated. As illustrated in Figure 3.4, talent intelligence spans multiple HR domains, including job architecture, labor market analytics, the shift toward skills-based organizations, and benchmarking capabilities.

Similar to workforce planning and people analytics, talent intelligence lacks a clear, universally accepted definition—in part because many HR technology vendors have co-opted the term to market their products. While this has fueled its visibility, it has also led to a fragmented understanding of what talent intelligence truly encompasses. At its core, talent intelligence is about extracting insights from internal and external data related to an organization's human capital, with a strong emphasis on labor market analytics. Talent intelligence can operate on both macro and micro levels:

- **Macro-level talent intelligence** examines labor market supply and demand across cities, countries, or regions to inform workforce strategies.
- **Micro-level talent intelligence** focuses on sourcing hard-to-find skills and individuals for specific roles or niche functions within an organization.

Much like people analytics and workforce planning, talent intelligence has evolved from multiple origins. Below are some of the key influences that shaped its development:

- **Executive Recruiting and Head-Hunting**—Not long ago, executive search firms were the gatekeepers of elite talent intelligence. A top headhunter's rolodex, their ability to reach exclusive senior candidates, and their deep insights into prevailing wages, employer reputation, and competitive hiring strategies were invaluable to corporations. These firms pioneered early talent intelligence databases, which are still used today to track high-potential executives and inform C-suite hiring strategies.
- **HR Technology Vendors and Consultants**—While the U.S. Bureau of Labor Statistics (BLS) and other government agencies provide rich labor market

data, their reports are often complex and difficult to interpret. Enter HR technology vendors: In the early 2000s, firms began aggregating and simplifying labor market data to provide benchmarks, job profiles, and insights into talent supply and demand. Early players such as Saratoga (HR benchmarks) and Lightcast (labor market insights, job profiles, and job postings) filled this gap, though adoption was slow. However, after the 2008 financial crisis, organizations rapidly embraced labor market analytics to inform workforce planning and recruiting. By the 2020s, the demand for talent intelligence skyrocketed, driven by skills shortages, demographic shifts, and changing immigration policies, as highlighted in Lightcast's "The Rising Storm" research report (2021).

- **Strategy, Mergers and Acquisitions (M and A)**—Business, much like war, is rarely a fair fight. Corporate strategy teams have long understood that human capital is a competitive advantage, even if it isn't always acknowledged explicitly. In M and A, private equity, and venture capital, the value of a company doesn't only reside in its financials—it's in its people. If a competitor employs the only 20 engineers in the world with expertise in a breakthrough technology, acquiring that company outright might be more effective than trying to outcompete them. Likewise, understanding why one company consistently outperforms another in EBITDA, margin, or stock price often boils down to hidden factors, such as human capital insights. Investors and insiders know this—and if you want to operate at a strategic level, so should you.

- **Corporate Real Estate**—Unlike other talent intelligence origin stories, corporate real estate has historically been considered an operational function, not a strategic one. In the early 2000s, however, business leaders began recognizing location strategy as a critical workforce variable. Trends such as corporate headquarters relocations (e.g., to lower-cost states), globalization (e.g., outsourcing to developing nations), and skill-based geographic expansions (e.g., opening R and D centers in tech hubs) reshaped corporate real estate decision-making. The impact was so significant that when one company moved, competitors often followed—as seen in the highly publicized Amazon HQ2 selection process, which was driven almost entirely by talent intelligence data.

THE GROWING ROLE OF TALENT INTELLIGENCE

Talent intelligence was not born out of HR—it was born out of necessity. Organizations realized that understanding talent at a macro and micro level was a competitive differentiator, not just an HR function. In today's business landscape, talent intelligence is no longer optional—it is a critical input for workforce strategy, hiring, and business decisions. Companies that fail to integrate labor market insights into their planning risk falling behind competitors who leverage talent intelligence to identify new opportunities, mitigate risks, and optimize their workforce. As we move forward, talent intelligence will continue to evolve, blending elements of AI, people analytics, workforce planning, and business strategy. Those who master it will not only shape the future of HR but also influence the strategic direction of their entire organization.

REAL-WORLD EXAMPLE

"Who's Going to Do the Work and The Demographic Drought" with Ron Hetrick, Vice President, Staffing Strategy and Senior Labor Economist at Lightcast

(Paraphrased for length from Ep. 93 of "Directionally Correct, A People Analytics Podcast")

Leveraging Labor Market Data for Strategic Talent Decisions

Ron Hetrick, Vice President of Staffing Strategy and Senior Labor Economist at Lightcast, sheds light on how organizations can harness labor market data to make smarter talent decisions in an era defined by shifting demographics and evolving skills. Lightcast's platform integrates internal organizational data with external labor market insights to provide a 360-degree view of talent availability, competition, and emerging trends. This approach helps organizations answer critical questions, such as where to locate new offices, how to set competitive compensation, and how to align talent strategies with broader labor market conditions.

The Rising Storm

"The Rising Storm: Building a Future-Ready Workforce to Withstand the Looming Labor Shortage" is a 2024 report by Lightcast that examines the impending labor shortage in the United States. The report projects a deficit of six million workers by 2032, primarily due to Baby Boomer retirements, declining birth rates, and reduced labor force participation. Industries such as healthcare, hospitality, and service sectors are expected to be most affected. To address this challenge, Lightcast recommends strategies including globalization, automation, immigration, and workforce development, emphasizing the need for immediate action from both public and private sectors to build a future-ready workforce.

Mapping the Global Labor Market

Ron describes Lightcast's ambitious goal of mapping the global labor market by analyzing over 10 million job postings daily. This data provides insights into:

1   Emerging Skills and Roles: Tracking trends such as the rise of "prompt engineering" following the surge in generative AI applications like ChatGPT. Lightcast identifies how new skills appear across industries and job roles, often revealing unexpected areas of demand.

2   Labor Market Trends: Highlighting where talent is concentrated, what skills are in demand, and how job titles and requirements vary by region and industry.

3   Talent Strategies: Offering companies detailed recommendations on where to find the right talent, which markets to target, and what combinations of skills are gaining traction.

Demographic Challenges and Skill Fluidity

Hetrick underscores the importance of external data in navigating labor shortages driven by demographic shifts. Many companies have traditionally relied on internal data to inform their talent strategies, but Lightcast broadens this perspective by offering external benchmarks and market intelligence. This is particularly important in a fluid skills market where the emergence of new roles, such as those related to generative AI, can quickly reshape demand.

For example, when "prompt engineering" emerged as a desirable skill, Lightcast immediately integrated it into its skills library, allowing companies to track its trajectory across industries and roles. The ability to pinpoint such trends in real-time enables organizations to stay competitive in attracting and retaining talent.

Integrating Internal and External Perspectives

A key takeaway from Hetrick's insights is the power of combining internal organizational data with external labor market information. By doing so, companies can move beyond insular decision-making and develop comprehensive strategies that address both immediate needs and long-term workforce planning. This integration allows organizations to:

- Identify talent hotspots: Find optimal locations for new offices or call centers based on skill availability and economic conditions.

- Benchmark compensation: Set competitive pay rates by comparing internal salary data with external market benchmarks.

- Adapt to market trends: Adjust hiring strategies to align with emerging skills and shifting labor market dynamics.

Key Takeaways for Addressing Workforce Challenges

- 360-Degree Talent View: Combining internal and external data provides a holistic view of talent availability, enabling smarter decisions.

- Tracking Emerging Skills: Real-time monitoring of new skills and roles, like "prompt engineering," helps companies stay ahead in competitive markets.

- Global Labor Market Mapping: Leveraging advanced analytics and taxonomies allows for apples-to-apples comparisons of talent trends across regions and industries.

- Proactive Workforce Planning: External data offers critical context to internal insights, helping organizations anticipate demographic and economic shifts.

- Skill Fluidity: Regular updates to skills libraries ensure organizations remain agile and responsive to evolving market demands.

Hetrick's work at Lightcast exemplifies how labor market data can empower organizations to navigate demographic challenges, skill shortages, and rapid technological change. By leveraging data to anticipate trends and align strategies, companies can remain competitive in an increasingly dynamic and uncertain labor landscape.

Implementing People Analytics

Referring back to the quote at the beginning of this chapter—*"The more you know, the less you use"*—it becomes clear that people analytics, workforce planning, and talent intelligence all share a common purpose at their core. Despite their different origins and evolving definitions, they are all ultimately about extracting value from human capital data to drive better decision-making. This data takes many forms—it can be employee records, candidate pipelines, or workforce trends emerging from high schools, universities, and vocational programs. It can scale from national demographics and birth rates down to individual cognitive and behavioral traits. In reality, all of this is people analytics—a discipline that extends far beyond traditional HR functions and into the very fabric of how organizations compete and thrive.

Now that you understand the foundation, the next step is implementation. In the following sections, we will explore how to build a people analytics strategy that drives measurable impact, the critical components you need to establish, and how to position your organization to win with data-driven human capital decisions. But first, we must acknowledge the organizational realities that people analytics teams must face; namely, the necessary roles of navigating organizational politics and power.

REAL-WORLD EXAMPLE

"How to Navigate Organizational Politics" with Amit Mohindra, People Analytics leader at Takeda, Apple, Mckesson (among others) and Stanford Lecturer

(Paraphrased for length from Ep. 29 of "Directionally Correct, A People Analytics Podcast")

The Unavoidable Role of Politics in People Analytics

Dr. Amit Mohindra, a veteran people analytics leader and lecturer, emphasizes the necessity of understanding and embracing organizational politics to succeed as a people analytics leader. Based on insights from his research and experience, he shares that many founding people analytics leaders regret underestimating the influence of politics in their roles. The misconception that people analytics can operate as a neutral and objective function often leaves leaders unprepared for the political dynamics that shape decision-making in organizations.

Understanding Organizational Politics

Dr. Mohindra defines organizational politics as the attainment, retention, and expansion of power, which includes decision-making rights, budget control, and resource allocation. To thrive in a politically charged environment, people analytics leaders must:

1   Map Power Structures: Identify both formal and informal power dynamics. While organizational charts reveal formal roles, informal influencers—such as gatekeepers or key collaborators—often wield significant control.

2   Recognize the Power of Data: People analytics teams often have access to data that can shape decisions, expose inefficiencies, and influence the perception of leaders. This makes them powerful, even if they don't initially hold much formal authority.

3   Use Data Responsibly: Leaders must carefully decide which analyses to prioritize, how to frame results, and what narratives to present, as these choices can significantly impact organizational outcomes.

The Strategic Importance of Playing the Game

Amit underscores the need for people analytics leaders to engage in the "game" of organizational politics. Neutrality is a myth; by the nature of their role, people analytics leaders are stakeholders with influence over key decisions. To protect their teams and ensure their insights drive positive change, leaders must:

• Build alliances and identify supporters who will advocate for their work.

- Stay vigilant about detractors or individuals who may seek to undermine their efforts.
- Understand that higher levels of the organization are often populated by individuals adept at navigating political games.

The Pitfalls of Neglecting Organizational Politics

Failing to navigate organizational politics can have significant consequences, including the risk of people analytics teams being deprioritized or disbanded. Mohindra notes the common adage, "If you're not at the table, you're on the menu," emphasizing the importance of maintaining visibility and influence within the organization. Recent trends of people analytics teams being downsized illustrate what can happen when leaders fail to secure their place in the broader organizational power structure.

Key Takeaways for Navigating Organizational Politics

1 Embrace Politics: Recognize that organizational politics is inevitable and learn to navigate it effectively.
2 Map Power Dynamics: Understand both formal and informal power structures to identify key influencers and gatekeepers.
3 Leverage Data Strategically: Use your access to data thoughtfully to frame narratives and influence decision-making.
4 Build Alliances: Foster relationships with advocates and protect your team's influence within the organization.
5 Stay Vigilant: Be aware of potential detractors and the competitive nature of higher organizational levels.

Balancing Power and Objectivity

While people analytics is inherently seen as data-driven and objective, Mohindra argues that subjectivity is unavoidable due to the choices made during analysis and reporting. Leaders must wield this power responsibly, ensuring that their insights are used ethically and for the greater good of the organization.

Dr. Mohindra's insights highlight the nuanced role of people analytics leaders as both analysts and political players. To succeed, they must combine technical expertise with political savvy, leveraging their unique position to drive meaningful change while navigating the complex realities of organizational life.

Power

To succeed in people analytics, one must possess more than technical expertise—knowledge, credibility, influence, and power are all essential. It is not enough to generate insights; one must also have the authority and influence to act on them. At its core, politics is about power—the ability to shape decisions, drive action, and influence outcomes. People analytics does not simply walk into HR and take over; gaining influence requires strategic acumen, persuasion, and a level of finesse that many analytical professionals may not naturally possess. This does not mean people analytics leaders should run HR or control the organization (although one day they could), but they should be the CHRO's most trusted advisor, guiding decision-making (or even making decisions ourselves), diagnosing problems, and driving change. This is not someone else's responsibility—it is ours.

Ask yourself: Do you have power? Are you truly able to make business decisions, or are you merely a "decision support" function? True power is the ability to act, not just advise. In most organizations, people analytics does not wield decision-making authority and often retreats when the opportunity arises. This must change. When you have the chance to step up and own a decision, take it. Making decisions and taking responsibility can be transformative—not just for your career, but for the future of people analytics as a business-critical function rather than an internal support service.

Jeffrey Pfeffer, a leading scholar on power dynamics in the workplace, makes this clear in his book 7 *Rules of Power* (2022). One of his rules? **"Use your power."** Yet, few people analytics leaders ever hear this advice. Use your power. Most new people analytics teams start from a position of powerlessness. The formation of a new team is a particularly vulnerable time, as existing HR stakeholders may see people analytics as a threat—a function that has something they don't: Data. This can lead to resistance, skepticism, and even active pushback from those who fear being exposed, outshined, or losing influence.

So, how can you tell if you truly have power? If you do, you likely already know it. But if you're uncertain, here are some key indicators:

SIGNS OF POWER IN PEOPLE ANALYTICS

- **P and L Responsibility**—Owning revenue or cost centers gives you authority.
- **Headcount and Team Size**—The larger your team, the more influence you hold.

- **Budget and Resources**—Having financial control signals power within the organization.
- **Technology Ownership**—Controlling critical tools and data infrastructure strengthens influence.
- **Direct Reporting to the CHRO**—A clear sign of strategic importance.
- **"Seat at the Table"**—Being involved in executive decision-making rather than just supplying data.

If you lack these signs of power, the real-world experiences of Amit Mohindra and Matthew Jackson provide valuable insights on how to build, sustain, and leverage power in people analytics. In the next section, we will explore how to bridge this gap and position people analytics as a driver of business success, rather than a passive observer.

REAL-WORLD EXAMPLE

"Power, Game Theory, and Using Network Analysis for Influence" with Matthew Jackson, Stanford Economics Professor

(Paraphrased for length from Ep. 89 of "Directionally Correct, A People Analytics Podcast")

Understanding Power Through Networks

Dr. Matthew Jackson, a Stanford Economics Professor, explores the dynamics of power and influence through the lens of game theory and network analysis. He emphasizes that power is not just about the number of connections or followers one has but about the strategic position one occupies within a network. Jackson defines power as the ability to get others to act in ways they wouldn't otherwise—what he describes as influencing behavior or coordinating actions.

The Medici Case: A Lesson in Network Power

One of Jackson's key examples is the rise of the Medici family in 15th-century Florence. Despite not being the wealthiest or most politically connected family, the Medicis strategically positioned themselves as connectors within the social and economic networks of Florence. They facilitated marriages and business dealings that placed them at the center of a star-like network, where many families were connected only through them.

In contrast, their rivals formed tight, clique-like structures with limited external connections. This centrality gave the Medicis extraordinary influence, allowing them to act as brokers of favors and coordinators of actions. Their ability to connect otherwise disconnected groups made them indispensable, establishing their dominance in Florentine society.

Power Beyond Social Media Metrics

Dr. Jackson critiques the modern view of power as defined by social media metrics like followers. While social media influencers may have large audiences, their ability to drive coordinated action or meaningful change is limited. True power, Jackson argues, comes from the ability to influence critical nodes in a network—key individuals or groups who can enact change. This highlights the importance of understanding the quality, rather than just the quantity, of connections.

Applications in Organizational Networks

In organizational contexts, Jackson emphasizes the importance of identifying and leveraging network dynamics to influence change. For example:

- Connector Roles: Employees who act as bridges between different departments or teams often wield disproportionate influence by enabling collaboration and information flow.
- Strategic Coordination: Leaders who can rally diverse groups to act toward a common goal hold a distinct form of power that goes beyond hierarchical authority.
- Network Mapping: Using network analysis, organizations can identify individuals or groups with strategic positions, such as connectors or brokers, to enhance decision-making and change initiatives.

Key Takeaways for Leveraging Networks in People Analytics

1 Power is Positional: True influence stems from strategic positioning within a network, not just the number of connections.
2 Connector Advantage: Acting as a bridge between disconnected groups enhances one's ability to coordinate and influence.
3 Network Analysis in Organizations: Mapping organizational networks reveals key players and potential bottlenecks, informing leadership strategies.
4 Beyond Metrics: Influence is about driving action and coordination, not just visibility or audience size.
5 Historical Lessons in Power: The rise of the Medici family demonstrates how network centrality can translate into real-world influence and dominance.

Practical Implications for People Analytics

People analytics leaders can apply Jackson's insights to better understand organizational power dynamics. By leveraging network analysis, they can identify influencers, design more effective communication strategies, and foster collaboration across silos. This approach not only enhances decision-making but also empowers organizations to navigate complex social and professional networks effectively.

Dr. Jackson's work underscores the strategic value of network positions and offers a roadmap for organizations to harness these insights to build influence, drive change, and achieve strategic goals.

People Analytics Strategy

"A strategy is a carefully crafted plan to murder your competition"—Jeff Lyons (Porter, 1985)

As illustrated by Figure 3.5, your people analytics strategy should always be anchored in business strategy. It must first align with your organization's broader strategic priorities and then fit within the overarching HR strategy before being formulated. However, strategy is not crafted in a vacuum—the structure, resources, and operating model of the people analytics team will determine what is possible. A small, underfunded team cannot execute the same strategy as a large, well-resourced one, and failing to account for these constraints will lead to unrealistic expectations and unmet objectives.

For leaders tasked with building and scaling a people analytics function—assuming you have the headcount, budget, and executive support to do so—the challenge often lies in determining where to focus investments. People analytics operating models vary widely, influenced by industry (high-margin vs. low-margin businesses), organizational structure (centralized vs. embedded analytics teams), and company size (smaller firms often have leaner teams). To design an effective strategy, begin with a fundamental question:

- *What is people analytics' true purpose in this organization?*

The answer depends on the specific context of your company. Table 3.1 gives an example from a large, global retailer, demonstrating how its people analytics strategy is structured to meet its unique business needs.

The Myth of a "One-Size-Fits-All" Operating Model

In recent years, there has been a push to standardize people analytics operating models—an effort that, while well-intentioned, risks oversimplification and commoditization. Every consulting firm and thought leader seems to offer a universal framework, yet real-world application rarely follows these blueprints exactly.

FIGURE 3.5 Strategy and Operating Model

| Business Strategy | HR Strategy | People Analytics Strategy | Infrastructure and Operating Model |

What Table 3.1 offers as an illustrative example is that a successful people analytics function must be highly customized—a bespoke, organization-centric approach rather than a "cookie-cutter" solution. No two organizations should have identical people analytics strategies. At best, they may "rhyme" with one another, but rigidly copying another company's model will only lead to mediocre, least-common-denominator outcomes.

This need for customization is rooted in principal agent theory (Harvard Law School, 2024)—a long-standing concept in organizational behavior. People analytics teams must ensure their goals align with the success of the organization rather than pursuing pet projects or research initiatives with limited business impact. This requires a delicate balance between delivering short-term value and executing long-term strategic initiatives. It also means responding to the demands of the CHRO, the business, and internal stakeholders, even when those demands challenge existing priorities.

TABLE 3.1 Example Strategy from a Large, Global Retailer

Business Strategy	HR Strategy	People Analytics Strategy	Infrastructure and Operating Model
• Expand the business to dominate online retail • Vertically integrate operations • Quantify everything • Focus on execution	• Decentralize HR into every vertical • Focus on raising the bar for talent • Quantify everything HR does • HR must have operational mindset	• Decentralize people analytics into every business unit • Quantifying the value of talent is paramount • Create the mechanisms to quantify all HR processes • Produce analytics focused on throughput and efficiency	• All data infrastructure must be built and maintained in-house • The data models and dashboards must be tailored to the HR processes they support • All tasks that can be automated, should be • Minimal consultation and human touch provided

The "Laggard's Advantage" in People Analytics

What does a high-performing people analytics team look like? The best advice for strategy formulation is to deliver value to the business first and evolve as you grow. Think of the mobile phone revolution in Africa. Many regions in Africa skipped the technical debt of 2G and 3G networks and jumped straight to 4G (Trustonic, 2022). This phenomenon—sometimes called the laggard's advantage (Jahanmir and Lages, 2015)—allows organizations to bypass inefficient legacy processes and leap directly to best-in-class solutions. For people analytics leaders, the lesson is clear:

- *"Be world-class where your company needs you to be world-class, and ignore everything else—until you have the time and resources to expand."*

In other words, avoid overproduction (building complex models no one uses) and avoid underproduction (failing to deliver meaningful insights). The key is to focus only on what works and drives impact. But how do you measure what's working? The answer lies in three pillars:

1 **Science**—You cannot claim something works unless you can scientifically prove it.
2 **Data**—Without data, there is no way to validate impact.
3 **Execution**—Insights without action are wasted effort.

The Role of Leadership & Operating Principles

An often-overlooked factor in the success of a people analytics team is the leadership style and operating principles of its leader. Through experience, a set of guiding principles has emerged, helping teams focus on what truly matters and driving value quickly.

PEOPLE ANALYTICS OPERATING PRINCIPLES
- **Alignment**—Always prioritize what is best for the business; sometimes, you must go slow to go fast.
- **Scalability**—Build solutions that serve 100 people once, rather than solving the same problem 100 times.
- **Innovation**—Commit to continuous improvement—personally and professionally—by striving to be 1 percent better every day.
- **Credibility**—Always measure twice and cut once; lost credibility is nearly impossible to regain.

These principles embody the core tenets of evidence-based practice (Briner, 2019)—the foundation upon which a strong people analytics team should operate. A successful people analytics strategy is not about following a predefined playbook—it is about deeply understanding your organization, aligning with business needs, and executing with precision. The path to success is not in chasing the latest trends, but in focusing on where you can create the most value, as quickly and effectively as possible.

In the next section, we will explore how to operationalize this strategy— from designing the right team structure to securing executive buy-in and delivering measurable business impact.

Three Key Problems Your Strategy Must Solve

For a people analytics strategy to be truly effective, it must address and resolve three fundamental challenges that every team encounters:

1 **Building the Business Case Before Showing Results (The Chicken-and-Egg Problem)**

2 **Balancing Demand vs. Supply of People Analytics**

3 **Data Infrastructure and Engineering**

Without a clear solution for these obstacles, even the most well-crafted strategy will struggle to succeed.

The Chicken-and-Egg Problem

"Why can't HR provide the data we need, when every other function can?"

If you've ever heard this question directed at your people analytics team, you're not alone. Many teams launch their strategy with the goal of securing more funding, headcount, and technology—only to face pushback from leadership when justifying these investments. The common challenge is:

"Why should we invest more in people analytics when we haven't yet seen measurable ROI yet?"

And so, the paradox emerges—the team needs resources to deliver impact, but impact must be proven before securing resources. Unlike Finance, Marketing, or IT, which are often better funded and more deeply embedded in decision-making, people analytics is frequently understaffed, underfunded, and expected to prove value across too many workstreams with too few resources.

So how do you break this cycle? The most effective solution is to demonstrate undeniable business value before rolling out your strategy. Even if it means stretching existing resources, prioritizing high-impact projects, or deprioritizing legacy reporting tasks, delivering tangible ROI early is crucial.

For example, at a previous organization, I committed to bringing in $50 million in business value before introducing a new people analytics strategy. With that kind of dollar figure on the table, business and HR leaders were eager to hear the vision and invest in the future of the function. You should consider making a monetary commitment as a part of your key KPIs or OKRs in the coming year. By doing so, you have a commitment to accountability of your results, while at the same time you will get the attention of business leaders and many will be more willing to invest in your projects.

Balancing Demand vs. Supply

In Amit Mohindra's seminal article, "Three Laws of Workforce Analytics" (2015), he outlines the rapid rise in demand for people analytics once the team starts delivering results. His First Law states:

- *"The demand for workforce analytics grows exponentially."*

Once a people analytics function proves its value, demand surges—but supply (i.e., resources and headcount) rarely keeps pace. People analytics teams are unlikely to scale the team proportionally to meet growing demand, and suddenly, a team that once struggled for credibility is now drowning in requests. This challenge is largely shaped by operating model choice. Most people analytics teams fall into one of three models:

- **Services Model**—Functions as an internal consulting or shared-services group, responding to analytics requests from HR and business units on a case-by-case basis.
- **Platform Model**—Focuses on building and maintaining a self-service data infrastructure, enabling leaders across the organization to access and analyze people data independently.
- **Product Model**—Treats analytics like a scalable product, delivering dashboards, tools, and insights as pre-packaged solutions for stakeholders.

Of these, the services model struggles the most with demand vs. supply, as it relies on manual execution. Teams are continuously reacting to requests, leading to burnout and bottlenecks. The platform and product models are better suited for scalability, but they introduce another challenge—HR leaders often want high-touch, consultative support, and that is something automated tools may lack. The solution? A hybrid approach:

- **Prioritize scalable solutions**—Automate repeatable requests, freeing up bandwidth for strategic work.

- **Align analytics priorities with business needs**—Focus on the most impactful projects, not just the loudest requests.

- **Embrace "strategic neglect"**—Learn to say no to low-value work. Paradoxically, the ability to decline requests increases the power and stature of the people analytics function.

Data Infrastructure & Engineering

Regardless of how sophisticated your strategy sounds, if your data infrastructure is weak, execution of projects will likely fail. Most smaller people analytics teams lack:

- A modern data lake or enterprise-grade data warehouse
- A business intelligence (BI) tool that integrates with HR data
- Adequate data engineering talent to handle ETL (Extract, Transform, Load) processes, data pipelines, and system integrations

This creates a major bottleneck—teams want to deliver insights but are forced to spend excessive time on data wrangling, cleaning, and troubleshooting. The problem is compounded by the shortage of skilled data engineers—they are expensive, in high demand, and HR often struggles to attract top technical talent. Many new people analytics teams fall into the trap of spending years building out infrastructure before delivering value—a fatal mistake.

The key to not falling victim to this cycle is balancing immediate impact with long-term investment.

- **Short-term solution:** Layer data quality and infrastructure improvements into ongoing business needs, rather than treating infrastructure as a standalone project.

- **Long-term solution:** Embed the costs of a Gen AI-ready, future-proof data infrastructure into your ROI projections, ensuring leadership sees data engineering as a business-critical investment rather than an HR expense.

But remember—you don't have two years to prove your worth. The clock is ticking, and delaying impact is not an option. Every successful people analytics strategy must overcome these three core obstacles:

- **Breaking the Chicken-and-Egg Problem**—Deliver impact before asking for resources.

- **Managing Demand vs. Supply**—Build scalable solutions and set boundaries to prevent burnout.

- **Solving the Infrastructure Challenge**—Deliver insights early, while gradually building data maturity.

Mastering these challenges will ensure that your strategy is not just theoretical—but a practical, business-aligned roadmap that drives measurable impact. In the next section, we will dive deeper into how to operationalize this strategy, ensuring that people analytics, workforce planning, and talent intelligence are positioned as an indispensable driver of business success.

REAL-WORLD EXAMPLE

"The Mighty Ducks Problem of People Analytics" with Rob Stilson, employee listening expert at HP

(Paraphrased for length from Ep. 48 of "Directionally Correct, A People Analytics Podcast")

The "Mighty Ducks" Dilemma in People Analytics

Dr. Rob Stilson, an employee listening expert at HP, introduces the "Mighty Ducks" problem in people analytics, drawing an analogy to the 1992 Disney movie. The film's producers faced a key decision: Should they train actors to play hockey or hockey players to act? Similarly, Rob argues, the field of people analytics faces a challenge in deciding whether to train businesspeople to understand research or train researchers to operate effectively in business environments.

Balancing Speed and Rigor in People Analytics

Dr. Stilson highlights a growing concern in people analytics: the business world's demand for fast, scalable, and actionable insights often prioritizes speed over rigor. This has led to a trend where organizations rely heavily on data scientists who may lack foundational knowledge in critical areas like industrial-organizational (I/O) psychology, bias mitigation, or legal defensibility.

Organizations sometimes attempt to "fill the gap" by offering data scientists short seminars on topics like bias or adverse impact. However, Stilson argues that this checkbox approach undermines the depth of expertise needed to ensure ethical, defensible, and people-focused analytics.

The Call for Researchers to Evolve

To address this challenge, Rob advocates for I/O psychologists and people analytics professionals to embrace programming, automation, and large-scale data practices. By developing technical skills and staying current with advancements in data science, researchers can drive conversations about ethical and impactful analytics rather than risk being sidelined.

The Branding Issue in People Analytics

Stilson also points to a branding problem in the field. Many professionals in analytics roles are unaware of the contributions of I/O psychologists or even the definition of people analytics. This lack of awareness limits the influence of those with a deep understanding of human behavior and organizational dynamics. Stilson emphasizes the need for the field to better communicate its value to broader audiences.

Key Takeaways from the "Mighty Ducks" Problem

1   Training Matters: Organizations must decide whether to focus on training researchers in business skills or teaching business professionals about research rigor.

2   Technical Skills for Researchers: I/O psychologists and people analytics professionals should adopt technical skills like programming and automation to remain competitive and relevant.

3   Avoiding Check-the-Box Solutions: Ethical and legally defensible analytics require more than cursory training for data scientists; deep expertise in bias mitigation and people-focused analysis is essential.

4   Field Branding: People analytics needs better branding to highlight its unique contributions and ensure it is recognized as a critical function.

The Path Forward

Stilson's insights serve as a wake-up call for people analytics professionals to adapt and evolve. By bridging the gap between rigorous research and scalable business practices, the field can ensure it remains a vital contributor to organizational decision-making. Much like the Mighty Ducks team, success requires striking the right balance between technical skills and a focus on human impact.

The Role of Workforce Planning & Talent Intelligence in a People Analytics Strategy

As mentioned earlier, people analytics, workforce planning, and talent intelligence are all branches from the same tree of adding value to businesses through the strategic use of human capital labor data for competitive success.

Workforce Planning

Workforce planning plays a fundamental role in ensuring that an organization has the right people, with the right skills, in the right place, at precisely the right time to achieve its strategic objectives. It involves anticipating both current and future talent demands, identifying gaps in capability or capacity, and developing targeted solutions to fill those gaps. When integrated with people analytics, workforce planning becomes even more powerful, allowing organizations to predict headcount needs, proactively address succession challenges, and optimize workforce costs. By combining historical HR data with predictive modeling, businesses can reduce guesswork and make data-driven decisions about hiring and resource allocation.

Talent Intelligence

Talent intelligence complements workforce planning by focusing on external data sources—such as labor market trends, competitor insights, and broader industry benchmarks from providers such as Lightcast—to provide a holistic view of the talent landscape. This external perspective enables organizations to monitor new skill requirements, shifts in competitive hiring practices, and emerging roles critical for future success. For example, a surge in demand for AI-related skills could alert an organization to invest more heavily in employee upskilling programs or refine its campus recruitment strategy. By analyzing these external signals, organizations can refine their internal workforce plans and remain agile in a rapidly changing market.

REAL-WORLD EXAMPLE

"Talent Intelligence and Is the Future Skills-Based?" with Mark Hanson, VP of Skills Strategy and People Analytics at Lightcast

(Paraphrased for length from Ep. 83 of "Directionally Correct, A People Analytics Podcast")

What is a Skills-Based Organization?

Mark Hanson, VP of Skills Strategy and People Analytics at Lightcast, highlights the growing trend of skills-based organizations as a transformational approach to talent management. Unlike traditional models that focus on job titles and descriptions, a skills-based approach dives deeper into the specific capabilities required to perform a job effectively. This level of precision enables organizations to better manage talent, anticipate workforce needs, and adapt to rapidly evolving demands.

Why Adopt a Skills-Based Approach?

Mark argues that a skills-based approach is becoming essential due to several factors:

1   Shrinking Talent Pools: As global talent markets tighten, companies can no longer rely on large pools of qualified candidates. Precision in screening, matching, and developing talent is critical.

2   Emerging Roles: New technologies like ChatGPT and large language models are creating entirely new job categories, requiring organizations to identify and develop previously unknown skills.

3   Future-Readiness: Understanding the granular skills within the workforce helps organizations anticipate future demands and align their strategies accordingly.

The "Build, Buy, Borrow, Bot" Framework

A skills-based approach enables companies to implement the "Build, Buy, Borrow, Bot" framework for talent management:

- Build: Identify and develop skills within the existing workforce through targeted learning and development programs.

- Buy: Recruit talent externally for specialized or in-demand skills that cannot be developed internally.

- Borrow: Leverage contingent labor or temporary staff to meet short-term needs.

- Bot: Automate repetitive or low-value tasks, freeing up human talent for higher-value work.

This framework provides a structured way to optimize talent strategies, especially in a tight labor market where every resource counts.

The Role of Skills in Workforce Transformation

Hanson emphasizes that while skills are a critical part of modern talent management, they are not a silver bullet. Skills must work alongside other mechanisms, such as:

- Competency Models: Skills complement rather than replace broader frameworks that capture behaviors, attitudes, and contextual factors.
- Assessments and Interviews: Measuring and validating skills through rigorous assessments and structured interviews remains crucial for effective hiring and development.

The Impact of Emerging Technologies on Skills

Hanson highlights how tools like ChatGPT have reshaped the skills landscape, creating demand for roles like "prompt engineers" and accelerating the adoption of AI in daily work. These technological advances highlight the need for organizations to quickly adapt to new skill demands and integrate emerging technologies into their talent strategies.

Key Takeaways for Skills-Based Talent Management

1 Precision Over Vague Descriptions: Moving from general job descriptions to precise skills allows organizations to better match talent to roles.
2 Adapting to New Technologies: The rapid emergence of new tools and roles, such as those related to generative AI, requires a dynamic approach to identifying and building skills.
3 Integrated Talent Strategies: The "Build, Buy, Borrow, Bot" framework provides a comprehensive method for managing talent in a complex and competitive labor market.
4 Skills Are Part of a Larger System: While skills are crucial, they must be integrated with competency models, hiring practices, and assessments to create a holistic talent strategy.
5 Future-Proofing the Workforce: Organizations that adopt skills-based strategies are better positioned to anticipate and respond to the changing demands of the workforce.

Hanson's insights make a strong case for the future of skills-based organizations. By adopting this approach, companies can not only navigate current challenges but also position themselves to thrive in an era of continuous technological and economic change.

We're Better Together

When workforce planning and talent intelligence operate in tandem with people analytics, organizations gain a powerful, end-to-end view of the talent pipeline. On one hand, workforce planning highlights how best to deploy existing employees and address internal skill shortages. On the other, talent intelligence reveals the real-time dynamics of external talent pools, allowing organizations to adjust their hiring and development strategies in response to market shifts. This unified approach mitigates risks like skill mismatches and unexpected talent shortages, ultimately safeguarding business continuity and performance. People analytics serves as the wrapper around all three to combine the internal lens, the external lens, the competitive landscape and the analytics sophistication necessary to add business value.

Collectively, workforce planning and talent intelligence are indispensable components of a forward-looking people analytics strategy. By combining internal HR data, predictive models, and external market insights, organizations can align their human capital decisions with long-term business goals. Moreover, this alignment fosters collaboration across HR, finance, operations, and executive leadership, ensuring that talent investments are not just reactive but serve as a competitive advantage. Through a strategic blend of workforce planning and talent intelligence, companies can proactively manage their workforce, stay attuned to industry disruptions, and drive sustainable growth.

To successfully implement a people analytics strategy that encompasses both workforce planning and talent intelligence, you must integrate internal HR data with external labor market insights to provide a comprehensive view of your talent landscape—including within your data infrastructure and architecture. As you begin to align your workforce planning approach to the business and HR strategies, ensure that internal data sources—such as HCMs, ATS, LMS, employee listening, digital exhaust (see page 223)—and external data sources—such as labor market information, industry benchmarks, and competitor analyses—create a robust, data-driven foundation for decision-making. This does not happen organically. It must be intentional with the business and HR strategies in mind. This integrated perspective will allow your people analytics function to proactively anticipate skill shortages, identify emerging roles critical for future success, and optimize recruiting and retention strategies.

Lastly, prioritize data governance and technology infrastructure to handle the increased complexity of combining internal and external data streams.

Develop clear processes for cleansing, maintaining, and validating data so that your insights remain reliable and actionable for all stakeholders. Concurrently, embed user-centric design into analytics products—whether you operate in a Services, Platform, or Product operating model—so that business leaders, HR partners, and front-line managers can easily derive value from dashboards and predictive models. By maintaining a balanced focus on both quick wins (e.g., addressing immediate workforce planning needs) and strategic, long-term enhancements (e.g., building advanced talent intelligence capabilities), your people analytics strategy can remain both nimble and enduring, even under the pressures of demand growth and infrastructure challenges.

Summary

Implementing a successful people analytics strategy requires more than just collecting data—it demands a structured approach that ensures business alignment, scalability, and long-term impact. This chapter outlines the foundational disciplines of people analytics, workforce planning, and talent intelligence, showing how they work together to create value. It also provides practical guidance on overcoming common challenges, such as securing executive buy-in, navigating organizational politics, and building scalable analytics capabilities.

Key Takeaways

1 **Master the Core Disciplines, Not Just Trends**
   People analytics success does not come from chasing every new tool or fad. Instead, it is built on four foundational disciplines:
   o **People Analytics** (HR data analysis and decision-making)
   o **Behavioral Science** (applying psychology to workforce decisions)
   o **Workforce Planning** (aligning talent supply with business needs)
   o **Talent Intelligence** (using labor market insights for strategic advantage)

2 **Shift from Passive Reporting to Proactive Impact**
   Many organizations treat people analytics as a thermometer—passively measuring HR trends—when it should be a thermostat, actively shaping talent and business strategies.

3 Understand the Origin Stories of People Analytics
People analytics has evolved from multiple fields, including:

o **HR Technology:** The shift from paper records to digital data storage created vast new datasets.

o **Recruiting Analytics:** Early efforts focused on optimizing hiring processes.

o **Behavioral Science and I/O Psychology:** Brought scientific rigor and predictive modeling to HR.

o **Data Science:** Introduced AI, machine learning, and predictive analytics into HR decision-making.

4 The Role of Workforce Planning: Aligning Talent with Business Strategy
Workforce planning is the oldest and most structured people analytics discipline, originally developed in government, finance, and operations-heavy industries. It involves three key approaches:

o **Strategic Workforce Planning:** Long-term forecasting (3–5 years ahead).

o **Operational Workforce Planning:** Mid-term planning (90–180 days).

o **Headcount Planning:** Annual budgeting and hiring strategy.

5 Talent Intelligence: Turning External Data into Competitive Advantage
Unlike traditional HR analytics, talent intelligence focuses on external labor market data, including:

o Competitor hiring trends and workforce structure.

o Skills supply and demand in specific geographies.

o Emerging talent trends and market shifts.

6 Navigating Organizational Politics in People Analytics
Data is power, and people analytics teams must navigate internal politics wisely to secure influence. Strategies include:

o **Mapping Power Structures:** Identifying key decision-makers and informal influencers.

o **Building Executive Alliances:** Securing high-level champions for analytics initiatives.

o **Using Data Responsibly:** Framing insights in ways that drive action without creating resistance.

7 **People Analytics Must Transition from Decision Support to Decision-Making**

Traditional people analytics teams operate as "scorekeepers," passively reporting metrics. To increase impact, they must:

o Drive strategic decision-making, not just provide data.

o Secure a seat at the table by demonstrating financial impact.

o Make business cases that tie people analytics to revenue growth.

8 **Overcoming the Three Biggest Challenges in People Analytics Implementation**

o **The Chicken-and-Egg Problem:** People analytics teams must prove their value before they receive investment—this means demonstrating impact without additional resources at first.

o **Balancing Demand vs. Supply:** Once credibility is established, demand for analytics grows exponentially. Teams must scale effectively without burnout.

o **Data Infrastructure and Engineering:** A strong data foundation is critical. Many teams fail by focusing too much on reporting and not enough on data quality, automation, and self-service analytics.

9 **The "Laggard's Advantage": Skipping Inefficient Legacy Practices**

Just as some regions skipped landlines and adopted mobile networks immediately, new people analytics teams can bypass inefficient legacy models by adopting:

o Self-service analytics platforms.

o Cloud-based data architecture.

o AI-driven workforce insights.

10 **Aligning People Analytics with Business Strategy**

A people analytics function should not exist in isolation—it must be directly tied to business priorities. Successful teams:

o Start with business challenges rather than HR problems.

o Embed ROI measurement into every project.

o Ensure all analytics insights lead to direct action.

People analytics is not just about data—it's about power, influence, and business impact. Teams that master workforce planning, talent intelligence, and data-driven decision-making will become strategic drivers of competitive advantage. The opportunity is clear: those who implement scalable, business-aligned people analytics strategies will shape the future of HR and workforce management.

References

Briner, R. (2019). The Basics of Evidence-Based Practice. cullenscholefield.com/wp-content/uploads/2020/07/Briner%202019%20The-Basics-of-Evidence-Based-Practice.pdf (archived at https://perma.cc/K6NX-7RLJ).

Harvard Law School (2024). Principal Agent Theory. PON—Program on Negotiation at Harvard Law School. www.pon.harvard.edu/tag/principal-agent-theory/ (archived at https://perma.cc/VE7S-LAVE).

Jahanmir, S. F. and Lages, L. F. (2015). The Lag-User Method: Using Laggards as a Source of Innovative Ideas. *Journal of Engineering and Technology Management*, 37, 65–77. doi.org/10.1016/j.jengtecman.2015.08.002 (archived at https://perma.cc/M4SS-KE2V).

Lightcast (2021). The Rising Storm, a Lightcast Demographic Drought … Lightcast. lightcast.io/resources/research/the-rising-storm (archived at https://perma.cc/X7X9-42WM).

Lightcast (2024). Talent Intelligence Where Internal and External Data Intersect. Lightcast.io. lightcast.io/why-lightcast/talent-intelligence (archived at https://perma.cc/K6SR-NS8R).

Mohindra, A. (2015). The Three Laws of Workforce Analytics. LinkedIn. www.linkedin.com/pulse/three-laws-workforce-analytics-amit-mohindra (archived at https://perma.cc/GX5W-L99G).

Mohindra, A. (2021). Adoption of People Analytics: The Role of Founding People Analytics Leaders. Dissertation, University of Southern California.

Napper, C., Hines, S. and Culshaw, T. (2023). Talent Intelligence as Competitive Intelligence. Directionally Correct. www.podbean.com/eas/pb-v2wr8-151f6ce (archived at https://perma.cc/R472-HZ2R) Ep. 63.

Napper, C., Hines, S. and Hanson, M. (2024). Talent Intelligence & Is the Future Skills-Based? Directionally Correct. www.podbean.com/eas/pb-mer7w-159868e (archived at https://perma.cc/Z98H-XDSF) Ep. 83.

Napper, C., Hines, S. and Hetrick, R. (2024). Who's Going to Do the Work & The Demographic Drought. Directionally Correct. www.podbean.com/eas/pb-p32sz-1628c2f (archived at https://perma.cc/3LDL-A6SY) Ep. 93.

Napper, C., Hines, S. and Jackson, M. (2024). Power, Game Theory, and Using Network Analysis for Influence. Directionally Correct. www.podbean.com/eas/pb-dfpbd-15ddecc (archived at https://perma.cc/3XCK-6MJ2) Ep. 89.

Napper, C., Hines, S. and Mohindra, A. (2022). How to Navigate Organizational Politics. Directionally Correct. www.podbean.com/eas/pb-nwtdd-151f6f1 (archived at https://perma.cc/29JC-QF4F) Ep. 29.

Napper, C., Hines, S. and Stilson, R. (2023). The Mighty Ducks Problem of People Analytics. Directionally Correct. www.podbean.com/eas/pb-jvy69-151f6dd (archived at https://perma.cc/7EZD-BTRN) Ep. 48.

Pfeffer, J. (2022). *7 Rules of Power*. BenBella Books.

Porter, M. E. (1985). *Competitive Advantage: Creating and Sustaining Superior Performance: With a New Introduction*. New York: Free Press.

Trustonic. (2022). The Benefits of Cell Phone Migration to 4G in South Africa. www.trustonic.com/opinion/cell-phone-migration-in-south-africa-the-benefits-of-migrating-to-4g/ (archived at https://perma.cc/NP8G-PA69).

U.S. Bureau of Labor Statistics (2024). U.S. Bureau of Labor Statistics. https://www.bls.gov/ (archived at https://perma.cc/FF4H-5PR4).

PART TWO

Gen AI

4

Introduction to People Analytics and Generative AI Use Cases

This chapter sets the stage by defining key concepts and discussing the transformative potential of integrating AI with people analytics. It emphasizes how these technologies not only reshape HR and business strategies but also drive significant improvements in efficiency and operational effectiveness.

> *(Disclaimer: The world of Gen AI is changing quickly. This the best attempt at writing something evergreen in regard to the use of Gen AI in people analytics.)*

> *"You seek a great fortune, you three who are now in chains. You will find a fortune, though it will not be the one you seek. But first… first you must travel a long and difficult road, a road fraught with peril. Mm-hmm. You shall see thangs, too wonderful to tell."*—Blind Seer, *Oh Brother Where Art Thou?* (2000)

In the first section of the book, we dedicated much of the time to focusing on how to add value to the business using people analytics in a very tangible and pragmatic manner. In this section of the book, we expand upon that notion to include how advances in Gen AI will help augment, but also disrupt, how people analytics will gain and maintain strategic relevance for HR and the business more generally. But, before we get started it is necessary for you to be familiar with some words and terms to better understand Gen AI.

What is Generative AI?

Generative AI refers to artificial intelligence systems that can create new content—such as text, images, code, and even audio and video—rather than merely analyzing or classifying existing data. This technology took a major leap forward with the development of transformers, a type of deep learning architecture introduced in 2017 by Vaswani et al. in their paper "Attention Is All You Need." The key innovation of transformers is the attention mechanism, which allows models to weigh the importance of different words in a sequence, enabling them to capture long-range dependencies more effectively than earlier AI models like recurrent neural networks (RNNs). This breakthrough paved the way for large language models (LLMs) like OpenAI's ChatGPT series, which upon its release became the fastest adopted technology in history, using massive datasets and billions of parameters to generate human-like responses across diverse topics.

For people analytics, generative AI represents a paradigm shift. Traditionally, HR and workforce data were analyzed through structured reports and statistical models, requiring manual interpretation and significant effort to extract insights. With generative AI, organizations can leverage LLMs to automate analytics, predict workforce trends, and generate actionable insights in real-time. AI-powered chatbots and copilots can assist HR professionals in drafting job descriptions, summarizing performance reviews, and even offering personalized career development suggestions, but Gen AI is about so much more than just chatbots. As AI continues to advance, forward-thinking and innovative AI governance will be crucial to ensuring positive decision-making in the workplace—an area where people analytics professionals will play a key role in shaping the future.

Primer: LLMs, RAG, and AI Agents

Large Language Models (LLMs) are sophisticated AI models that can understand and generate human language. They are trained on massive datasets of text, images and code, learning to identify patterns and relationships between words and phrases. This allows them to perform a wide range of tasks, including generating text, translating languages, writing different kinds of creative content, and answering your questions in an informative way.

Retrieval-Augmented Generation (RAG) improves LLMs by fetching relevant information from internal sources during text generation, ensuring more accurate and contextually relevant responses. RAG systems consist of a retriever that searches for relevant information and a generator that utilizes this information to produce the output.

AI Agents are autonomous entities that perform actions on behalf of users, often based on received inputs or objectives. They can range from simple rule-based systems to sophisticated models that leverage deep reinforcement learning. Agentic RAG combines RAG with AI Agents, where agents control or request specific retrieval tasks in real-time, providing more control over the retrieval process. This allows for more dynamic and contextually aware interactions, as agents can actively decide which information is relevant and adjust the generation process accordingly (Hassan and Hassan, 2024).

In essence:

- **LLMs** are the brains, understanding and generating language.
- **RAG** provides LLMs with the memory and local knowledge base.
- **AI Agents** give LLMs the ability to act upon that knowledge and interact with the world and other agentic systems.

In the MIT Sloan Review "Practical Guide to Gaining Values from LLMs" (Ramakrishnan, 2024), getting a return from generative AI investments requires a systematic approach to analyzing appropriate use cases. Leveraging LLMs and Gen AI in people analytics requires a clear strategy centered on high-impact use cases and thoughtful replacement of existing systems. To extract tangible value, organizations must focus on areas where Gen AI excels, such as automating repetitive tasks, uncovering hidden insights in unstructured data, and generating prescriptive recommendations. By targeting specific

TABLE 4.1 Practical Guide to Understanding Gen AI

Feature	LLMs	RAG	AI Agents
Core Function	Understand and generate human language	Enhance LLMs with external knowledge	Act autonomously to achieve goals
Key Components	Neural networks, massive datasets	Retriever (finds relevant info) and Generator (produces output)	Perception, action, decision-making
Focus	Language processing and generation	Improving LLM accuracy and context	Goal-oriented behavior & interaction
Key Benefit	Powerful language capabilities	Accesses real-time information	Automates tasks and makes decisions
Example	ChatGPT, Gemini, Claude	Enhancing search engines, customer service	Self-driving cars, virtual assistants

applications, businesses can realize immediate efficiency gains and enhanced decision-making capabilities in people analytics.

Investing in Gen AI for people analytics should also prioritize the four operating principles of people analytics mentioned in the last chapter: Alignment, Scalability, Innovation, and Credibility. Start with projects aligned to demonstrate value quickly and secure buy-in from key business stakeholders. As you scale, it's also critical to align your investments to innovative efforts for the business, such as leveraging Gen AI to solve strategic challenges like reducing turnover or improving workforce agility. Lastly, ensure that your models are trained on high-quality data while adhering to ethical guidelines around privacy and error mitigation to ensure the credibility of your work. By embedding these technologies into how you operate rather than treating them as standalone tools, organizations can unlock the full potential of Gen AI, transforming how HR teams analyze data, make decisions, and drive business outcomes.

Trends in People Analytics Skills 2015–Present

The integration of Gen AI into HR represents a revolutionary shift, requiring people analytics teams to evolve their capabilities and lead the transformation. However, technological shifts are only as effective as the skills of the practitioners implementing them. If people analytics is to drive real change, it must develop the technical fluency necessary to embed AI, automation, and data-driven decision-making into HR's core functions. This raises an important question: Have people analytics professionals meaningfully advanced their technical skills over the past decade? The answer, unfortunately, is more complex and negative than you might hope.

Using Lightcast skills data, my research focused on isolating the major themes in the trend of skill gains in the technical areas of people analytics by practitioners over the last 10 years. The findings were stark. Overwhelmingly, practitioners acquired skills in Microsoft Excel and Research. At first glance, this may seem like progress—after all, more people analytics professionals are developing research and Excel-based analytical capabilities than just pulling reports out of HR tools. But is this truly an advancement of the function, or are we simply reinforcing the traditional HR skill set with better data hygiene? While research and Excel skills are valuable, they do not push the boundaries of analytics for which this book recommends.

Figure 4.1 shows the trend in people analytics skills from 2015 through the beginning of 2025. Here are the top findings:

- **Microsoft Excel and Research skills** are the two most common skills and have also seen two of the largest increases in frequency between 2015 and 2025.

- **Data Visualization and SQL skills** saw the two largest increases in frequency between 2015 and 2025, making them the third and fourth most common skills in people analytics today.

- **Data Science, R, and Python skills** had very few adopters in 2015, and their growth over the last decade has been nearly identical. By 2025, these skills rank fifth, sixth, and seventh in frequency.

- **Machine Learning and Artificial Intelligence skills** were practically nonexistent in 2015 and have had the lowest growth and lowest prevalence in 2025 compared to the other skills on this chart.

FIGURE 4.1

Advanced skills haven't been widely adopted by people analytics practitioners

Share of people analytics practitioners in the US with specific skills

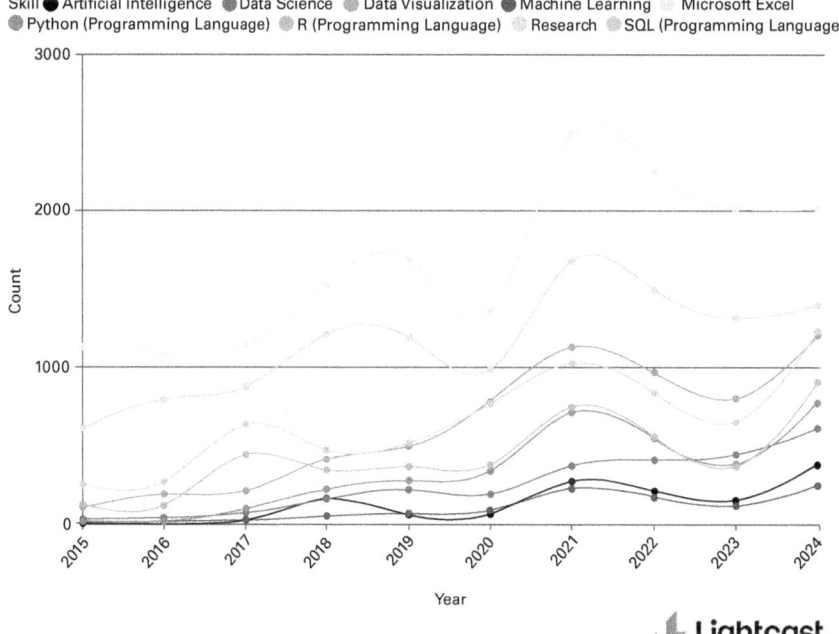

Skill ● Artificial Intelligence ● Data Science ● Data Visualization ● Machine Learning Microsoft Excel
● Python (Programming Language) ● R (Programming Language) Research ● SQL (Programming Language)

SOURCE Lightcast

The fact that people analytics has primarily grown in Research and Excel skills over the last decade is deeply concerning. While it's encouraging to see increased adoption of SQL and Data Visualization skills, one could argue that this simply reflects the expansion of *dashboarding* as the dominant interpretation of people analytics—a trend that has regretfully defined the last ten years. While dashboards and reporting have their place, they are not the future of the function, nor even where we should be in the present. They are a reflection of where we've been, not where we need to go.

The most transformative skills—Python, R, Data Science, and, more importantly, Machine Learning and AI—remain the lowest in frequency and have experienced some of the weakest gains over the last decade. **That is a major red flag.** If people analytics is to evolve into a truly strategic function capable of driving business outcomes, we must accelerate adoption of these advanced capabilities. We are on the cusp of an AI-driven revolution in HR, yet our field has done little to prepare for it. This book will be the catalyst for changing that trend. The time to start is now.

If we do not see these skill trends dramatically shift over the next three years, people analytics will fall behind—and once that happens, there may not be a path to catch up. The people analytics function is at risk of being perceived as a basic reporting and dashboarding function rather than a true driver of business impact. This is a make-or-break moment, and without a significant investment in developing machine learning, AI, and coding expertise, we risk becoming obsolete in an era where every other business function is rapidly advancing.

Put simply: We must eat our own dog food. If we expect HR to evolve into a more data-driven, AI-powered function, then people analytics must lead the way—not lag behind. What we see today just isn't cutting it, and frankly, it wasn't what I expected at all before conducting this research. The time for incremental progress is over. If we don't take radical steps now, we won't be the ones shaping the future of work—we'll be struggling to keep up with it.

How to Add Value in People Analytics with Gen AI

The future is no longer on the horizon—it's here. Generative AI is already transforming people analytics, augmenting existing capabilities, accelerating insights, and, in some cases, outright replacing traditional methods. Early research, such as Noy and Zhang (2023), suggests AI can increase knowledge worker productivity by up to 50 percent, while Sapient Insights (Sapient

Insights Group, 2025) reported that companies leveraging Gen AI in HR have seen a 7–8 percent lift in business outcomes. This shift presents both an opportunity and a challenge for people analytics professionals. To stay relevant and add value, practitioners must evolve their roles. The key? Challenging the status quo.

- Don't accept processes simply because "that's how they've always been done."
- Ask better questions. Challenge assumptions. Find new and better ways to operate.
- Push the profession forward by embracing innovation and positioning people analytics as a driver of strategic decision-making.

People analytics is still a relatively young field with room for improvement. Those who take an active role in shaping its future will ensure the discipline remains indispensable. This brings us to a critical question: What role will people analytics practitioners play in a Gen AI-driven future?

I would argue that two roles will be critical: **The Inquisitor and The Change Agent.**

The Changing Value Chain of People Analytics

As you can see in Figure 4.2, at its core, people analytics follows a three-step process:

1 Ask a strong research question or hypothesis.
2 Analyze data to diagnose, predict, or explain an answer.
3 Take action based on insights to create real-world impact.

FIGURE 4.2 The Simplified People Analytics Cycle

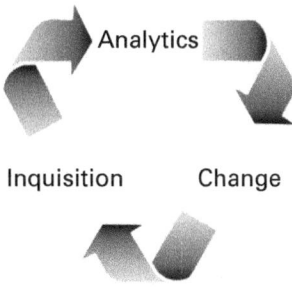

Analytics

Inquisition   Change

Historically, Step 2 (data analysis) was the most difficult and differentiated skill in people analytics. Teams invested heavily in advanced analytics, visualization, data science, and statistical modeling because these skills were rare and highly valued. But here's the reality: generative AI is rapidly automating and commoditizing Step 2 (DC News, 2023). With AI models like ChatGPT and Claude, you can already:

- Load and clean datasets in minutes.
- Generate visualizations and dashboards automatically.
- Write Python or SQL code for advanced modeling.
- Develop predictive models and deploy analytics solutions with minimal human input.

And the capabilities are only improving. Within a few years—likely by 2026, if not sooner—the most technically demanding step in people analytics, the analysis step, will become the easiest. The very thing that once made people analytics unique—data analysis—is becoming a commodity. So where does that leave people analytics professionals? The answer lies in the two steps AI cannot replace: Asking the right business questions and driving real change. This is where The Inquisitor and The Change Agent come in.

REAL-WORLD EXAMPLE

"Is Machine Learning Better than Human Intuition?" with Jennifer Diamond Acosta, Global Skills Strategy Lead at Kenvue

(Paraphrased for length from Ep. 85 of "Directionally Correct, A People Analytics Podcast")

The Power of Human Intuition in Predictive Analytics

Dr. Jennifer Diamond Acosta, Global Skills Strategy Lead at Kenvue, provides a compelling case for the enduring value of human intuition in predictive analytics. During a SIOP symposium in 2015, Acosta's organization conducted a simple exercise: Asking managers to predict how likely an employee was to quit within the next year. Surprisingly, the managers' intuition outperformed sophisticated machine learning models designed to predict turnover and retirements.

This example highlights that human intuition, informed by direct experience and context, can rival or even surpass data-driven predictions. However, Acosta emphasizes that intuition and machine learning aren't adversaries—they're complementary tools. When combined, they offer a stronger, more nuanced approach to prediction.

The Complementary Nature of Intuition and Machine Learning

Jennifer underscores the value of integrating human judgment with algorithmic insights. While machine learning excels at identifying patterns and processing vast datasets, human intuition provides context, nuance, and an understanding of factors that may not be captured in data. For instance, managers might pick up on subtle behavioral cues or organizational dynamics that a machine learning model would overlook.

The key, Acosta argues, is to treat human intuition and machine learning as components of a unified system. By combining predictions from both sources, organizations can achieve stronger, more reliable forecasts. This hybrid approach not only improves accuracy but also ensures that predictions are relevant to the business context.

Key Takeaways for Balancing Intuition and Machine Learning

1 Value of Human Intuition: Human intuition, informed by direct experience, can rival sophisticated machine learning models in predictive accuracy.

2 Complementary Strengths: Combining intuition and machine learning leads to stronger and more nuanced predictions by leveraging the strengths of both approaches.

3 Focus on Relevance: Predictive models should prioritize understanding the *why* behind employee behavior, not just the *who*.

4 Hybrid Prediction Models: Integrating human and machine insights reduces redundancy and explains more variance, improving overall decision-making.

Acosta's insights illustrate that in the age of AI, human intuition remains a vital asset in people analytics. By blending intuition with machine learning, organizations can create a more comprehensive and actionable understanding of workforce dynamics, ensuring that predictive analytics delivers meaningful value.

The Inquisitor

Who is going to ask the right business questions? Who is simultaneously knowledgeable enough to be at the nexus point of the three key points of people analytics: The business context and problems, how HR functions, and the idiosyncratic and challenging nature of HR data? People analytics teams, of course.

With Gen AI in people analytics, the onus is on the researcher to solve the "problem of induction" when it comes to scientific inquiry. The "problem of induction," articulated by philosopher David Hume, questions the justification for assuming that future events will resemble past experiences, which is the foundation of inductive reasoning. It highlights that there is no logical necessity linking past observations to future occurrences, making inductive inferences inherently uncertain. People analytics functions must become a function of synthesis of the business context, HR context, and HR data capabilities and be the "first mover" in determining what business problems to tackle, what research questions to ask, and what hypotheses to test. People analytics practitioners are best positioned to do this. We must be the inquisitors. We must ask the right questions and be in-tune with the business.

This is serious business. The future of the relevance of people analytics to the business depends upon it, and it is why I makes the argument that the leader of people analytics will be best positioned to be the Chief of HR (i.e., CHRO or CPO) in the future. It's not that people analytics leaders *want* to be the head of HR—because if you ask them, they don't—it's that the skillset necessary to be the CHRO in the age of AI will necessitate the skills that only the leaders of people analytics and HR technology maintain. This includes:

- Knowledge of HR data to solve business problems
- Knowledge of the applications of Gen AI
- Knowledge of technology and systems of how to apply the first two bullets to create processes and workstreams that enable HR strategy to execute business strategy

In the past, the HR business partner (or sometimes compensation) was the straightforward path to the C-Suite of HR. As a result of Gen AI, I would argue those functions will be the least-equipped to handle the transformation that HR, and all business functions, are going through in the next few years. If heads of HR thought "digital transformation" was difficult, they are in for a whole new level of disruption as the maturation of AI HR technology takes over the HR function. However, leaders of HR technology are not usually equipped to take up the mantle to lead the HR function due to their lack of business acumen, lack of interest in power and influence, and their general disinterest in HR leadership more broadly.

However, it is not enough for people analytics to assume a leadership postion in HR through asking the right business questions; nor is it enough to analyze the data to understand the problem.

The Change Agent

Someone must be willing to take action based on the results. Who is going to take action based on the results of the commoditized data analysis that is coming? The Change Agent.

Luminaries of people analytics, Alexis Fink and Alec Levenson (Levenson, Stevenson, and Fink, 2021) say that people analytics and OD must be two sides to the same coin to be effective. People analytics experts are professionals at diagnosing organizational problems with data, and OD professionals are experts at taking the diagnosis and influencing and enacting real change in the workplace to make a difference. Therefore, people analytics needs to expand its skillset to assume more OD-like responsibilities—and/or likely hire some OD people as well—and acquire the core competence of change management as Gen AI proliferates the HR function.

As was said in Chapter 1, people analytics must be more than merely "decision support." It must become comfortable and acquire skill at wielding power and influence in the HR function. People analytics should be at the forefront of making real business decisions, owning the consequences, and putting change into action. We must be the change agents. And, we must acquire the power to bring about that change.

We must know that we are no longer the neutral arbiters of data. When leading people analytics, we are a stakeholder, not just a data provider. We are in the arena. The decision-making arena, that is. Risk, uncertainty, accountability. If these words are foreign or scary to us, then we must change ourselves. If it is not already clear, I am putting forward a prediction for the future of HR. One in which people analytics is the future of HR. Maybe people analytics is all that's left of HR after Gen AI fully takes hold. Someone in HR needs to be asking the right questions, and someone needs to be the one accountable for making the change. That should be us. Peter Drucker once famously said *"The best way to predict the future is to create it"* (National University, 2016). With the Gen AI age looming upon HR, it's our turn to create the future we want to see, with people analytics at the center of HR's influence and strategic relevance. In ten years, I believe only revenue-generating functions will exist in the business. Therefore, people analytics must transform HR into a revenue generating function or risk being left behind.

REAL-WORLD EXAMPLE

"How is AI Disrupting HR and What Can Be Done?" with Vin Vashishta, world-renowned AI expert and thought leader, author of *From Data to Profit*

(Paraphrased for length from Ep. 103 of "Directionally Correct, A People Analytics Podcast")

AI's Impact on Jobs in HR

Vin Vashishta, a globally recognized AI expert and author of *From Data to Profit*, provides a candid perspective on the disruption AI is bringing to HR. He emphasizes that AI is not merely augmenting roles but automating tasks that were previously thought to require human involvement. Specifically, compliance-based and transactional tasks—like approval workflows, payroll questions, and documentation creation—are prime targets for automation. While this brings efficiency and error reduction, it poses a serious challenge to job security within HR, particularly in roles focused on low-value, repetitive tasks.

The AI Hype Cycle and Gradual Transformation

Vashishta notes that while the initial hype around generative AI (Gen AI) has cooled, the technology continues to improve. Organizations are realizing that implementing AI isn't as simple as plugging in data and expecting instant results. However, advancements in AI products and tools will steadily replace large portions of transactional work, such as responding to routine employee queries, creating documentation, and managing bureaucratic processes.

The true transformation, Vashishta argues, will not be an overnight shift but a gradual restructuring of roles over the next few years. The implications are significant: as organizations adopt AI, they'll need fewer employees for tasks that are fully automated, and roles will consolidate around high-value, strategic work.

What's at Risk?

Vin highlights the vulnerability of HR roles that spend most of their time on repetitive, transactional work. For example:

- Approval workflows: Entirely automatable through AI, reducing human involvement.
- Payroll and compliance inquiries: Chatbots and AI-powered agents will handle these functions, bypassing traditional HR channels.
- Documentation and bureaucratic processes: AI will streamline or eliminate the need for manual creation and management.

Even though automation frees employees to focus on higher-value tasks, the sheer reduction in transactional work means fewer roles overall. Vashishta estimates that fully implemented AI could reduce HR teams by as much as 70 percent.

Opportunities for Transformation in HR

While the outlook may seem bleak, Vashishta sees opportunities for HR to evolve into a more strategic and impactful function. Freed from repetitive tasks, HR professionals can:

1 Focus on Optimization and Strategy: Spend more time on process improvements and implementing AI models to optimize organizational workflows.

2   Shift to Value Creation: Transition from compliance-driven tasks to roles that drive organizational transformation and efficiency.

3   Improve Candidate and Employee Experiences: Dedicate time to high-touch activities like personalized engagement, better talent acquisition strategies, and career development programs.

However, even as these opportunities grow, the need for HR professionals will shrink due to the overall reduction in transactional work. Organizations will need fewer but more skilled professionals to manage these high-value activities.

The Broader Impact Across Industries

Vashishta warns that the disruption won't be limited to HR. Similar transformations are occurring across industries, leading to incremental but significant job losses over time. For example:

- A 10 percent annual reduction in roles due to AI could lead to a substantial shift in the job market over five years.

- Fewer job openings and increased layoffs will create a competitive environment where more people are vying for fewer roles.

Key Takeaways for AI in HR

1   Automating Transactional Work: Routine HR tasks like payroll inquiries, approvals, and documentation will disappear as AI takes over.

2   Shrinking HR Teams: Even with a focus on higher-value work, fewer people will be needed to manage what remains.

3   The Need for Upskilling: HR professionals must pivot to roles that focus on optimization, strategy, and employee experience to stay relevant.

4   Long-Term Workforce Impact: AI adoption will lead to widespread job reductions across industries, intensifying competition for available roles.

5   Strategic Focus for HR: Organizations must transition HR into a value-creation function, emphasizing continuous improvement and innovation.

Vashishta's insights serve as a call to action for HR professionals and organizations to prepare for the coming wave of AI-driven transformation. By embracing AI's potential while addressing its challenges, HR can redefine its role and maintain relevance in a rapidly evolving workplace.

Top Use Cases for Gen AI in People Analytics

In this book, I will do my best to avoid the age-old "build vs. buy" debate on new technology. As you read the potential use case of Gen AI in people analytics, just assume that these can either be built or bought. It must be understood, though, that there are technology providers in the marketplace that are intent on commoditizing all Gen AI applications, and even if you decide to build your own solution, chances are you aren't building your own "foundation" models of Gen AI; therefore, you're buying somewhere along the technology value chain. That said, here are the top use cases for what Gen AI will be capable of in the near term and longer term.

Near term

What are the top use cases for implementing Gen AI in the near term in people analytics? These are in no particular order:

- No more pivot tables or descriptive analysis
- Never build another dashboard again, and no more SQL queries, running reports, or data visualization
- No more surveys and open- ended feedback
- No more prediction, more prescription
- Knowledge management—No more documentation (or code-management)!

Let's explore each of these in more detail:

No more pivot tables or descriptive analysis. Generative AI can instantly process and interpret large datasets without requiring tedious manual aggregation or pivot table work. This frees analysts to focus on strategic insights and recommendations, as the system automatically handles number-crunching and trend identification.

Never build another dashboard again. With AI-driven data visualization, UX formatting, and interactive reports, creating static dashboards, reports, and queries has become obsolete. Instead of monitoring a collection of charts, stakeholders can query the AI directly for insights, automatically receiving the exact metrics or visualizations they need in real time.

No more surveys and open-ended feedback. Generative AI can gather and interpret sentiment through continuous listening across communication channels (e.g., email, Slack, and more). This eliminates the need for traditional surveys by continuously surfacing employee concerns and ideas, providing richer context for decision-making. I/O psychologists should be adopting these techniques as we speak.

No more prediction, more prescription. Rather than simply predicting future outcomes, of which the building of predictive models is already commoditized by Gen AI, AI systems can recommend specific actions to improve employee experiences and business results based on the model and even cite research examples for what and why to do it. This shift to prescriptive analytics positions HR teams to proactively intervene and optimize workforce strategies before issues escalate.

Knowledge management—No more documentation (or code-management). Generative AI can ingest and comprehend vast amounts of organizational knowledge, making it instantly accessible without the need for constant manual documentation updates. As employees ask questions, the AI provides relevant, up-to-date answers—significantly reducing the burden of creating and maintaining knowledge bases and code repositories. Thank goodness.

Longer term

What are the most plausible and likely use cases for implementing Gen AI in the longer term in people analytics according to my logic and deduction? These are in no particular order:

- Hyper-personalized talent sourcing
- Automated candidate end-to-end candidate screening
- Dynamic skills gap analysis and upskilling recommendations
- Automated career path modeling
- Automated workforce and succession planning scenario modeling
- Voice-of-the-Employee summaries from communication forums
- Organizational Network Analysis for collaboration optimization
- AI-assisted compensation benchmarking, pay adjustments, and fair pay analysis
- Workforce redeployment simulations

Let's also explore these potential outcomes:

Hyper-personalized talent sourcing. What if all talent sourcing was at least starting by an AI agent? Gather and analyze large volumes of candidate data from traditional resumes, social media, and professional networks to identify the best-fit talent for open roles. Use advanced language models to parse subtle cues in candidates' backgrounds (e.g., niche technical skills, leadership traits) and generate shortlists by matching candidate profiles to job requirements, factoring in not just keywords but context and inferred skills, likely from data sources like Lightcast.

Automated candidate end-to-end candidate screening. Why do humans assess candidates if we know how much they suffer from a variety of biases? Automate the entire hiring process by creating standardized questions and screening rubrics. Automatically craft role-specific, competency-based interview questions tailored to each candidate's resume and background. Then, the AI agent can assess and summarize each candidate's responses in real time, highlighting potential red flags or areas that need deeper exploration, or go all the way to making the selection decision.

Dynamic skill gap analysis and upskilling recommendations. It is incredibly difficult to assess skills, make recommendations, and take action at scale. Continuously track and measure employees' skill sets to identify evolving gaps across the organization, based on data sources like Lightcast. Generate tailored upskilling pathways in real-time. For example, the AI could suggest relevant courses, projects, or mentorship programs for each employee, and continually refine these recommendations based on performance data and employee feedback.

Automated career path modeling. Now that you've assessed skill gaps and given plans to map and track upskilling, the next logical step is career path modeling. Map out potential career trajectories and internal mobility options for different roles and employees. Create "what-if" scenario-based career paths by analyzing employees' skills, performance metrics, and historical promotion data. AI-generated path models can show employees exactly which milestones they need to achieve for their next promotion.

Automated workforce planning and succession scenario simulations. Workforce planning is the "macro" output of the simulation of your organization and succession planning is the "micro" or person-by-person simulation and application of what should happen. Identify potential successors for key leadership positions and create succession roadmaps. Use generative models to simulate various organizational scenarios—like a major merger, rapid expansion, or retirement wave—and produce "best fit" suggestions for macro and micro scenarios based on leadership competencies, performance history, and organizational culture factors.

Voice-of-the-Employee summaries from communication forums. Employees need to feel real-time support and need to know "you spoke, we listened, we changed." Simply avoiding surveys and relying on digital exhaust is not enough to understand employee sentiment. Leaders must know what actions to take and when to take them. Create concise summaries of thousands of messages, automatically grouping themes (like dissatisfaction with a specific tool or excitement about a new product), and suggest recommended actions for leaders to take and measure the real-time results and efficacy of the response.

Organizational Network Analysis (ONA) for collaboration optimization. ONA is another talent program that is fun to analyze but incredibly difficult to take action upon at scale. Using Gen AI, map how employees collaborate across departments to identify hidden influencers and team bottlenecks. Use generative capabilities to interpret communication patterns and propose organizational adjustments—e.g., recommending cross-functional pods or highlighting overlapping responsibilities that slow collaboration. Optimize organizational collaboration at scale for the first time.

AI-Assisted compensation benchmarking, pay adjustments, and fair pay analysis. Compensation has always been the real craftsman or trade of HR, with very little common knowledge known about its processes and methodologies. This will no longer be the case. Review compensation levels against market rates, give raises and make pay adjustments, and set internal fairness measures with Gen AI. Generate tailored salary bands and compensation strategies by analyzing real-time market data, skill scarcity, and internal performance metrics from external data sources like Lightcast—providing interactive scenarios on how pay adjustments might reduce attrition or attract top talent. Compensation will be a mystery no longer.

Workforce redeployment simulations. With all the Gen AI disruption in HR and throughout the business, workforce redeployments will be necessary and critical. Plan for large-scale redeployment needs (e.g., expansions into new markets, acquisitions, work displacements) by examining internal talent capacity and comparing with external talent supply and demand. Suggest various redeployment scenarios—who to move, how to cross-train them—and predict organizational impact, helping leaders experiment with different workforce structures before they make costly real-world moves.

Implications

Strategic talent management has long been one of the key activities HR does to differentiate its strategic value to the business. When the "Long Term" use cases described above come to fruition, the function frequently called "Talent" (i.e., the combination of Talent Management, Talent Acquisition, and sometimes other functions) and the employee talent lifecycle, will be fully automated by Gen AI, with people analytics teams at the helm driving the workflow automation, analytics, and change necessary to make it happen. As you can see, every single step in the talent management chain can be automated or at least augmented by Gen AI applications. All of these applications are already ready or in various stages of development by HR technology firms. The future is here, it is just not evenly distributed. We'll discuss this more in the third section of the book, *How to Win.*

However, one key variable necessary to make these use cases a reality cannot be commoditized, and that variable is **data**. The most valuable data is rare, organization-specific, difficult to source and resistant to commoditization, offering unique insights that cannot be easily replicated or replaced. And as any economist knows, the thing that can't be commoditized ends up being the only thing of real value. In the age of AI, unique data will be the true source of value derived from HR functions. This is why people analytics will be at the helm of the change of power in HR, and why data providers become of extreme value the more exclusive and proprietary data they are able to provide and tailor to organizations. Software and technology, including HR technology, will be commoditized, but the unique data will be a premium as will those who control it.

REAL-WORLD EXAMPLE

"Gen AI's Impact on People Analytics Functions" with Luka Babic, former CEO of Orgnostic and VP of Product at CultureAmp

(Paraphrased for length from Ep. 40 of "Directionally Correct, A People Analytics Podcast")

Generative AI as a Transformational Technology

Luka Babic, former CEO of Orgnostic and VP of Product at CultureAmp, views Gen AI as a groundbreaking innovation poised to transform the people analytics field. Unlike other technological hypes, such as blockchain, Gen AI offers tangible and immediate benefits, fundamentally changing how organizations interact with data and analytics. Babic describes Gen AI as enabling a paradigm shift, where people analytics becomes more accessible, relational, and intuitive.

Revolutionizing People Analytics with Gen AI

Luka foresees Gen AI reshaping people analytics in several ways:

1   People Analytics GPT: Gen AI will act as a "people analyst in a box," enabling stakeholders to interact with analytics using natural language queries. This approach eliminates the need for technical expertise in querying or reporting, making analytics more user-friendly for HR professionals.

2   Simplified UX: By allowing users to ask questions in plain language and receive answers instantly, Gen AI will demystify analytics and make it as easy as conversing with a colleague.

3   Real-Time Insights: Users will be able to test hypotheses, generate reports, and perform complex analyses on demand, all through conversational interfaces.

4   Prescriptive Analytics: Training Gen AI models on domain-specific knowledge (e.g., HR research, benchmarks) will enhance prescriptive analytics, offering actionable insights informed by both organizational and benchmark data.

Gen AI as the "New Bundle" of Knowledge

Babic draws parallels between Gen AI and the historical evolution of information access. He likens it to the bundling and unbundling cycles of information dissemination: encyclopedias bundled knowledge, search engines unbundled it into links, and now Gen AI re-bundles it into direct, actionable answers. This streamlined approach allows HR professionals to skip the step of sifting through search results or complex dashboards, creating a more efficient and impactful workflow.

Opportunities and Challenges in the AI Era

Babic maintains an optimistic outlook, emphasizing the opportunities Gen AI creates for creativity, strategy, and the humanities. While some fear that AI could render certain roles obsolete, Babic argues that social sciences and liberal arts will play a critical role in interpreting, contextualizing, and applying Gen AI-driven insights. He envisions a future where philosophers, policy experts, and creatives thrive in guiding ethical AI adoption and bridging gaps that machines cannot address.

Key Takeaways for Generative AI in People Analytics

1 Democratizing Analytics: Gen AI simplifies access to people analytics, enabling stakeholders to query data and generate insights without technical expertise.

2 Enhancing User Experience: Conversational interfaces transform analytics from a cryptic tool into an approachable, relational system.

3 Prescriptive Insights: Domain-specific training of Gen AI models will provide prescriptive analytics, combining organizational data with benchmarks to offer actionable recommendations.

4 Creative and Strategic Roles: While some roles may diminish, new opportunities will emerge for human creativity and strategic thinking, particularly in interpreting and applying AI-driven insights.

5 Streamlined Knowledge Access: Gen AI serves as the next evolution of bundled information, delivering direct answers rather than requiring users to navigate complex resources.

Babic's insights highlight how Gen AI will redefine people analytics by making it more accessible and impactful. Organizations that embrace this transformation stand to gain not only operational efficiencies but also the ability to unlock new strategic opportunities in workforce management and beyond.

How Will Gen AI Impact the People Analytics Operating Model?

The integration of Gen AI into people analytics represents a fundamental transformation—not just an evolution—of how organizations leverage data to drive workforce decisions. As Gen AI reshapes the landscape, people analytics functions must adapt across four key dimensions: The technology that powers insights, the consultation that translates data into business impact, the strategic decision-making that influences outcomes, and the broader ecosystem that ensures integration into HR and business operations. This shift will redefine the role of people analytics, requiring new skills, new ways of working, and a proactive approach to embedding AI-driven insights into the fabric of organizations. The following sections outline the four key components of this transformation and how people analytics teams can prepare for the Gen AI-powered future.

1 **Right Technology**—A Gen AI-enabled people analytics platform.

2 **Impactful Consultation**—Consulting on strategic business problems.

3 **Strategic Decision-Making**—Influence, change management, and execution.

4 **Enabling Ecosystem**—Integration into the broader business and HR context.

Four Key Components

1. Right Technology: Whether you build or buy, Gen AI will revolutionize the core technology underpinning people analytics platforms. By automating data preparation, analysis, and visualization, Gen AI platforms will enable faster, more robust insights with minimal manual intervention. Additionally, Gen AI-powered platforms will generate dynamic narratives and recommendations tailored to specific business scenarios, allowing organizations to scale analytics capabilities without technical expertise required by users. This will allow teams to focus on higher-value tasks rather than spending time on transactional data procedures.

2. Impactful Consultation: While Gen AI excels at handling repetitive and transactional tasks, consulting on strategic business problems will remain a domain requiring human expertise. People analytics professionals will leverage Gen AI to quickly synthesize data and identify patterns, but the interpretation of nuanced insights and their alignment with organizational goals will depend on the human influence. By enabling analysts to focus on complex, high-impact questions, Gen AI will enhance the value of consultation rather than replace it.

3. Strategic Decision-Making: Gen AI will amplify the strategic impact of people analytics by facilitating influence and change management. It can simulate the outcomes of various HR strategies, generate scenario-based analyses, and provide decision-makers with tailored insights that bridge data into actionable business strategies. The people analytics team will be pivotal in contextualizing these insights, ensuring they resonate with stakeholders, and driving execution to institutionalize data-driven decision-making across the business. People analytics will need to pivot from decision support to decision-making in this context. This component, along with impactful consultation, will be the key differentiator for people analytics' function value in the future.

4. Enabling Ecosystem: To fully realize the potential of Gen AI, people analytics must be deeply embedded in an ecosystem that prioritizes evidence-based management throughout HR. This is a fundamental shift in how HR is practiced. Automation of many HR functions will be necessary and prevalent. Gen AI will accelerate the cultural shift by democratizing access to insights, fostering greater collaboration between HR and business leaders. However, the people analytics team must take the lead in integrating these technologies into workflows, ensuring alignment with broader business objectives, and fostering trust in AI-driven recommendations. This integration will help build an agile, data-literate organizational culture that embraces change and innovation.

This is a revolutionary, not evolutionary, shift in how people analytics teams and HR functions work together. We are undergoing a radical shift in the nature of work. It will be necessary for people analytics teams and HR's skills to adjust to the changes that are here and to come.

Using Gen AI to Make Work More, Not Less, Human

The future of work, HR, and people analytics doesn't all have to be about automation, Gen AI, and somewhat dystopian in nature. We're stuck thinking that work happens on an assembly line. Our mental models of work haven't kept up. Essentially, assembly lines force humans to act like machines. That's the mental model we still use: People acting like machines are doing "work." People doing anything else are doing "not work."

In this way of thinking, Gen AI is the next form of the work-destroying dragon. However, I do not think AI will destroy human work at all. We think AI is going to force people to be human at work instead of acting like machines. *Machines can be machines. Humans can be humans.* This is due to the simple fact that work today is so highly integrated and dependent on other people that it won't be easy to automate. Here's a thought-experiment, inspired by Shuba Gopal (*see the "Real World Example" below, for reference*).

Thought experiment

Imagine your boss is a Gen AI web-application instead of a human. And it knows you. It has all the data about you available, right? It's been fed all the best advice on managing a team, and it knows that career development is a critical component of keeping employees engaged and motivated (Fraser-Thill and Gopal, 2023). About once a month, it asks "*What are your career goals or aspirations?*" Each time, you're stumped. You've got a lot of ideas but no clarity on how to grow professionally. Instead, you ask it back, "*I'd like to understand how I get to the next level in this organization.*" The Gen AI helpfully spits back a list of job requirements for the next level up in the career ladder for your type of work (much like we described above as use cases). You leave the conversation just as unclear about what it takes to grow your career, and more than a little annoyed that you don't have a human boss who might actually understand what you're saying. You didn't want an essay on moving up. You wanted advice, and frankly you wanted someone who cared.

To be clear, this scenario happens plenty even without Gen AI as your boss. In fact, there's a possibility that AI would be better at navigating this conversation than a human (Bersin, 2024). But the real reason these conversations don't go as well as we hoped in our minds is that everyone thinks about work in outdated ways.

The Unlikely Virtue of Managers

The manager role has been gutted in the last few years as companies are looking to remove layers, and they see managers as senseless bureaucracy. However, manager-augmenting Gen AI applications will cause good management to rise from the ashes. Why? Because in a world of highly specialized, deeply interconnected work, somebody has to be the connective tissue for the team (McKinsey, 2024). That's the managers' function, and as long as there are humans to manage they will want a manager who cares about them. Lose managers and suddenly the whole fabric of the organization comes undone. It's the difference between a team and a group. A manager makes a collection of individuals become an interdependent team, while a group is just the collection of individuals.

AI is certainly capable of creating linkages across disparate information sources, curating solutions, and recommending next steps. Isn't that what we're asking our managers to do in this new "connective tissue" model of work? However, Gen AI applications seemingly offer the obvious solutions to most problems. Most workers don't need their managers to offer obvious solutions. They need help with finding new solutions because their first pass solutions didn't work or because the problem itself is entirely new.

AI-augmented managers are the solution to keeping the humanity in work. There's new evidence that AI helps average workers significantly improve their work, while doing little for top performers (Brynjolfsson, Li, and Raymond, 2023). This is phenomenal news: It means we can finally help all the lousy managers become better managers. Managers in concert with AI can quickly get through the obvious, easy solutions to problems. Then, AI can nudge managers to come up with better answers. It can coach them through tricky interpersonal dynamics, mostly by squashing their knee-jerk reactions and helping them identify a more nuanced response. Reducing the downside, and increasing the upside (Bersin, 2021). It can also reduce the risk of burnout for managers themselves (Kellogg and Hadley, 2023). In this new mental model of work, AI does what it does best: Being the machine so people don't have to be. See? The future is not all bad, right?

REAL-WORLD EXAMPLE

"What Can Computational Biology Teach Us About People Analytics?" with Shuba Gopal, Principal at Glean Signals, and former Senior Scientist at the Broad Institute of MIT and Harvard

(Paraphrased for length from Ep. 95 of "Directionally Correct, A People Analytics Podcast")

The Value of Mid-Level Managers: The Phoenix and the Dragon

Dr. Shuba Gopal highlights the critical yet often overlooked role of mid-level managers in organizational success. Drawing from her article on the "phoenix and the dragon," Shuba explains that managers serve as the connective tissue for teams, facilitating coaching, resource allocation, and interdepartmental collaboration. With the rise of knowledge work, managers are no longer supervisors counting widgets on a factory line but are instead essential for fostering team effectiveness and addressing individual needs.

However, Dr. Gopal points out that most organizations fail to train managers for these responsibilities, particularly in academia and technical fields, where technical proficiency often supersedes managerial skill. She likens AI to the "dragon," a disruptive force that could either undermine or empower managers, depending on how it is implemented. The "phoenix" represents the potential rebirth and transformation of management practices through thoughtful integration of AI tools.

Applying Computational Biology to People Analytics

Shuba's expertise in computational biology offers valuable insights for tackling challenges in people analytics, particularly when dealing with small sample sizes. In computational biology, small sample sizes are common due to the rarity of certain diseases, necessitating advanced statistical methods to yield robust results. Gopal identifies two key methods that can enhance people analytics:

1   Permutation Testing:

- o   Permutation testing allows analysts to assess whether observed differences in data are statistically significant without relying on normal distribution assumptions.

- o   Gopal applied this method during her tenure at the Broad Institute, addressing gender pay equity in an organization with a small, flat structure and over 450 unique job titles for 1,100 employees. Permutation testing helped identify and correct apparent pay disparities that were initially skewed due to the dataset's complexity and non-normal distribution.

2   Simulations:

- o   Simulations are widely used in computational biology to model outcomes when additional data cannot be gathered. In people analytics, simulations can be particularly useful for understanding network dynamics and predicting outcomes like retention and promotion probabilities.

- o   By running simulations, organizations can explore hypothetical scenarios, test interventions, and better account for the variability and complexity of their workforce data.

Use Cases for Advanced Methods in People Analytics

Dr. Gopal emphasizes the applicability of permutation testing and simulations across various people analytics functions, such as:

- Pay Equity Analysis: Ensuring fairness in compensation by addressing skewed data distributions.

- Retention and Promotion Modeling: Building more accurate models to predict employee outcomes by accounting for non-normal data distributions.

- Network Analysis: Using simulations to understand team dynamics, collaboration patterns, and the impact of organizational changes.

Key Takeaways for Leveraging Computational Biology in People Analytics

1   Advanced Methods for Small Sample Sizes: Techniques like permutation testing and simulations, drawn from computational biology, are invaluable for robust analysis in small or complex datasets.

2   Reframing the Role of Managers: Managers must transition from task supervisors to team connectors, empowered by AI tools to focus on high-value, people-oriented responsibilities.

3   Practical Applications: These methods can be applied to challenges like pay equity, retention modeling, and organizational network analysis to improve decision-making.

4 Addressing Data Complexity: Permutation testing helps account for skewed distributions and complex organizational structures, ensuring accurate and fair insights.

5 Simulation for Scenario Planning: Simulations enable organizations to test interventions and explore hypothetical scenarios, offering strategic foresight in workforce planning.

Gopal's integration of computational biology techniques into people analytics demonstrates the potential for cross-disciplinary innovation. By adopting these methods, organizations can tackle complex challenges with greater confidence and precision, while also reimagining the role of managers in the AI era.

In this chapter, we have discussed how Gen AI will impact people analytics and how it operates more broadly. But, for Gen AI to be effective in the first place, your team must have the right data foundations in place. In the next chapter, we'll learn about the role data infrastructure plays in the success of a modern people analytics function.

Summary

This chapter explores the intersection of people analytics and generative AI (Gen AI), highlighting how these technologies are reshaping HR, workforce strategy, and business decision-making. As AI evolves, organizations must adapt not only to leverage its capabilities but also to maintain their strategic relevance. The chapter introduces key concepts, including large language models (LLMs), retrieval-augmented generation (RAG), and AI agents, while also identifying high-impact use cases and the skills transformation required for HR and people analytics professionals.

Key Takeaways

1 **Gen AI is a Transformational, Not Incremental, Shift in People Analytics**

   o Generative AI can automate, augment, and disrupt traditional people analytics functions, shifting HR's role from descriptive reporting to strategic decision-making.

   o AI models like OpenAI's ChatGPT series have transformed the field by making natural language-driven insights and automation possible.

2 **Core AI Technologies Powering People Analytics**

o **LLMs (Large Language Models):** Process and generate human-like text, enabling automation of HR tasks like job descriptions, performance reviews, and workforce forecasting.

o **RAG (Retrieval-Augmented Generation):** Enhances LLMs by incorporating real-time external knowledge, improving accuracy and relevance.

o **AI Agents:** Autonomous entities that act on insights, facilitating proactive decision-making and automation in workforce planning and talent management.

3 **People Analytics Must Move Beyond Dashboards and Descriptive Analytics**

o The last decade has seen over-reliance on dashboards rather than advanced analytics.

o While skills like Microsoft Excel and research have grown, AI, machine learning, and coding (Python, R, SQL) remain underdeveloped in HR functions.

o People analytics must evolve beyond static reporting to prescriptive and action-oriented insights powered by AI.

4 **The Future of People Analytics Lies in Asking the Right Questions, Not Just Analyzing Data**

o AI is rapidly automating data analysis, making question formulation and decision-making the most valuable skillsets.

o The Inquisitor Role: People analytics professionals must be the ones to ask the right business questions—ones that align with HR, business needs, and workforce data.

o The Change Agent Role: It's not enough to analyze data—people analytics must drive real change by implementing insights and influencing strategic decisions.

5 **AI is Reshaping HR Jobs—and People Analytics Must Lead the Transition**

o Routine, transactional HR work (e.g., payroll, compliance, approvals) will be automated by AI, leading to fewer but more specialized HR roles.

o HR professionals must transition to strategy, optimization, and experience design to stay relevant.

o People analytics will play a key role in managing AI-driven workforce transformations, including job displacement, skills gaps, and automation strategies.

6 Top Near-Term Use Cases for Gen AI in People Analytics

- o **Automated Data Processing:** No more pivot tables—Gen AI can instantly analyze large datasets and generate insights.

- o **Eliminating Static Dashboards:** AI-driven interactive analytics will replace manual dashboards.

- o **Real-Time Employee Sentiment Analysis:** AI can analyze digital communications to replace traditional surveys.

- o **Prescriptive HR Insights:** AI won't just predict turnover; it will recommend specific interventions.

- o **AI-Driven Knowledge Management:** Automates HR documentation and knowledge sharing.

7 Long-Term Disruptive Use Cases for Gen AI in People Analytics

- o **Hyper-Personalized Talent Sourcing:** AI will dynamically match candidates with jobs based on skills, experience, and behavioral traits.

- o **Automated End-to-End Candidate Screening:** AI will assess resumes, conduct interviews, and make hiring decisions.

- o **Skills Gap Analysis and Personalized Upskilling:** AI will map workforce skills gaps and recommend learning pathways at scale.

- o **Automated Career Path Modeling:** AI will forecast career trajectories and optimize internal mobility.

- o **AI-Driven Workforce and Succession Planning:** HR will simulate workforce scenarios using AI to optimize leadership pipelines.

8 People Analytics Must Evolve Its Operating Model for Gen AI

- o The traditional people analytics function must shift from descriptive reporting to decision-making.

- o Four key areas of transformation:

  a. **Right Technology:** AI-driven people analytics platforms will replace traditional BI tools.

  b. **Impactful Consultation:** Analysts must move beyond reports and become strategic advisors to business leaders.

  c. **Strategic Decision-Making:** AI enables predictive and prescriptive recommendations that drive organizational action.

  d. **Enabling Ecosystem:** HR must integrate AI into broader business strategies and become a driver of innovation, not a passive function.

9 AI Will Reshape Work—But Can Also Make Work More Human

o AI won't eliminate work—it will force a shift toward more human-centric work.

o Managerial roles will become more critical as they focus on guiding employees through AI-driven change.

o AI can augment leadership and coaching, allowing managers to focus on mentorship, team building, and strategic execution rather than administrative tasks.

10 The Future of HR is Data-Driven, and People Analytics Must Lead the Way

o HR's influence will be determined by its ability to harness data and AI for decision-making.

o People analytics must drive AI adoption, develop data fluency, and become central to business strategy.

o Organizations that fail to embed AI into workforce management will fall behind—those that succeed will position HR as a key driver of business outcomes.

The AI-driven revolution in HR is already underway, and people analytics is at the center of this transformation. The future of the field depends on its ability to evolve beyond dashboards and reporting into a function that drives real business decisions and change. Generative AI will not replace people analytics—but people analytics teams that fail to adapt will be replaced by those who do.

References

Bersin, J. (2021). AI-Enabled Coaching Is Hot. And There's Lots More To Come. Josh Bersin. joshbersin.com/2021/07/ai-enabled-coaching-is-hot-and-theres-lots-more-to-come/ (archived at https://perma.cc/LJ4M-GE3R).

Bersin, J. (2024) Coaching at Scale AI Democratizes Leadership Development. joshbersin.com/wp-content/uploads/2021/07/OD_21_06CoachingAtScale.pdf (archived at https://perma.cc/P5M6-B4V5).

Brynjolfsson, E., Li, D. and Raymond, L. (2023). Generative AI at Work. National Bureau of Economic Research. doi.org/10.3386/w31161 (archived at https://perma.cc/92J7-8LHN).

DC News. (2023). The Inquisitor and The Change Agent. Substack. directionallycorrectnews.substack.com/p/the-inquisitor-and-the-change-agent?r=ybtwi (archived at https://perma.cc/5SUW-UQ8X).

Fraser-Thill, R. and Gopal, S. (2023). How to Talk to Your Team About Their Career Development. Harvard Business Review. hbr.org/2023/03/how-to-talk-to-your-team-about-their-career-development (archived at https://perma.cc/CL7Q-AR3E).

Hassan, S. and Hassan, S. (2024). RAG, AI Agents, and Agentic RAG: An In-Depth Review and Comparative Analysis of Intelligent AI Systems. MarkTechPost. www.marktechpost.com/2024/09/22/rag-ai-agents-and-agentic-rag-an-in-depth-review-and-comparative-analysis-of-intelligent-ai-systems/ (archived at https://perma.cc/GF6V-NVJR).

Kellogg, K. C. and Hadley, C. N. (2023). How AI Can Help Stressed-Out Managers Be Better Coaches. Harvard Business Review. hbr.org/2023/06/how-ai-can-help-stressed-out-managers-be-better-coaches (archived at https://perma.cc/WC9G-2RDU).

Levenson, A., Stevenson, M. and Fink, A. (2021). Are OD and Analytics Twins Separated at Birth? Toward an Integrated Framework." In *Research in Organizational Change and Development* (Research in Organizational Change and Development, Vol. 29), edited by A. B. (Rami) Shani and D. A. Noumair. Emerald Publishing Limited.

McKinsey (2024). Middle Managers are the Heart of Your Company | McKinsey. www.mckinsey.com/capabilities/people-and-organizational-performance/our-insights/middle-managers-are-the-heart-of-your-company (archived at https://perma.cc/A4SX-T27S).

Napper, C., Hines, S. and Acosta, J. (2024). Is Machine Learning Better than Human Intuition? Directionally Correct. www.podbean.com/eas/pb-zjgh9-15c5373 (archived at https://perma.cc/75KZ-3XVR) Ep. 85.

Napper, C., Hines, S. and Babic, L. (2023). Gen AI's Impact on People Analytics Functions. Directionally Correct. www.podbean.com/eas/pb-59e78-151f6e5 (archived at https://perma.cc/2SZR-LBQX) Ep. 40.

Napper, C., Hines, S. and Gopal, S. (2024). What Can Computational Biology Teach Us About People Analytics? Directionally Correct. www.podbean.com/eas/pb-gfnzz-163fb48 (archived at https://perma.cc/5MVV-XGAS) Ep. 95.

Napper, C., Hines, S. and Vashista, V. (2024). How is AI Disrupting HR and What Can Be Done? Directionally Correct. www.podbean.com/eas/pb-rvw6y-16e4a68 (archived at https://perma.cc/KL3P-N6SV) Ep. 103.

National University. (2016). December 2016 News. www.nu.edu/chancellors-page/december-2016/ (archived at https://perma.cc/WA72-JQNF).

Noy, S. and Zhang, W. (2023). Experimental Evidence on the Productivity Effects of Generative Artificial Intelligence. *Science*, 381 (6654): 187–192. doi.org/10.1126/science.adh2586 (archived at https://perma.cc/SL53-QM2U).

Ramakrishnan, R. (2024). A Practical Guide to Gaining Value from LLMs. MIT Sloan Management Review. sloanreview.mit.edu/article/a-practical-guide-to-gaining-value-from-llms/ (archived at https://perma.cc/YR8Z-W3M6).

Sapient Insights Group. (2025). Home – Sapient Insights Group. sapientinsights. com (archived at https://perma.cc/MX8Y-BSRQ).

Vaswani, A., Shazeer, N., Parmar, N., Uszkoreit, J., Jones, L., Gomez, A. N., Kaiser, L. and Polosukhin, I. (2017). Attention Is All You Need. *arXiv*. arxiv.org/ abs/1706.03762 (archived at https://perma.cc/GWU7-QYN7).

YouTube Movies (2000). *O Brother, Where Art Thou?* YouTube. www.youtube. com/watch?v=vndkDwrZHCA (archived at https://perma.cc/5HC4-WX6H).

5

Building a Foundation: Data Infrastructure for AI

This chapter focuses on the importance of high-quality, AI-ready data infrastructure as the backbone of effective analytics. It discusses how robust data practices not only support but enhance strategic decision-making and operational reliability across business functions.

> *"We choose to go to the moon in this decade and do the other things, not because they are easy, but because they are hard"*—John F. Kennedy

Perhaps, with advances in Gen AI in the next five years, the prospect of creating the data foundations and infrastructure for your people analytics team will get much easier. However, for the entire history of people analytics getting "good data" is one of the most important and difficult tasks of a people analytics team. You can delay it, try to avoid it, try to create workarounds, proofs-of-concept, and pilot studies, but at some point if your organization wants to do credible work in people analytics—which has escalated in primacy due to the introduction of Gen AI applications in HR—it must make the investment in good data infrastructure. This takes time, energy, money, and resources. We consciously choose to do these things not because they are easy, but because they are hard... and because they are meaningful to the long-term success of people analytics at your organization.

But why is good data infrastructure more important now for Gen AI? In Chapter 4, we began with a short primer on LLMs, RAG, and AI agents. Whether it be foundation models of LLMs, or local models built with RAG, or AI agents built to deconstruct and automate specific tasks, data is at the core of powering the transformation of HR. The expression "data is the new oil" featured prominently in the "big data" revolution years. However, from my perspective, it was never really true in the HR and people analytics context. Leaders still largely made decisions based on intuition and not data, regardless of how valuable the data was. With the introduction of Gen AI, that has all changed, and data *really* is the new oil. The reality is that LLMs cannot function and improve without continuous streams of new, curated, logic and inference-informed data. Data is king, and your people analytics and HR technology infrastructure are what will power the revolution.

What Data Do You Need?

To understand what data you need, you first must understand the constituent elements that LLMs require to make sense of the world. The good news is many of these data elements are not new, and if your organization has been investing in good data practices for some time, you will be set up to succeed. Some good data practices would include: Combining data from multiple sources into a single data architecture; having logic-based tables in which the data resides; ensuring that the tables in which data reside are appropriately tied to the right classifications of data and tied to consistent data definitions; calculations and metrics based on the data and standardized and consistently applied with the logic documented; data is tagged with the appropriate metadata elements; code repositories are built, maintained, and annotated for historical preservation and continuity of support; and most importantly, the data is scrubbed and audited for quality assurance.

This is a great start, and if your organization has not previously invested in data engineering (whether built or bought) and it wants to make the necessary transformation to an AI-led future, it needs to begin making those investments now. However, good data practices are not enough to be ready to layer LLMs on top of your data. Below are the concepts of what is needed in addition to good data practices to be LLM-ready.

Data Applications in People Analytics

As seen in Table 5.1, some of these data elements probably look familiar, but others are new to most people analytics practitioners, especially logic and context variables. But let's start with the familiar ones: Data, metadata, and code. Here are some example applications of those categories for LLMs.

1 **Data:** Employee satisfaction scores, tenure, and salary data derived from an HCM.

TABLE 5.1 Elements of data

Layer	Description	Purpose
Data	Raw information such as employee demographics, performance metrics, engagement scores, etc.	Provides the foundational dataset for analysis and model training.
Metadata	Information about the data, such as column descriptions, data types, source systems, timestamps, and confidentiality levels.	Ensures proper data understanding, governance, and traceability for accurate and ethical usage.
Code	Scripts, functions, or processes to preprocess, clean, and transform data (e.g., Python, SQL).	Automates and standardizes data preparation, ensuring consistency and reproducibility.
Context	Annotated information, narrative explanations, or labels that explain data relationships, organizational meaning, and business goals.	Helps the LLM understand the data's real-world relevance, making predictions and analyses meaningful.
Logic	Rules, algorithms, or decision-making frameworks applied to interpret and analyze data relationships (e.g., business rules, AI model logic).	Guides the LLM in applying appropriate reasoning or decision-making aligned with organizational goals and ethical considerations.

2 **Metadata:** Field descriptions (e.g., "Satisfaction Score: Scale from 1–10"), timestamp format, and confidentiality tags that are maintained on top of (or "tagged") to data itself.

3 **Code:** Python, SQL, or R scripts to clean missing values, normalize satisfaction scores, and create salary brackets or any procedure that consistently transforms data.

This layered structure of data ensures that LLMs can effectively process, analyze, and generate meaningful insights. Data infrastructure that captures these elements are typical. However, the logic and context layers are different and new. Here are some example applications of those categories for LLMs.

1 **Context:** Annotation indicating that satisfaction scores may correlate with turnover rates and should be analyzed with caution regarding causality. You may even provide linkages to previous research done on the topic.

2 **Logic:** Define business rules, such as "employees with less than 1 year of tenure and low engagement scores are flagged for retention risk analysis." Explaining in "if-then" language so that LLMs can understand the logic.

Context data and logic data are typically new for most people analytics team's architecture. This type of data enables the LLM to execute intelligent decision-making frameworks or simulate scenario-based insights. It also focuses on incorporating structured reasoning and algorithms to enhance the LLM's analytical capabilities and operational impact. If an LLM is going to be able to act like an analyst, it must be equipped with the same logic and context an analyst would need to do their jobs effectively.

Historically, a people analytics analyst would need to combine domain knowledge of HR, with analytics rigor and organizational context to effectively analyze data then tell a story. With the appropriate data architecture in place and the right LLM wrapper, an analyst's role will move to that of the prosecutor. Imagine you were a prosecutor in a courtroom and wanting to interrogate the data. What context and logic would be necessary to get the answers you need without any human input into the analysis? All of that context and logic will need to be associated with the data so that LLMs, RAG, and AI agents will be at their full capacity in the future.

Example Using Survey Data

Today at most organizations, when a scientifically valid and reliable survey is conducted, an analyst is responsible for digging into the data to determine key themes and insights on which leaders can take action. Some of this information may be provided out-of-the-box by a survey tool, such as basic averages, counts, and demographics. However, what is called "linkage analysis"—or tying survey responses to other organizational priorities or phenomena—is usually only completed by analysts with sophisticated statistical expertise, typically in I/O psychology. However, if the data is properly constructed in the future, the analyst will be able to interrogate the data with basic prompts and very little if any statistical expertise will be needed.

Example Prompt: *"Please show me what are the percent favorable engagement scores by employee tenure"*

- A dip in engagement scores is seen in employees with a tenure between 18 months and three years

2nd Prompt: *"Please use this survey and our previous survey from last year's responses to see what changed in the employee experience from those employees* *who used to be engaged who are now not engaged at the 18 months to three year tenure range. Please dig into their open ended survey feedback to tell me why this dip may be occurring. Please summarize the responses and outline some key quotes as to what may be causing this dip."*

As you can see, the first prompt is quite broad, but it is through the second prompt where the real inquisitive value of the analyst will be. However, now that you've seen how clever prompting will bring about more insights, let's go through the data architecture assumptions that must be valid for this analysis to be executable using Gen AI.

ASSUMPTIONS:

- **Data**—You have engagement survey responses for this survey and the one a year prior, as well as open-ended feedback. You have tenure data from your HCM tied to the data.

- **Metadata**—You have a repository of survey items that are categorized into fields like "engagement" and "open-ended responses" and descriptions and definitions are provided for what this means.

- **Code**—You have the appropriate annotations of your code scripts to pull in logic like tenure calculations and percent favorable. Also, you have the right unique identifiers that allow for data to be merged from two surveys and your HCM together into one place from your data warehouse.

- **Context**—In addition to the data and metadata of the survey responses and open-ended feedback, any methodology as to why certain items are combined with others to make engagement, the semantic expectations associated with the open-ended question, any research the survey may be based upon, the key findings and action plans from the previous surveys, and even the organizational reasoning for why they are doing the survey and what they intend the outcome of the survey to be.

- **Logic**—Related to the code, consistent definitions and calculations such as what percent favorable means should be documented, but also if-then logic statements such as "if scores go down by X percent, then the motivation of that team decreases as a consequence."

Once you have all of this information, the life of the analyst will be materially improved, and moving from insights to action will be much clearer and quicker; however, you'll see it's going to take some work investing in data infrastructure to get to that point.

REAL-WORLD EXAMPLE

"How to Do Data Engineering for People Analytics and Gen AI at AWS" with Michael Hutchins, Principal Product Manager and Data Engineer for People Analytics at Amazon Web Services

(Paraphrased for length from Ep. 98 of "Directionally Correct, A People Analytics Podcast")

Data Engineering at the Heart of People Analytics

Michael Hutchins, Principal Product Manager and Data Engineer at AWS, provides a behind-the-scenes look at the pivotal role of data engineering in people analytics. His team focuses on understanding the employee experience from hire to alumni status, translating complex business problems into technical requirements, and building data architectures to support insights. Hutchins emphasizes that clean, annotated, and well-prepared data is the unsung hero of effective analytics, especially in the era of Gen AI.

Building Data Infrastructure for Generative AI

Hutchins explains that preparing data for generative AI, such as large language models (LLMs), requires a paradigm shift from traditional data practices. Key differences include:

- Annotated Code and Data Dictionaries: Beyond merely normalizing datasets, LLMs require detailed annotations and clear data definitions to understand and generate insights. For example, each data attribute must be well-documented to ensure the model can interpret it effectively.

- Data Lakes and Warehouses: Modern data architectures, such as data lakes, must integrate comprehensive, tagged information to support infinite potential use cases. This contrasts with narrowly scoped datasets used for specific research purposes.

- Dynamic Scope Management: The complexity of large-scale organizations necessitates narrowing down the scope of LLMs to solve specific problems while still allowing for future expansion.

Generative AI in People Analytics: Practical Applications

Hutchins outlines the practical steps for applying LLMs to people analytics, such as understanding drivers of attrition. Starting with foundational data (e.g., timestamps, employee attributes, and tenure), the process involves layering business context—like geographic mobility or transportation access—to hypothesize about potential attrition factors. This iterative process highlights the synergy between technical data engineering and contextual business knowledge.

Challenges in Scaling Gen AI for Enterprise Use

Hutchins identifies a monumental delta between building Gen AI models for internal research versus production-level systems designed for enterprise-wide use. Internal models are purpose-built for specific studies, while production systems must accommodate nearly infinite use cases across departments and domains. This challenge underscores the need for robust, flexible, and future-proof data architectures.

Narrowing Use Cases and Managing Expectations

In large organizations, managing the scope of Gen AI is critical. Hutchins suggests starting small—focusing on narrow, well-defined problems like attrition—and then expanding incrementally. Clear communication about what the system excels at (e.g., analyzing employee turnover patterns) versus its limitations ensures users can derive value while avoiding unrealistic expectations.

Key Takeaways for Data Engineering in People Analytics

1   Data Preparation is Key: Clean, annotated, and well-documented data forms the foundation of effective analytics and is essential for Gen AI applications.

2   Modern Data Architectures: Data lakes and warehouses must integrate annotated and tagged information to support enterprise-scale AI.

3   Contextual Insights: Business context enriches technical data, making it possible to generate actionable insights into complex problems like attrition.

4   Iterative Approach: Start with narrow use cases and expand the scope as the system matures, balancing focus and flexibility.

5   Scope and Communication: Clearly define what the system can and cannot do, ensuring alignment between capabilities and user expectations.

Hutchins' insights reveal the critical role of data engineering in unlocking the potential of generative AI for people analytics. By combining technical expertise with business context, organizations can build scalable systems that provide meaningful and actionable insights.

Investing in Data Architecture for AI Opens Up Multitudes

Investing in data architecture for Gen AI in people analytics will no longer be optional—it's a strategic imperative. As organizations increasingly rely on data to make informed decisions about their workforce, a robust and scalable data architecture becomes the foundation for unlocking transformative capabilities. With Gen AI, this foundation can support advanced applications such as automating business intelligence (BI), streamlining data engineering workflows, and enabling the creation of AI agent clusters that mimic human-like decision-making. The organizations that invest now are positioning themselves to not only stay competitive but to lead the charge in reimagining future business impact at their organizations.

What About Generative BI, Not AI?

One of the most immediate opportunities lies in automating business intelligence. Traditional BI processes are often time-consuming and rely heavily on manual intervention to generate insights from people data. A modern data architecture tailored for Gen AI can transform these workflows, enabling real-time analytics and predictive modeling at scale. Imagine a system where data from disparate HR platforms is automatically harmonized and visualized, allowing HR leaders to shift from reactive reporting to proactive decision-making. This automation not only reduces time-to-insight but also empowers organizations to uncover trends and risks that would otherwise remain hidden.

Generative Business Intelligence (or Gen BI) represents a paradigm shift in how businesses interact with data, transforming the traditionally complex process of building dashboards and data models into a more intuitive, conversational experience and using BI as code (Rilldata, 2024). This evolution leverages the principles of BI-as-Code, where dashboards and metrics are defined declaratively. Such definitions provide structured context for generative AI to operate effectively. Instead of requiring expertise in SQL or data engineering, Gen BI enables users to articulate their needs in natural language, allowing AI to generate dashboards, metrics, and data models. This innovation bridges the gap between technical and non-technical users, democratizing data insights while maintaining accuracy and efficiency.

In people analytics, the integration of Gen AI and Business Intelligence provides transformative applications that redefine workforce data analysis and decision-making. For example, Gen AI-powered dashboards can automatically generate insights on employee engagement, turnover trends, or productivity metrics by analyzing structured HR data—many people analytics vendors are already working on this. Through a metrics layer, Gen BI systems can contextualize business-specific definitions, such as average tenure or revenue per employee, allowing for advanced modeling of workforce outcomes. With conversational interfaces, HR leaders can dynamically refine dashboards—requesting breakdowns by department, region, or tenure—without the need for technical intervention. This accelerates the ability to derive actionable insights, enabling leaders to make data-driven decisions about talent strategies, organizational design, and workforce planning.

The broader implications of Gen BI lie in its ability to merge the strengths of traditional BI with the accessibility of AI-driven tools, creating a seamless, iterative analytics workflow. Declarative definitions not only enhance maintainability and governance, but also empower AI to comprehend and adapt to complex business logic. This positions organizations to achieve faster time-to-insight, optimize resource allocation, and adapt swiftly to evolving business needs—all while reducing technical bottlenecks.

AI Agent Clusters & Automated Data Engineering

Beyond BI, investing in data architecture unlocks the potential for AI agent clusters and automated data engineering. AI agent clusters, powered by Gen AI, can simulate complex decision-making scenarios, from workforce planning to optimizing employee engagement strategies. Meanwhile, automated data engineering can handle data cleaning, integration, and transformation tasks—areas historically plagued by inefficiency and human error. Together, these innovations create a virtuous cycle of efficiency and insight, driving people analytics to its next evolutionary stage.

AI agent clusters will transform people analytics and all of HR into a proactive, strategic function by leveraging multiple specialized AI agents that collaborate to optimize talent acquisition, workforce management, and employee experience (Talent Intelligence Collective, 2024). These clusters enable HR to predict skill needs, engage with potential candidates preemptively, and personalize recruitment strategies based on market trends and organizational goals (Lightcast, 2023). Beyond recruitment, they dynamically monitor performance, recommend personalized career paths, and even match employees with AI or human mentors. By automating routine tasks and providing actionable insights, AI agent clusters liberate people analytics professionals to focus on decision-making, ensuring AI aligns with organizational values and enhances human potential.

Specific to people analytics, AI agent clusters will revolutionize data-driven insights by identifying workforce trends, predicting turnover risks, and modeling future talent needs. For talent intelligence, these agents analyze global labor markets to pinpoint emerging skills and recruitment opportunities while crafting personalized outreach to top candidates. Workforce planning benefits significantly from this approach, as clusters simulate scenarios, automate skill gap analysis, and suggest solutions such as targeted hiring or training programs. By integrating real-time analytics, proactive insights, and personalized strategies, AI agent clusters empower organizations to make informed, agile decisions, ultimately fostering a more adaptive, engaged, and productive workforce.

Generative AI is also set to revolutionize data engineering in people analytics by automating complex tasks, enhancing scalability, and enabling faster, more accurate insights into workforce data (Wilson, 2024). Traditionally, data engineers spend significant time wrangling disparate data sources, building pipelines, and maintaining data models. Gen AI will streamline these processes by generating SQL queries, automating ETL (Extract, Transform, Load) workflows, and creating data models with minimal manual intervention. It can also adapt dynamically to new data sources, ensuring real-time integration and consistency across HR systems. Moreover, by leveraging natural language interfaces, Gen AI allows HR professionals to articulate their analytical needs directly, enabling automated generation of dashboards, metrics, and reports tailored to business objectives. This reduces dependency on technical expertise, accelerates time-to-insight, and empowers HR teams to focus on strategic decision-making, such as identifying patterns in employee engagement, forecasting workforce needs, and mitigating turnover risks. Ultimately, Gen AI enhances the efficiency and impact of people analytics by bridging the gap between technical data management and taking action in the real world.

People Analytics Requires Gen AI-Ready Data Engineering

People analytics is evolving rapidly, and Gen AI-ready data engineering is the cornerstone of its future. As organizations aim to unlock deeper insights into their workforce, the demand for scalable, clean, and AI-ready data pipelines has never been higher. Gen AI, with its ability to generate nuanced narratives, automate workflows, and drive predictive analytics, thrives on high-quality data. Without robust data engineering to prepare, clean, and integrate information from disparate systems, the promise of Gen AI in people analytics remains out of reach. This critical foundation separates organizations that achieve groundbreaking insights from those that struggle with incomplete or unreliable data (SeattleDataGuy, 2025).

However, the path to Gen AI-ready data engineering isn't one-size-fits-all—companies must decide whether to build or buy. Organizations that choose to build their infrastructure often have the internal technical expertise and long-term vision to customize data pipelines to their unique needs. This approach allows for maximum control but comes with significant upfront investment in time, talent, and technology. Conversely, companies that opt to buy prebuilt solutions can accelerate their adoption of Gen AI, leveraging third-party platforms designed for seamless integration and rapid deployment. While faster to implement, these solutions may require trade-offs in flexibility and long-term scalability. This build-versus-buy decision ultimately reflects each company's strategic priorities, technical maturity, and appetite for innovation in the rapidly shifting landscape of people analytics.

The Gen AI-Enabled Full HR Tech Stack

Below is a high-level overview of the core elements that typically make up a data infrastructure for an internal people analytics function, followed by a contrast of the "build vs. buy" approach when it comes to Gen AI. While the particular design of your data stack will vary depending on your organization's scale, data maturity, and strategic goals, these components—and the considerations that come with them—tend to be common across most modern people analytics teams.

1. DATA SOURCES AND INGESTION

A Gen AI-enabled full HR tech stack requires diverse and interconnected data sources, including HRIS platforms, applicant tracking systems (ATS), learning management systems (LMS), external labor market data tools like Lightcast, performance management tools, and employee engagement platforms. Data ingestion pipelines must seamlessly integrate these sources, ensuring real-time or near-real-time updates while maintaining data accuracy and consistency. Additionally, robust APIs and ETL processes are critical for harmonizing structured and unstructured data, preparing it for Gen AI-powered analytics and decision-making. Here are some examples:

- **Primary HR Systems:** Core Human Capital Management (HCM) platforms (e.g., Workday, SAP SuccessFactors, Oracle HCM), payroll systems, external labor market data tools (e.g., Lightcast), applicant tracking systems (ATS), performance management tools, learning management systems, etc.

- **Employee Engagement Systems:** Surveys (e.g., Glint, Culture Amp), feedback tools, recognition platforms, learning management systems.

- **Operational Systems:** Collaboration tools (Slack, Teams), scheduling platforms, labor-management systems (for hourly workforce), etc.

- **3rd-Party Data:** External benchmarking data, market compensation data, recruitment marketing data, etc.

Key considerations for data ingestion using AI

- **Data Quality:** Ensure that each source's data is as clean and standardized as possible before ingestion.

- **Frequency and Volume:** Plan how frequently data should be pulled. Real-time or near real-time might be needed for certain analytics, while weekly or monthly extracts may suffice for others.

- **Ingestion Methods:** APIs, flat-file transfers (SFTP), event streaming, or manual uploads.

- **Security and Privacy:** Handle PII (Personally Identifiable Information) and sensitive HR data carefully, encrypt in transit and at rest, and ensure compliance with regulations (GDPR, CCPA, etc.).

Build vs. Buy Contrast

- **Build:** You may develop custom data pipelines (e.g., using Python scripts, etc.) that connect directly to HR systems' APIs. This offers greater flexibility but requires internal data engineering resources and maintenance.

- **Buy:** Managed ETL/ELT services (e.g., Fivetran, Workato) or vendor-specific connectors. There will be vendor-specific DaaS data sources, like that of Lightcast, and the ability to overlay that data with your in-house data systems. These solutions reduce the need for in-house development but can come with subscription costs and less customization.

2. CENTRAL DATA REPOSITORY (DATA LAKE/DATA WAREHOUSE)

The central data repository in a Gen AI-enabled HR tech stack, whether a data lake or data warehouse, serves as the unified hub for all workforce data. It stores both structured and unstructured data, ensuring it is secure, scalable, and optimized for fast querying and analysis by Gen AI tools. This repository enables seamless data access, supports advanced modeling, and ensures compliance with data governance and privacy regulations critical in HR contexts. Here are some examples:

- **Data Lake:** A storage repository that holds raw (or lightly processed) data in various formats (structured, semi-structured, unstructured) at scale.

- **Data Warehouse:** A more structured environment optimized for querying and analytics. Often sits on top of or alongside a data lake for refined and aggregated views.

Key considerations for your central data repository and AI

- **Storage Format:** If using a data lake, consider formats that handle large volumes efficiently.

- **Access Patterns:** HR data is often needed for ad hoc analytics. A warehouse with well-defined schemas (star/snowflake schemas) can speed up query performance.

- **Governance and Security:** Segment employee data by region or role-based access control to meet privacy and compliance needs.

- **Scalability:** As the business grows, you'll need storage and compute resources to scale seamlessly.

Build vs. Buy Contrast

- **Build:** Implement an open-source or cloud-managed data lake (e.g., AWS S3, Azure Data Lake) plus an in-house data warehouse solution (e.g., self-managed SQL or Hadoop ecosystem). This can be cost-effective at large scale but requires strong engineering expertise.

- **Buy:** Use fully managed cloud data warehouse services (Snowflake, BigQuery, Azure Synapse) or people analytics vendor-provided analytics data stores. This offloads infrastructure scaling and maintenance but comes at a premium and may lock you into a particular vendor ecosystem.

3. DATA INTEGRATION & TRANSFORMATION LAYER (ETL)

The data integration and transformation layer (ETL) in a Gen AI-enabled HR tech stack orchestrates the flow of data from multiple sources into a unified format ready for analysis. This layer performs critical tasks such as data cleaning, deduplication, normalization, and enrichment to ensure consistency and usability across the entire system. By automating these processes, the ETL layer enables real-time updates, reduces manual effort, and ensures the data is optimized for Gen AI-powered insights and decision-making. Here are some examples:

- **Data Processing:** Tools or workflows that clean, standardize, and merge data from multiple sources into an integrated data model.

- **Orchestration and Scheduling:** Ensuring data pipelines run reliably and on time (e.g., RestAPIs, etc.).

- **Data Modeling:** Creating logical models (e.g., "employee," "position," "event") that accurately capture workforce metrics.

Key considerations for ETL with AI

- **Consistency and Data Integrity:** Align fields (e.g., "Manager ID," "Location," "Job Family") across disparate systems.

- **Version Control:** Keep track of changes in transformation scripts, especially as new data fields or sources are introduced.

- **Error Handling and Monitoring:** Build alerting systems for pipeline failures or unexpected data anomalies.

Build vs. Buy Contrast

- **Build:** You have full control over transformations and can use open-source frameworks. This requires an in-house data engineering culture, and ideally a fully dedicated data engineering team.

- **Buy:** A "low-code" or "no-code" data integration platform. Faster to implement, but can be less flexible in handling complex transformations or data modeling nuances.

4. DATA GOVERNANCE AND PRIVACY

Data governance and privacy in a Gen AI-enabled HR tech stack ensure that workforce data is managed securely, ethically, and in compliance with regulations such as GDPR and CCPA. Robust access controls, encryption, and anonymization protocols safeguard sensitive employee information while maintaining the utility of data for analysis. Governance frameworks and audit trails are essential to building trust and accountability, especially as Gen AI processes inherently sensitive and high-stakes HR data. Here are some examples:

- **Policies and Compliance:** Adhere to local labor laws, GDPR, CCPA, and other regulations concerning employee data.

- **Access Control:** Granular roles and permissions to ensure only authorized stakeholders can view and manipulate sensitive information.

- **Metadata Management:** Document data definitions, lineage, and usage policies to maintain clarity across teams.

Key considerations for data governance and privacy with AI

- **Sensitive Data Handling:** Pseudonymization or anonymization steps may be required for certain analytics use cases (e.g., diversity and inclusion reporting).

- **Auditability:** Logs and audit trails for data access and modifications.

- **Cultural Adoption:** Effective governance requires both technical frameworks and organizational buy-in.

Build vs. Buy Contrast

- **Build:** Develop custom governance frameworks for your organization based on its internal processes, stakeholders, and risk tolerance. This requires dedicated data governance roles and internal oversight.

- **Buy:** Many HCM and analytics platforms offer built-in governance modules or partner with specialized compliance solutions. Simplifies compliance processes but may lack custom features or domain-specific governance rules.

5. ANALYTICS AND VISUALIZATION LAYER

The analytics and visualization layer in a Gen AI-enabled HR tech stack translates complex data into actionable insights through intuitive dashboards, interactive reports, and predictive models. This layer leverages Gen AI to uncover trends, simulate workforce scenarios, and generate natural-language narratives, making insights accessible to HR professionals and executives alike. By presenting real-time analytics and AI-driven recommendations, it empowers organizations to make informed, data-driven decisions that align with their strategic goals. Here are some examples:

- **BI and Dashboarding:** Tools such as Power BI, Tableau, or Looker for dynamic dashboards and standard "people metrics" reporting (headcount, turnover, engagement, performance, etc.).

- **Advanced Analytics and ML:** Data science tools/environments (e.g., Python, R, Databricks) for predictive models (e.g., flight risk, high-performer retention), workforce optimization, and scenario planning.

- **Self-Service Capabilities:** Portal or analytics environment where HR business partners and managers can build or interact with their own reports.

Key considerations for analytics and visualization with AI

- **Data Literacy and Training:** Internal stakeholders need enough support to interpret dashboards or run simple analyses themselves.
- **Performance and Security:** Large historical datasets can slow down queries, so ensure the BI layer is optimized.
- **Collaboration:** A single source of truth and consistent metrics definitions across the organization.

Build vs. Buy Contrast

- **Build:** A custom analytics platform (e.g., building advanced models in-house, hosting your own notebooks, custom front-end dashboards). This allows the highest level of customization for analytics tailored to your specific business questions but requires robust data science and engineering talent.
- **Buy:** Off-the-shelf analytics solutions for people analytics (e.g., Visier, One Model, eqtble/Paradox, CultureAmp People Analytics, etc.), and new Gen AI native entrants (e.g., Arbor, Included, etc.). These come with prebuilt dashboards, metrics definitions, and best-practice workflows. Faster to deploy, but you may sacrifice some control or customization.

6. DATA SCIENCE AND SPECIALIZED TOOLS

The data science and specialized tools layer in a Gen AI-enabled HR tech stack focuses on advanced modeling, predictive analytics, and algorithm development tailored to workforce insights. It integrates machine learning frameworks and natural language processing tools to enable sophisticated analyses, such as employee churn prediction or skills gap assessments. By providing a platform for customized AI development and experimentation, this layer ensures organizations can continuously innovate and adapt their people analytics capabilities to meet evolving business needs. Here are some examples:

- **Statistical and Predictive Models:** Turnover prediction, workforce planning, recruiting funnel optimization, measuring the ROI of training, etc.
- **Natural Language Processing (NLP):** Text analytics for engagement surveys, open-response feedback, or exit interviews.
- **Organization Network Analysis:** Tools that leverage collaboration data (emails, calendar, Slack) to reveal communication patterns and influence networks.

Key considerations for data science tools with AI

- **Talent and Skills:** Data scientists, machine learning engineers, and business translators who understand HR use cases. This talent has grown in supply, but is still small.

- **Compute Resources:** GPU/CPU capacity for large-scale modeling, especially with unstructured or big data. This likely will only be a concern for extremely advanced teams.

- **Ethical and Bias Concerns:** Predictive models can create or perpetuate biases. And there are so many kinds of statistical biases. Strong governance, interpretability, and fairness checks are critical.

Build vs. Buy Contrast

- **Build:** In-house modeling capabilities can differentiate your company and yield proprietary insights. This can be more expensive (people, technology, time) but extremely powerful if you have the right talent in-house.

- **Buy:** Many vendors offer out-of-the-box predictive models for HR metrics (e.g., churn, internal mobility). It's fast to get started but may not be highly tailored to your unique workforce or policies. (*Note: AI will likely commoditize this layer in the near future*)

Summary: Build vs. Buy HR Tech Stack for People Analytics

The decision to build or buy a Gen AI-enabled HR tech stack for people analytics hinges on factors like organizational resources, customization needs, and time-to-value. Building allows for tailored solutions that align perfectly with unique business goals but requires significant investment in technical expertise, infrastructure, and ongoing maintenance. Buying off-the-shelf solutions accelerates deployment and provides access to proven platforms, but it may involve compromises in flexibility and scalability as business needs evolve.

Build Pros and Cons

- **Pros:**
  - Maximum flexibility to tailor solutions to unique data sources and business contexts.
  - Potentially lower long-term costs if you have strong engineering capabilities and large scale.
  - Ownership of intellectual property and methodology.
  - Can integrate seamlessly into existing enterprise data strategy.

- **Cons:**

    o Requires skilled data engineers, data scientists, and technical HR domain experts—often in short supply.

    o Longer time-to-value; building from scratch can take months or years to fully mature.

    o Ongoing maintenance burden and risk of technical debt.

Buy Pros and Cons

- **Pros:**

    o Faster implementation with preconfigured HR metrics, dashboards, and best practices.

    o Less technical overhead and risk. The vendor handles upgrades, security patches, etc.

    o Can scale or change vendors more easily if business needs evolve.

- **Cons:**

    o Less customization: you're often locked into how the vendor structures data and metrics.

    o Potentially higher recurring costs: subscription models can become expensive at scale.

    o Data portability concerns if you ever need to switch platforms.

    o May limit the development of deep in-house analytics expertise.

Constructing your people analytics data infrastructure is a step-by-step journey. By carefully evaluating each layer—data ingestion, storage, transformation, analytics, and governance—and deciding whether to build or buy, you can create an integrated ecosystem that meets both current HR insights needs and can flexibly adapt to future business demands.

REAL-WORLD EXAMPLE

"The People Data Supply Chain for AI in HR" with Richard Rosenow, VP of People Analytics Strategy at One Model

(Paraphrased for length from Ep. 97 of "Directionally Correct, A People Analytics Podcast")

The Evolving Role of People Analytics in HR

Richard Rosenow, VP of People Analytics Strategy at One Model, introduces the concept of the "People Data Supply Chain," a framework that highlights the interconnectedness of data, operations, and technology within HR. As organizations amass a growing number of data sources—ranging from learning and development (L and D) to talent acquisition (TA) and compensation (Comp)—the need for cohesive management of these systems has given rise to a new type of HR role.

Richard notes the emergence of roles such as "Head of Workforce Systems," which oversee operations, technology, strategy, and analytics horizontally across the HR function. These roles bridge gaps between traditional HR verticals, creating a unified approach to managing data and enabling more strategic decision-making.

Navigating Data Complexity and Politics in HR

HR is grappling with increasingly messy and fragmented data sources, making it difficult to aggregate and normalize information across systems. Richard highlights the importance of a centralized leader who can navigate organizational politics and prioritize resources effectively. Without this role, people analytics leaders often face friction with other HR teams, such as TA and Comp, which can delay or derail initiatives due to siloed data ownership and competing priorities.

By placing a leader over the "horizontals" of HR—operations, technology, data, and analytics—organizations can address these challenges more effectively. This leader not only integrates disparate data sources but also has the political authority to resolve conflicts and ensure alignment across HR verticals.

The Strategic Role of People Data in AI Initiatives

Rosenow emphasizes the critical need for clean, unified data as the foundation for successful AI applications in HR. AI tools, such as those used for predictive analytics or workforce planning, require high-quality inputs to generate meaningful insights. The "People Data Supply Chain" ensures that data is prepared, normalized, and aggregated in a way that enables AI to function effectively.

Moreover, the integration of these data sources allows for greater agility and innovation in people analytics. A centralized leader who manages this supply chain can identify gaps, set priorities, and unlock the potential of AI-driven insights across the organization.

Key Takeaways for the People Data Supply Chain

1   New Leadership Roles in HR: The rise of "Heads of Workforce Systems" reflects the growing need for leaders who can integrate operations, technology, data, and analytics across HR.

2   Data Integration is Critical: Managing messy, fragmented data requires a centralized leader to aggregate, normalize, and make sense of diverse sources.

3   Addressing Organizational Politics: A leader overseeing HR horizontals can navigate political dynamics, resolve conflicts, and prioritize initiatives effectively.

4   AI Readiness Depends on Data Quality: Clean, unified data is the foundation for AI applications in HR, enabling predictive insights and innovative solutions.

5   Protecting People Analytics Leaders: A horizontal leader can shield and empower people analytics teams by resolving friction with traditional HR verticals and advocating for their needs.

Richard Rosenow's insights highlight the transformative potential of the People Data Supply Chain for AI-driven HR strategies. By addressing data fragmentation, organizational politics, and leadership gaps, organizations can unlock the full value of people analytics and position themselves for success in the age of AI.

Provenance of Data

To Richard Rosenow's point in the real-world example, as people analytics evolves it may ultimately report to a "Workforce Systems Leader." However, people analytics and the strategic value it brings should be central to the people data supply chain and its associated governance. The successful application of Gen AI in people analytics hinges on establishing an emphasis on data provenance and chain of custody for HR data. Unlike traditional approaches to HR data governance, which often involve distributed responsibilities among various stakeholders, Gen AI's reliance on precise, high-quality data necessitates centralized control. People analytics teams, as stewards of this data, must assume ownership from end to end, ensuring that every data point's origin, transformation, and usage are meticulously categorized (e.g., data, metadata, code, logic, context). This level of control not only safeguards data integrity but also positions people analytics as the authoritative source capable of delivering the reliable insights Gen AI requires to thrive in HR applications.

The prevailing model of distributed governance, where various stakeholders share responsibility for HR data management, risks introducing fragmentation, inconsistencies, and delays. Gen AI exacerbates these risks because its effectiveness depends on accessing comprehensive datasets that are harmonized and free of discrepancies. In this context, a centralized governance model, where people analytics acts as the "ultimate decider" may be better suited to usher in the age of generative AI in HR. By centralizing control, people analytics teams can enforce uniform standards, streamline data integration, and quickly adapt to the evolving requirements of AI-driven systems, thereby ensuring readiness to harness the full potential of Gen AI.

Moreover, elevating people analytics to the role of primary decision-maker in data governance aligns with the demands of modern HR practices. Gen AI applications require not only vast amounts of data but also an unbroken chain of custody to maintain compliance and trust. People analytics, as the authority, can ensure adherence to ethical and legal standards while fostering innovation. By consolidating power and responsibility, the field can provide the clarity and direction needed to transition HR from its traditional, fragmented data governance models into a unified, AI-empowered future.

Data Hierarchies

To do people analytics effectively, you often need a "decoder ring" of sorts to manage disparate data, parts of the business, and functions. With the introduction of AI, this will be even more important to give LLMs the organizational context they need to do effective analysis. In my previous article "The Four Horsemen of Hierarchy," I explored the complexities of managing four key organizational hierarchies that serve as the "decoders"—Organizational, Cost Center, Functional, and Social Influence—and their implications for people analytics and HR practices. These hierarchies provide structure, help organizations make sense of their operations, and reduce the cognitive burden of understanding organizational data. While hierarchies are invaluable for organizing employees and data, they present unique challenges when reconciling their differences across functions like HR, Finance, and people analytics.

The **Organizational Hierarchy**, the most traditional and widely understood structure, defines reporting relationships and serves operational purposes like approvals and data visibility. It is integral to HR technologies but often diverges from the perspectives of other hierarchies, particularly Finance. The **Cost Center Hierarchy**, managed by Finance, organizes expenses and accountability but often conflicts with organizational and functional hierarchies, creating reconciliation challenges for HR and people analytics.

The **Functional Hierarchy** (and sometimes the **Location Hierarchy** as well) groups employees based on roles and tasks, such as marketing or analytics, enabling organizations to identify skill sets, optimize productivity, and manage layoffs strategically. Meanwhile, the **Social Influence Hierarchy**, a more fluid and less formal structure, captures hidden networks of influence within an organization. Tools like organizational network analysis

(ONA) can illuminate these networks, offering untapped insights into decision-making, communication, and inclusion.

Poorly managed hierarchies can become the bane of people analytics teams, leading to reconciliation issues, matrixed reporting challenges, and inefficiencies in handling organizational changes. Effective adoption of Gen AI practices in HR and people analytics hinges on maintaining coherent hierarchies. This requires close collaboration between HR and Finance, thoughtful application of modern technologies, and alignment on business decisions to address hierarchy-related complexities and leverage data-driven insights effectively.

Building AI Capability in HR

Building AI capability in HR is essential for getting the right investments and focus on workforce data and unlocking the potential of people analytics using Gen AI. As HR professionals increasingly rely on data to drive strategic decisions, AI will provide the tools to analyze and interpret vast amounts of information with unprecedented speed and accuracy. However, we must ensure that HR leaders can make informed investments in Gen AI solutions tailored to their needs. Without these foundational insights, organizations risk wasting resources on technology that fails to align with their unique structures and goals, hindering the realization of AI's transformative potential in HR.

To build this capability effectively, people analytics leaders need to focus on fostering collaboration between HR, IT, and Finance teams to establish a unified data strategy. Investments in upskilling HR professionals with AI literacy and integrating modern people analytics data can empower them to derive actionable insights. Additionally, piloting small-scale Gen AI projects will demonstrate value and build confidence in AI-driven approaches. By emphasizing the practical benefits—such as enhanced decision-making, personalized employee experiences, and improved HR practices—HR professionals can align stakeholders around the importance of investing in people analytics and Gen AI, ensuring these technologies become strategic enablers of organizational success.

REAL-WORLD EXAMPLE

"Gen AI Training Classes for People Analytics" with Serena Huang, founder of Data with Serena and previous People Analytics Leader at PayPal

(Paraphrased for length from Ep. 92 of "Directionally Correct, A People Analytics Podcast")

From Corporate Leadership to Solo Entrepreneurship

Serena Huang, founder of Data with Serena and former People Analytics Leader at PayPal, shares her journey transitioning from corporate leadership to running her own speaking and training company. Her work focuses on bridging the gap between analysts and executives, addressing the disconnect between data presentation and decision-making. Analysts often struggle to tell concise, compelling stories, while executives, impatient for actionable insights, may overlook the nuances of the data. Huang trains both groups to foster curiosity, improve storytelling, and enhance the overall analytics experience.

Generative AI Training: A Growing Demand

Serena has developed a Gen AI workshop aimed at helping organizations embed AI tools into their workflows. While many companies have adopted Gen AI, they often lack the internal training infrastructure to make these tools impactful. Simply assigning employees to online courses is insufficient; training must be practical, embedded in day-to-day tasks, and tailored to specific roles. Her workshops focus on how to use Gen AI to boost productivity and shift how work is done, particularly in people analytics.

Three Core Applications of Gen AI in Organizations

Huang identifies three primary areas where organizations are leveraging Gen AI, which she refers to as the "Three C's":

1   Communication: AI automates tasks like email creation by analyzing successful templates and generating personalized content. While not new, these capabilities are now more accessible and effective for individual users.

2   Collaboration: Gen AI streamlines meeting preparation, note-taking, and follow-up actions, saving significant time and effort. Tools like AI-powered assistants in platforms like Zoom have transformed how teams manage their workflows.

3   Culture Building: Gen AI supports HR teams in brainstorming team-building activities and other cultural initiatives, democratizing creativity by providing accessible and immediate suggestions.

The Role of Gen AI in People Analytics

Huang highlights how Gen AI is transforming people analytics. Tools that once struggled with rudimentary sentiment analysis are now being replaced by free, more advanced AI technologies. For instance, instead of manually analyzing survey comments and numbers, teams can use Gen AI to generate insights efficiently. This evolution prompts a shift in focus for people analytics professionals—from data crunching to delivering higher-value insights and strategy.

Challenges and Opportunities in Gen AI Adoption

While Gen AI offers a significant productivity boost, it also raises concerns about leaner teams as automation reduces manual tasks. For individuals in data analytics centers of excellence (COEs), mastering Gen AI tools can be a career advantage, helping them adapt to changing roles and expectations.

Key Takeaways for Gen AI in People Analytics

1   Bridging Analyst–Executive Gaps: Training analysts to tell compelling stories and encouraging executives to stay curious enhances collaboration and decision-making.

2   Embedding Practical Training: Effective Gen AI training must integrate into employees' daily workflows to drive adoption and behavior change.

3   The Three Cs Framework: Gen AI is driving transformation in communication, collaboration, and culture building, with immediate benefits for teams and leaders.

4   Revolutionizing People Analytics: Advanced AI tools free up time for higher-value work, prompting a shift in focus for people analytics professionals.

5   Adapting to Automation: As AI reduces the need for manual tasks, analytics professionals must embrace new skills and roles to remain relevant.

Huang's work demonstrates how Gen AI can revolutionize people analytics and organizational workflows when paired with practical, tailored training. Her approach emphasizes not just technological adoption but also the human side of analytics—improving storytelling, fostering curiosity, and unlocking the full potential of data in HR.

But data infrastructure and architecture are only the beginning steps in getting ready to scale Gen AI in people analytics. What comes next? It is what has long been considered the true mountain that people analytics looked to climb. Prediction. Let's see around the corner in the next chapter.

Summary

This chapter explores the critical role of AI-ready data infrastructure as the backbone of effective people analytics. With the rise of Gen AI, ensuring high-quality, structured, and well-governed data is no longer optional—it is essential for enabling meaningful insights, automating decision-making, and scaling AI-driven HR solutions. The chapter outlines best practices for data management, the key elements of AI-ready data architecture, and real-world examples of how leading organizations are preparing their data for the future of people analytics.

Key Takeaways

1 **Data Infrastructure is the Backbone of AI**
   - o People analytics has long struggled with data quality and accessibility.
   - o Gen AI applications amplify the need for structured, high-integrity data.

2 **Data is the New Oil—Now, More than Ever**
   - o Unlike in past "big data" revolutions, AI applications *require* constant streams of well-structured data.
   - o Leaders who previously relied on intuition must now embrace data-driven decision-making.

3 **Essential Data Layers for AI Readiness**
   - o **Data:** Raw employee demographics, performance metrics, and engagement scores.
   - o **Metadata:** Data descriptions, source information, timestamps, and confidentiality labels.
   - o **Code:** Scripts for cleaning, transforming, and normalizing datasets.
   - o **Context:** Annotations and business logic that help AI models interpret data correctly.
   - o **Logic:** Rules and frameworks for decision-making, ensuring AI models apply structured reasoning.

4 **People Analytics Must Evolve with AI**
   - o AI-ready data structures allow analytics teams to shift from data wrangling to high-impact strategy.
   - o Analysts will act more like "prosecutors," interrogating AI-driven insights rather than manually analyzing data.

5 **AI-Enabled Survey Analysis Example**
   - o Traditional analysis requires human interpretation of survey results.
   - o AI can automate insights generation, linking employee engagement scores with tenure and sentiment analysis.

6 **Real-World Example: AWS People Analytics**

- o Amazon Web Services (AWS) focuses on annotated code, data dictionaries, and data lakes to support AI.

- o AI models require detailed documentation and dynamic scope management to be scalable across HR functions.

7 **The Strategic Importance of Gen BI (Generative Business Intelligence)**

- o Traditional Business Intelligence (BI) is becoming automated with AI-driven dashboards and real-time analytics.

- o AI can generate insights dynamically, reducing dependency on technical expertise for data interpretation.

8 **AI Agent Clusters and Automated Data Engineering**

- o AI agent clusters optimize workforce management by predicting skills gaps and retention risks.

- o Automated data pipelines improve data quality, allowing AI models to generate more accurate insights.

9 **The Role of People Analytics in Data Governance**

- o Successful AI implementation requires centralized data ownership within people analytics teams.

- o Data provenance and chain of custody are essential for ensuring ethical and compliant AI usage in HR.

10 **Preparing for the Next Frontier: AI-Powered Predictions**

- o Building data infrastructure is only the first step in enabling AI-powered people analytics.

- o The next challenge is moving from insights to predictive analytics, allowing organizations to anticipate workforce trends and optimize decision-making before issues arise.

By investing in high-quality data infrastructure today, organizations can future-proof their people analytics function and unlock the full potential of AI in HR.

References

DC News. (2025). The Four Horsemen of Hierarchy. Substack. directionallycorrectnews.substack.com/p/the-four-horsemen-of-hierarchy?r=ybtwi&utm_campaign=post&utm_medium=web&triedRedirect=true (archived at https://perma.cc/G33K-SLSB).

Lightcast (2023). What are Lightcast Skill Projections | Lightcast Knowledge Base. kb.lightcast.io/en/articles/8496296-what-are-lightc ast-skill-projections (archived at https://perma.cc/2GHC-9A8H).

Napper, C., Hines, S. and Huang, S. (2024). Gen AI Training Classes for People Analytics. Directionally Correct. www.podbean.com/eas/pb-32qq5-16165c5 (archived at https://perma.cc/L7PW-QLWT) Ep. 92.

Napper, C., Hines, S. and Hutchins, M. (2024). How to do Data Engineering for People Analytics and Gen AI at AWS. Directionally Correct. www.podbean.com/eas/pb-fbbd6-16709fc (archived at https://perma.cc/2FP9-ABCC) Ep. 98.

Napper, C., Hines, S. and Rosenow, R. (2024). The People Data Supply Chain for AI in HR. Directionally Correct. www.podbean.com/eas/pb-ft9vz-165cebe (archived at https://perma.cc/WHM9-3LMY) Ep. 97.

Rilldata.com. (2024). Rill | BI-as-Code and the New Era of GenBI. www.rilldata.com/blog/bi-as-code-and-the-new-era-of-genbi?ref=blef.fr (archived at https://perma.cc/V842-M9YH).

SeattleDataGuy (2025). Is It Time to Say Goodbye to Data Engineers? Substack.com. seattledataguy.substack.com/p/is-it-time-to-say-goodbye-to-data (archived at https://perma.cc/K2VP-SGS6).

Talent Intelligence Collective (2024). The Future of HR: AI Agent Clusters as Proactive Advisory Partners. Linkedin.com. www.linkedin.com/pulse/future-hr-ai-agent-clusters-proactive-advisory-56sle?utm_source=share&utm_medium=member_ios&utm_campaign=share_via (archived at https://perma.cc/V3MC-D9YW).

Wilson, Z. (2024). How Gen AI Will Impact Data Engineering. blog.dataengineer.io/p/the-2025-ai-enabled-data-engineering (archived at https://perma.cc/4Q9E-BT6X).

6

Leveraging AI for Taking Predictive Action

This chapter explores the use of AI to enhance predictive modeling capabilities and implementation, with case studies illustrating how these advanced insights drive proactive decision-making not just interesting insights.

"If you're going to build an ark, you better do it before it starts to rain— Helms (2017)

In the world of people analytics, the quote above serves as a stark reminder of the power of foresight and the risk in not possessing it. With the advent of AI, we no longer have to guess when the clouds will gather or how severe the downpour might be. Instead, we must read the weather patterns of our workforce and make the right predictions, take action, and see value before the first raindrops hit. This chapter will explore how AI empowers us not just to predict the storm, but to decide when, where, and how to deploy our predictive capabilities—and in some cases, prevent the rain altogether.

Prediction

Can you see into the future? What is prediction, and who is the best at it? Over the last fifteen years, data science has been all the rage in people analytics when it comes to trying to achieve what is sometimes called the pinnacle of people analytics: **Prediction**. Can we predict the future with accuracy, precision, and reliability? Forget trying to predict the future. Can we even predict the present reliably using data points from the past?

Before we discuss how Gen AI can help make predictions, let's first explore the complexities of making predictions, and add wisdom to how predictions are made from two unexpected places: **Historians and demographers** (DC

News, 2023a). Are there lessons that can be learned from those disciplines that could be applied to the prediction problems that people analytics teams face? We, in people analytics, can countenance methods for prediction beyond statistics and machine learning.

Demography

So let's start with demographics. A common phrase that is often shared in the space of demography is: **Demographics are destiny.** But why are demographics destiny for the global population, a particular country or city, or even an organization? The great thing about demographics is that they are relatively reliable and predictable. Barring war, famine, or migration, you can succinctly model the future demographics of a country based on only a few factors, such as birth rates, excess mortality, and life expectancy. Using these few variables and parameters to extrapolate and predict complex phenomena is appealing.

Demographics can help people analytics and especially workforce planning to understand the unmovable factors of an organization's demographics and labor market availability for talent at competitors, within geographies, and even at a societal level (Lightcast, 2024). As an example in the workforce context, if an organizational problem requires someone with 20 years of experience to fix, you will have to wait exactly 20 years to get them up to speed. **Demographics are destiny, even in organizations.** Workforce planning and studying demographics are the perfect predictive match. Much like you can model a country's demographics with only a few variables, you can also model the future composition of a workforce very accurately using only a few variables, such as turnover rates, hiring rates, skill mixes, and tenure demographics. This can be a secret weapon for prediction of future events for a people analytics and workforce planning function.

EXAMPLES OF PREDICTION USING DEMOGRAPHICS

If the demographic and workforce planning variables of your workforce are available, you can very accurately predict the future composition of your workforce. Here are two quick examples:

- **Did your organization hire double, or triple, the number of new college grads this year?** This may fix a talent shortage today. But, in 18 months, the new college grads are all going to be expecting promotions, and in four years they'll expect to be moving into management roles—all at the same time. Is your organization ready for that? Probably not based on historical promotion and first-time manager patterns. And these insights are known today, before you hire them, and you don't have to wait four years to know the impact on your organization.

- **Is there a brain-drain of experienced workers happening in your organization due to the impact of layoffs?** This may be seen as a great cost-cutting and "efficiency" measure, but when the next "growth" cycle hits, that is exactly the time when the intellectual capital you lost will come back to haunt your organization. As an example, in 2014, Malaysian Airliner MH17 went missing over eastern Ukraine. Many of the world's top HIV/AIDS researchers were on the plane on their way to the International AIDS Conference in Melbourne, Australia. Their passing was seen as a major blow to the research of HIV/AIDS and set the field's progress back in countless ways for years to come. The wisdom to be gained from this example is that *sometimes unique and organization-specific knowledge cannot be replicated*. Demographics are destiny.

Even without AI, your organization is likely to have questions like these, and people analytics will be expected to have the answers.

History

Critical thinking is a very important skill for people analytics, but is very difficult to acquire. One idea for building critical thinking is to learn history. Using history, we can study how humans react in complex situations and when situations are not ideal—without having to experience those situations ourselves. You don't always have to learn "the hard way." Understanding the complexities of human nature requires critical thinking in spades. Why you should understand history is often highlighted by two quotes:

- *"Those who don't learn from history are doomed to repeat it"* and *"History doesn't repeat itself, but it does rhyme"*

If you want to understand more about how to navigate politics in your organization? Read history. If you want to understand more about the *real* psyche of human beings and the great and/or terrible things they are capable of? Read history. How this relates to prediction is simple: **Human beings change, but human nature stays the same.** The lessons we learned from similar circumstances in the past can help us explain and predict the present. If you want to do a good job of predicting the future, or even understanding the present, in your organization, consider the approach of the historian. A historian primarily consults three techniques to derive insights about the past: *Primary source materials, historical interactions between individuals,* *and counterfactuals*. Before we discuss how you can act like a historian to make predictions, let's learn a little more about the historian toolkit:

- **Primary Sources**—These are the raw materials of history. They are documents, objects, or other materials created by people who lived during the time period being studied. Primary sources can provide historians with first-hand accounts of events, as well as insights into the thoughts, feelings, and experiences of people from the past.

- **Interactions Between Individuals**—Historians look into the interactions between historical individuals. They do this by examining documents, such as letters, diaries, and biographies, that provide insights into the thoughts, feelings, and motivations of these individuals. They also look at the context in which these interactions took place, such as the political, social, and economic conditions of the time.

- **Counterfactuals**—These are hypothetical statements about what might have happened if something in the past had been different. Historians can use counterfactuals to explore the different possible outcomes of historical events. This can help them to better understand the causes and consequences of these events and to identify the key turning points in history.

Now that we know the toolkit of the historian, here are the ways we can apply the same tactics to prediction in people analytics:

- **Consulting primary sources = Consult historical trends in the data**—Forecasting the future is difficult. But what if instead of trying to forecast the future, you look into past events for similar examples? Chances are, if you consult long-term historical trends or previous internal research at your organization, you can find similar circumstances that can instruct what are some possible future outcomes to consider. Alternatively, you could take the economist approach and build a *naive model* (Andrew, 2022), which says the future will be like the present. You'll be surprised how accurate that model is.

- **Interactions between individuals = Stakeholder interviews and organizational network analysis (ONA)**—Data will often tell you "what happened," but it's often more difficult to discern "why something happened." Human beings are synthesis machines. Just ask them and they can easily tell them why something happened. You can use stakeholder interviews (*i.e., qualitative data*) before building any models of a problem. Additionally, you can use ONA to see the hidden networks of organizations. These interactions can make or break the relevance and accuracy of your models. Diagnose before you predict and your predictions will improve dramatically.

- **Counterfactuals = Consider causal relationships**—Whether it be the historian Niall Ferguson's use of counterfactuals to understand the past in *Virtual History: Alternatives and Counterfactuals* (2011), or Judea Pearl and Dana Mackenzie's advocacy for the causal revolution in sciences using causal models in the *The Book of Why: The New Science of Cause and Effect* (2020), people analytics should be considering "What if" scenarios in their models. What if the past had been different, what would the present look like? What if we changed the present and pulled different "levers" of impact in our organization, how can that impact the future? This is especially helpful for trying to understand how making changes to your employee value proposition (EVP) will impact the future talent prospects of your organization.

Needless to say, understanding history provides a unique insight into prediction in people analytics. But what about more "traditional" methods of prediction in people analytics? Those have been mostly associated with data science.

Data Science & Gen AI

Data science has claimed to help leaders "see around the corner" for many years now in business. However, perhaps we've maxed out the upside of where data science can have an impact in people analytics; much like the impact of *Moneyball* (2011) techniques has hit a point of diminishing returns in professional sports. The most sophisticated data science modeling techniques (e.g., XGBoost, Random Forests, Neural Networks, etc.) were deployed years ago in most progressive people analytics teams. The low hanging fruit of data science is gone. Before the introduction of Gen AI, it's why you saw the proliferation of AutoML, and the ability of people analytics vendors to deploy data science models out of the box with no expertise needed. Data science is now pretty much completely commoditized—it's the infrastructure layer that hasn't kept up pace for commoditization, which we discussed in the last chapter.

Now with Gen AI, we have a world of new possibilities in people analytics. The real "killer app" of generative AI is in automation, *not prediction*. Most people are still highly uncomfortable with generative AI making predictions and decisions for employment-related outcomes. **And they should be.**

They are, however, very comfortable with using generative AI to automate tasks, such as using generative AI to create dashboards almost immediately. If you asked any tenured people analytics practitioner if they never had to create another dashboard again, they would say: "Yes, please!" Automation is where the serious productivity gains will be made in people analytics with Gen AI. Most data scientists are scrambling to learn about transformers, LLMs, and generative AI because *these skills aren't currently in their toolkit.* For the moment, generative AI talent is hard to find.

A Word of Caution on Prediction

First, let's quit equating prediction with "magic." Many HR leaders were taken in and enthralled with people analytics in the early years because they were sold that people analytics would help predict the future. They took this to mean "magic" and it was not. The more nuanced explanation was that people analytics and prediction would give HR leaders a crash course in science, probabilistic thinking, and uncertainty. Needless to say, this was a dissatisfying learning journey for most HR leaders. What HR leaders should find the most value in people analytics is: "What happened," "Why did it happen," and "What should I do about it?" Notice that the key question was left out, "What will happen," because it's likely not reliably knowable. There is a famous quote that illustrates this point effectively:

"All models are wrong, some are useful"—George Box (1987)

This quote is taken to mean that some models can help you understand the future, but they are all wrong in the end. Take this as a thought exercise: If all you had ever seen were white swans, would you know to look for a black swan? This is the thesis behind Nassim Taleb's now-famous book *The Black Swan* (2007). The book focuses on the extreme impact of rare and unpredictable outlier events—and the human tendency to find simplistic explanations for these events, retrospectively. Said differently, how do you predict the unpredictable? How do you react to events that you have never considered?

Black Swans

Newton's third law states that *"for every action in nature there is an equal and opposite reaction."* This holds true for fields other than physics as well, including people analytics. Events outside the workplace sometimes have impacts inside the workplace as well. Reactions to these events have coun-ter-reactions, and sometimes even third-order consequences. Here's a quick example to illustrate the point:

1 **First Order "Black Swan" Event**—The Covid-19 pandemic, which no one expected or predicted.

2 **Second Order Consequence** *(in the Workplace)*—A first of its kind global experiment with remote work, overnight in March of 2020.

3 **Third Order Consequence** *(in the Workplace)*—The whole "will they, won't they?" return-to-office (RTO) debate ongoing at many organizations even years later.

The Covid pandemic was a "black swan" event. Yet, it and its second and third order consequences monopolized people analytics team agendas for almost three years. No one predicted it. It just happened. All the people analytics models that made predictions about the future that were built in 2019 and early 2020 were wrong; likely very few, if any, were useful. People analytics rose to its highest prominence and headcount to date during the pandemic, and now we have since experienced a reshuffling since the pandemic faded from relevance. Every action has a reaction.

The last few years have been rife with exogenous, "black swan" events (e.g., Covid, Capitol protests in 2021, BLM movement, Middle East crisis, Crypto boom and bust, Silicon Valley Bank crash, Trump assassination attempt, etc.). Many of them had unintended consequences in the workplace that affected people analytics outcomes. Did you incorporate the impacts of any of the following events into your models before they occurred? Probably not.

REAL-WORLD EXAMPLE

"Turnover Prediction and Machine Learning Ethics in People Analytics" with Ryan Hammond, VP of Total Rewards and People Operations at Datavant, former People Analytics Leader at Nike, Syndio, and HiQ Labs

(Paraphrased for length from Ep. 82 of "Directionally Correct, A People Analytics Podcast")

The Journey of HiQ Labs: Pioneering but Too Early

Ryan Hammond reflects on his time at HiQ Labs, a company that was ahead of its time in using data and machine learning to predict employee attrition risk. HiQ operated on the bleeding edge of people analytics, offering insights that were not yet widely understood or accepted. This early entry into the market posed challenges, as organizations struggled to see the value of these innovations, often perceiving them as too radical or outside the "Overton Window" of acceptable business practices. HiQ's lack of comparable competitors also made its offerings seem illegitimate, creating adoption barriers despite the technology's potential.

Ethical Considerations in Turnover Prediction

HiQ's flagship product predicted attrition risks by analyzing professional profiles from public platforms like LinkedIn and Indeed. While this data was entirely professional and publicly shared, the granular insights—such as individual-level predictions—raised ethical concerns. Hammond highlights that providing such detailed data could lead to uncomfortable and potentially harmful interactions, like managers confronting employees based on inferred job-seeking behavior.

HiQ quickly learned the importance of framing their predictions differently. Rather than focusing on individual-level insights, they shifted toward aggregate patterns, such as identifying skills or job categories at risk. This approach not only alleviated ethical concerns but also provided actionable insights that organizations could address at a broader level, avoiding unnecessary tension or invasive scrutiny.

Push vs. Pull Factors in Turnover Prediction

HiQ discovered that their predictive models were less about employees' internal dissatisfaction (push factors) and more about external opportunities (pull factors). Dr. Hammond coined this as measuring "recruiter pressure"—the likelihood of an employee being targeted by recruiters due to factors like their public-facing professional profile. For example, having a picture on a LinkedIn profile significantly increased the likelihood of recruiter engagement. This insight revealed how external market dynamics, rather than internal dissatisfaction, were often the driving force behind turnover.

The Shift in Labor Market Dynamics

Ryan observed a transformative shift in how professional hiring was mediated by platforms like LinkedIn, Indeed, and ZipRecruiter. Before public-facing profiles became widespread, recruiting was more passive. Now, with professional data readily available, employees face constant recruiting pressure, even without actively seeking new roles. HiQ's ability to measure and quantify this pull factor proved to be a valuable tool for organizations navigating this new reality.

Key Takeaways for Ethical Machine Learning in People Analytics

1   Timing and Legitimacy: Innovations must align with market readiness and have comparable alternatives to gain legitimacy. Being too early can hinder adoption.

2 Ethical Framing: Avoid granular, individual-level predictions that could lead to ethical and interpersonal conflicts. Aggregate insights provide value without overstepping boundaries.

3 Focus on Pull Factors: Understanding external recruiting dynamics (pull factors) offers organizations actionable insights while maintaining employee trust.

4 Transparency and Boundaries: Clearly define the sources and limitations of data used in predictive models. Avoid non-professional or personal data to maintain ethical integrity.

5 Adapting to Labor Market Changes: Analytics functions must evolve to address the shifting dynamics of hiring and the increasing external pressures employees face.

Ryan Hammond's insights emphasize the delicate balance between innovation and ethics in people analytics. As predictive technologies become more powerful, organizations must prioritize transparency, employee trust, and actionable insights that respect individual autonomy.

When to Use Predictive Analytics

Sometimes it's important to criticize the over-use of complex methods in people analytics, although that will likely become rarer once Gen AI is broadly adopted. It's not appropriate to throw the baby out with the bathwater and suggest to never use predictive analytics in HR. That would be unwise. Predictive analytics have a time and place, which we will discuss.

However, before you know *when* to use predictive analytics, you must know *what* predictive analytics are. Whole textbooks have been written about these topics, so this section condenses and simplifies quite a bit of information. Some statisticians/data scientists may criticize the way I have categorized predictive analytics into three categories as a distinction without a difference. Nonetheless, I will explain the three categories of predictive analytics in the social context.

Three Kinds of Predictive Analytics

This section explores three primary approaches: **Multivariate Statistical Models**, which focus on explaining relationships between variables; **Machine Learning Algorithms**, designed for making accurate predictions; and **Time Series Analysis**, which specializes in forecasting trends over time. Together, these methods form the foundation for making predictions in people analytics.

MULTIVARIATE STATISTICAL MODELS—EXPLANATORY MODELS

Multivariate, explanatory models—sometimes called *inferential* models—are the currency of the academic world. It cannot be stressed enough how many variants of these models there are. Moreover, some of the most common multivariate, explanatory models are regression-based. Two of the most accessible models to the layperson are multiple linear regression and logistic regression. The simplest way of distinguishing these two models is: *Are you trying to explain a dependent variable (DV) that is continuous or categorical in nature by using other independent variables (IV)?* Continuous variables use linear regression and categorical variables use logistic regression. Typically, these methods are used on cross-sectional data to diagnose the influence of multiple independent variables on a single dependent variable.

MACHINE LEARNING ALGORITHMS—PREDICTIVE MODELS

Machine learning models are the currency of the data science world. There are many variants of these models as well. The easiest way to simplify these models, in practice, is taking data from Time 1 (T1) and extrapolating it to make predictions in Time 2 (T2). This is done by training algorithms on Training and Testing data at T1 to refine the prediction, and then projecting the prediction onto Training, Validation, and Testing data at T2 with new data. As an example, unlike using exploratory models for predicting attrition, where predicting someone should leave is actually considered model error, making predictions using machine learning models on T2 data, and validating the accuracy of such predictions, can be a reliable method for making future-based decisions in the HR domain for predicting attrition. If you really want to know how all these algorithms work, the *go-to guide* of machine learning is this free text: *The Elements of Statistical Learning* (Hastie et al., 2004). Craig Starbuck also does a good job of applying these concepts to people analytics in his 2023 book *The Fundamentals of People Analytics: With Applications in R*. Search for it online and give it a read.

TIME SERIES ANALYSIS—FORECASTING

Time is a key element of a forecast—it is a variable unto itself—which makes time series analysis distinct from other predictive models. Time being the focal variable is how to distinguish predictions from forecasts. The layperson usually connotes predictions and forecasts as interchangeable. They aren't. Forecasts are made using time series data. Two commonly used time series models are ARIMAs and survival analysis, although there are many more. The key to understanding time series analysis is that time, and its related components such as seasonality and time-based events (e.g., sales spiking around Christmas, etc.), are the variables that should influence the forecasts of the model. Considering inputs, like seasonality and lines of best fit (*in ARIMA models*) and group/category differences (*in survival models*), elucidate what the future should look like based on data from the past. One key assumption of forecasts, that is often violated in these models, is that the future is relatively stable and must look like the past, especially for these forecasts to be accurate. Hence, the point earlier about "*black swan*" events.

So How Do You Know When to Use Predictive Analytics in HR?

The short answer is, you determine if you are trying to figure out **"What will happen?"** Predictive analytics should be used in HR when there is a clear business question or problem that requires an understanding of the probabilities of the likelihood of future events to guide decisions, such as identifying turnover risks or optimizing talent acquisition strategies to plan for future hiring. Forecasting is most valuable when historical data is available, patterns need uncovering, and the potential impact of predictions aligns with organizational goals. Here are some recommendations for when to use predictive models:

WHEN TO USE:

- **Multivariate Models**—Explanatory models are best used when trying to determine *why* something happened (*diagnostic*), rather than what will happen. Common examples include using survey data to understand employee sentiment in relation to why people turnover, burnout, or become disengaged. This is most commonly used in the academic and diagnostic context.

- **Machine Learning Models**—Machine learning models are best when trying to make true, reliable, and accurate predictions. If the appropriate procedures are followed, machine learning can make predictions of HR phenomena using commonly available data (e.g., Human Capital Management systems, Applicant Tracking Systems, Learning Management Systems, etc.) and novel data (e.g., organizational network analysis, employee sentiment, etc.). Almost every people analytics function has built a turnover prediction model. Those are a nice start, but more sophisticated use cases for machine learning in HR include: Using text data from interviews to determine who was selected and will likely fail, or who wasn't selected who would have succeeded; predicting potential for promotion of junior employees; predicting team effectiveness using multiple data sources, including ONA data; and many others.

- **Time Series Models**—Time series models, such as ARIMAs, are best used when forecasting a trend into the future where time is a relevant variable to the forecast. For example, turnover rates can fluctuate based on the seasons or times of year (*i.e., vesting schedules, performance reviews, annual raises, etc.*); therefore, an ARIMA may be helpful at forecasting a turnover rate 6–18 months into the future. Another interesting example is to use a forecast to act as a control group (*or preemptive null hypothesis*) for a future event, when experimental conditions are not available. For instance, how would you know if your turnover reduction effort had its intended impact if you aren't able to run a full experiment? Create a forecast of what turnover would have been if you did nothing to reduce turnover, and then conduct stay initiatives to see if the turnover rate drops outside the confidence interval of your original forecast.

Other considerations for prediction include measurement error (e.g., Type1 and 2 error, i.e., false positives and negatives) and ethical considerations (e.g., prediction of certain topics can be creepy to employees, etc.). Additionally, you'll notice that none of these models tell you **"What should I do?"** with the predictions that are made. This is why "prescriptive analytics" are challenging. Reasonable minds can debate the leap from prediction to prescription.

REAL-WORLD EXAMPLE

"Revolutionizing Natural Language Processing and Machine Learning in Employee Selection" with Emily Campion, Assistant Professor of Management at University of Iowa, and Michael Campion, Professor at Purdue University

(Paraphrased for length from Ep. 58 of "Directionally Correct, A People Analytics Podcast")

Natural Language Processing in Employee Selection

Drs. Emily Campion and Michael Campion discuss how Natural Language Processing (NLP) is transforming employee selection by analyzing text data in innovative ways. By leveraging data from applications, structured interviews, and passive text inputs, NLP provides insights into candidates' skills and potential fit for a role. This shift not only enhances efficiency but also offers a more nuanced view of candidate attributes, reducing the need for repetitive and often wasteful application processes.

Efficiency and Cost Savings

Michael Campion highlights the dramatic efficiency gains achieved through NLP. Starting as early adopters in 2012, the Campions developed systems that automate the scoring of job applications and interviews with accuracy comparable to human evaluators. This approach saves companies hundreds of thousands of dollars annually while delivering results in a fraction of the time. One notable success story includes their work with a client where their NLP-based system saved $200,000 per session, with sessions conducted multiple times a year.

Reducing Adverse Impact and Improving Fairness

A significant breakthrough in their research was the ability to increase predictive validity while simultaneously reducing adverse impact—an uncommon combination. For instance, their work demonstrated how incorporating NLP into selection processes enhanced predictions beyond traditional measures like cognitive ability tests, which have been standard for decades. This finding underscores the potential of NLP to not only improve hiring accuracy but also foster greater fairness in selection processes.

Uncovering New Constructs with Additional Data

The Campions emphasize the value of additional data in improving predictions over relying solely on sophisticated statistical models. NLP opens the door to identifying new job-relevant constructs by analyzing candidates' language systematically. For example, text analysis can reveal nuanced traits like conscientiousness or openness to experience without relying on traditional self-report measures, which are prone to socially desirable responses and range restriction.

Personality and Behavioral Insights from Text

One innovative application of NLP is extracting personality traits indirectly from candidates' text responses. Instead of directly asking candidates about their traits—leading to biased self-assessments—NLP can infer personality based on behavioral patterns described across different situations. This approach holds promise for improving the predictive power of personality in selection processes, as it reduces the limitations of self-reported data.

Balancing Innovation with Ethical Considerations

While NLP offers powerful tools for selection, the Campions caution against construct proliferation—the tendency to create too many constructs without clear evidence of their relevance. They advocate for systematic and thoughtful exploration of new constructs to ensure they are both job-related and non-discriminatory. This balance is crucial in maintaining the ethical integrity of machine learning applications in hiring.

Key Takeaways for NLP in Employee Selection

1   Efficiency Gains: NLP can automate the scoring of applications and interviews with human-like accuracy, saving significant time and resources.

2   Improved Fairness: Incorporating NLP can increase predictive validity while reducing adverse impact, addressing common trade-offs in hiring.

3   New Insights from Text: By analyzing text data systematically, organizations can uncover previously overlooked constructs that are job-relevant and fair.

4   Enhancing Personality Measurement: NLP offers a more accurate and unbiased way to assess personality traits, reducing reliance on self-reported data.

5   Ethical Application: Balancing innovation with thoughtful construct validation ensures fairness and effectiveness in employee selection.

The Campions' pioneering work demonstrates the transformative potential of NLP in employee selection, showcasing how organizations can harness advanced technologies to improve efficiency, fairness, and predictive accuracy while maintaining ethical standards.

How to Use Gen AI for Predictions in People Analytics

As we have discussed, predictive analytics has long been a cornerstone of people analytics, enabling organizations to anticipate employee outcomes to varying degrees of success. With the advent of Gen AI, the landscape of predictive capabilities has evolved dramatically. Gen AI offers unparalleled flexibility, advanced learning capabilities and the ability to process and interpret vast amounts of structured and unstructured data. In this section we explore how Gen AI can be applied to predictive tasks in people analytics, highlighting the necessary preconditions for its effective use, the ways it differs from traditional methods, the transformative benefits it offers, as well as the critical cautions to consider.

Preconditions for Predictive Modeling with Gen AI

Before using Gen AI for predictions in people analytics, there are several key prerequisites to consider. These form the foundation for creating a robust and effective predictive model:

- **Data Quality and Accessibility:** Gen AI models require clean, structured, and comprehensive datasets to function optimally. In people analytics, this data often includes employee demographics, performance metrics, engagement surveys, training history, and retention patterns. For accurate predictions, this data needs to be of high quality, ensuring there are minimal gaps or inaccuracies. We covered what is needed extensively in the previous chapter.

- **Data Integration:** Many organizations house their people data in disparate systems, such as HRIS, LMS, and performance management tools and other business and operational data. Integrating data across these systems is essential for ensuring that Gen AI can learn from a unified, holistic view of the organization's workforce.

- **Clear Objectives:** Predictive models are most effective when they are used to answer specific business questions. Whether it's predicting employee turnover, identifying high-potential talent, or forecasting training effectiveness, it is crucial to have a clear understanding of the prediction goal. This helps in framing the problem in a way that the Gen AI model can address effectively.

- **Historical Data for Training:** To train Gen AI models, it's important to have a rich set of historical data that includes past trends and outcomes. These datasets serve as the basis for the model's ability to identify patterns, correlations, and potential predictors of future events.

How Gen AI Differs from Previous Prediction Methods

The main difference between traditional predictive methods in people analytics (such as machine learning, statistical forecasting, and regression models) and Gen AI lies in the nature and scope of the models themselves. Here are a few ways in which Gen AI stands out:

- **Advanced Learning Capabilities:** While traditional predictive models often rely on predefined rules and human intervention to determine variables of importance, Gen AI models (e.g., LLMs and transformers) can autonomously extract insights from vast datasets without the need for explicit programming. Gen AI can identify complex, nonlinear relationships in data that would be difficult to uncover with traditional methods.

- **Scalability and Flexibility:** Gen AI can process large-scale datasets quickly, making it easier to work with data from across an entire organization or even multiple organizations. This scalability is especially important in people analytics, where datasets can be vast and constantly changing. Gen AI is also flexible in adapting to different data types, whether structured (e.g., employee demographics) or unstructured (e.g., employee feedback, emails).

- **Real-Time Predictions:** Gen AI's ability to continuously learn and adapt means that predictions can be updated in real-time. For example, in employee retention forecasting, Gen AI can consider the latest inputs such as recent survey results or organizational changes, delivering up-to-date predictions on turnover risks.

- **Natural Language Processing (NLP):** Unlike traditional methods, Gen AI models can interpret unstructured data, such as employee feedback from surveys or performance reviews. This can help people analytics teams derive predictive insights from text data, such as predicting employee satisfaction or identifying the factors that influence engagement.

Benefits of Switching to Gen AI Methods

Switching to Gen AI methods for predictions in people analytics offers several compelling advantages:

- **Improved Accuracy:** By leveraging Gen AI's ability to learn from large, diverse datasets, organizations can achieve higher predictive accuracy. Traditional methods often depend on human assumptions about which factors drive predictions, but Gen AI can uncover hidden patterns and relationships that might otherwise go unnoticed.

- **Democratized Decision-Making:** With the ability to process and analyze data quickly, Gen AI enables faster decision-making, but also with a user interface that is easily approachable by HR users. For HR leaders, this means being able to predict turnover risks, identify talent gaps, or understand training needs with speed and precision, empowering them to take timely actions without needing extensive technical training.

- **Personalized Insights:** Gen AI models can go beyond aggregate predictions and provide personalized insights at an individual level. For example, instead of predicting overall turnover rates, Gen AI can identify specific employees who are most likely to leave, allowing HR to intervene proactively and tailor retention strategies. More on this in the "Cautions" section.

- **Continuous Improvement:** Gen AI models continuously evolve as they are exposed to new data. This makes them adaptable and able to improve over time, leading to more reliable and accurate predictions in the long run. Traditional models, in contrast, may require frequent manual updates and recalibrations.

Cautions and Considerations When Using Gen AI for Predictions

While the benefits of Gen AI in people analytics are significant, it is important to remain cautious and aware of the challenges and risks associated with its use:

- **Data Privacy and Security:** As with any use of data in HR, privacy and security are paramount when applying Gen AI in people analytics. Organizations must ensure that sensitive employee data is protected, and that the AI system complies with privacy laws such as GDPR or CCPA. This includes implementing safeguards against unauthorized access to personal data and ensuring transparency in how data is used.

- **Ethics and Culture:** The example was used earlier of the ability to democratize making individual-level predictions using Gen AI. This comes with many caveats. Are we using data that employees are aware of? Do they have informed consent to the data being collected and the actions taken? Who benefits, the employee or the company? All of these will be big questions to wrestle with from an ethical and company culture perspective.

- **Over-Reliance on Predictions:** While Gen AI can provide valuable insights, it's important for HR leaders to understand that predictions are not always perfect. Gen AI models can make errors, especially in complex, dynamic environments. Organizations should treat AI-generated predictions as one input among many and continue to rely on human expertise to make final decisions.

- **Interpretability:** Gen AI models, particularly deep learning models, can often be seen as "black boxes," meaning it can be difficult to understand how they arrive at specific predictions. This lack of transparency can be a concern for decision-makers who need to justify their decisions or explain them to other stakeholders. Organizations should consider using explainable AI techniques (e.g., SHAP values) for diagnostics on top of LLMs to enhance the interpretability of the predictions. Unexplainable Gen AI will have no place in organizations.

- **Fairness:** One of the most critical risks when using Gen AI for people analytics is the potential for bias and unfairness. If the data used to train the Gen AI model reflects historical unbalanced datasets (e.g., gender or racial differences in hiring or promotions), the predicted accuracy will likely suffer and be unfair at face value. It is crucial to ensure that datasets are representative, diverse, and ethically sound, and to use techniques such as fairness constraints during training to mitigate this risk.

- **Implementation and Change Management:** Switching to Gen AI-based methods for prediction requires a significant investment in time, training, and infrastructure. There may also be resistance to change, as employees and leaders may feel more comfortable with traditional methods. Ensuring smooth adoption requires proper training, clear communication, and ongoing support.

Gen AI represents a significant leap forward in the ability to make predictions in people analytics. By leveraging its advanced capabilities, organizations can unlock deeper insights, drive more personalized strategies, and achieve more accurate predictions. However, it's essential to approach Gen AI with caution, paying close attention to potential biases, ensuring data privacy, and understanding the limitations of AI-driven predictions. We need to be at the forefront of the transformation towards using Gen AI to remain leaders in the HR function, but we also need to be the wisest arbiters of this information as well.

Where to Start: Find the Right Use Case

Implementing Gen AI in people analytics may feel like a daunting task, especially given the technology's vast potential and transformative capabilities. You probably don't feel like an expert, so you may feel hesitant. With its ability to process massive datasets, uncover hidden patterns, and generate predictive insights, Gen AI offers so much positive potential. However, the key to success of integrating Gen AI into your people analytics strategy lies in starting with the right use case. Identifying a clear, impactful problem to solve ensures that your efforts are focused, achievable, and aligned with business goals, setting the foundation for success. This has been the theme of the entire book; let's not do people analytics for people analytics' sake, but let's make an impact—first.

Choosing the right use case is not just about feasibility—it's about finding opportunities where Gen AI can deliver tangible business value. The best starting point is to address a pressing organizational need, such as improving retention, enhancing employee engagement, or forecasting workforce demand—or an organization-specific business problem. By focusing on a specific, high-priority challenge, organizations can demonstrate the potential of Gen AI while building confidence and momentum for broader adoption. In this section, we'll explore how to identify and prioritize use cases that align with your goals, balance complexity and impact, and maximize the return on your Gen AI investment.

Gen AI Use Cases

We should use Gen AI to revolutionize the field of people analytics by unlocking new levels of productivity, refining predictive accuracy, and elevating the quality of HR and workforce insights. From automating repetitive tasks and generating tailored reports to providing real-time talent recommendations and predictive models, there are a broad spectrum of use cases that will enhance decision-making and strategy. In this section, we'll explore specific examples of how Gen AI is transforming people analytics, with better predictions, productivity gains, and quality work.

Better Predictions

As described earlier in the chapter, traditional methods of machine learning, such as Support Vector Machines or Ridge Regression, have performed quite well at predictive tasks in people analytics. However, early evidence suggests that the traditional top performing gradient descent machine learning algorithms (i.e., XGBoost and Random Forests) are being replaced by algorithms created by Gen AI in machine learning competitions such as Kaggle. LLMs are now writing their own predictive algorithms that are outperforming the best human-made algorithms. On one hand, this is quite impressive, and for the first time in years, people analytics predictions will likely improve and perhaps even asymptote towards near-perfect prediction. On the cautionary side, some of the current machine learning algorithms were already considered a "black box" of prediction and now that black box is "squared" (i.e., the predictive mechanisms will be a black box, and how the algorithm itself that was generated will be a black box—thus a black box squared). Regardless, this means that previously hindered predictions in people analytics could come to be a reality. Here are some examples of areas where better predictions will be employed using Gen AI algorithms:

- **Current Predictions**—Gen AI-generated algorithms will be able to improve any machine learning-based predictions your teams currently make. Noteworthy, these predictions can be made using prompts rather than traditional coding languages such as R or Python.

- **Previously Unavailable Predictions**—Despite your best efforts, many times in people analytics the "noise to signal" ratio is so unbalanced that accurate predictions are unable to be made on many topics. Two factors will likely contribute to potential accuracy improvements using Gen AI. First, as described before, with algorithmic improvements comes the ability to see more signals in the noise, and that leaves potential for predictions to be made where they were previously unavailable. Also, Gen AI-enabled data architecture will broaden the breadth of traditional datasets by which to make predictions. Better algorithms and previously untapped data will make for newly found predictions to be made.

- **Better Data**—Building on from the previous point, with better data architecture comes more opportunities for making predictions, and with minimal compute costs for making predictions, the nominal cost of making predictions will trend toward zero. Imagine using a single prompt to ask Gen AI: *"I have 10 outcomes I'm trying to predict [listing ×1, ×2, ×3,…], please find every combination of variables, including time components such as seasonality, that most accurately predicts those outcomes from our workforce data. Please indicate what variables were the key drivers of each prediction, visualize the results in charts, and dig into the relevant research from peer-reviewed journals to show why these variables accurately predict the outcomes. Please list the top five recommendations based on the peer-reviewed research findings for addressing our organizational problems for each prediction. Also, please suggest data points we don't currently have in our systems that would improve the predictions, and how I might get these data points at my organization."*

The Inquisitor and The Change Agent proposed in Chapter 4 are real. What was just described within that prompt could be the equivalent of the whole team's worth of analysis over many months' worth of work today. Gen AI's predictive capability completely disrupts the people analytics value chain. Now, people analytics teams spend the majority of their time analyzing data, but the volume of sheer compute and data analysis will allow for lifetimes and careers worth of analysis to be completed in minutes if not seconds. We must ask the right questions, we must build the right data architectures, and we must refocus our efforts on taking action based on what we find. The prediction and analysis step is completely commoditized.

If you know almost all analysis is commoditized, all that is left to improve is getting better data for your predictive models. Many people analytics teams neglect external factors to their organization when making internal predictions. That is like fighting with one hand behind your back. If you are not combining external labor market data, benchmarks, trends, role-specific supply and demand, and broad economic sentiment from providers such as Lightcast into your data warehouse, how can you possibly query such data using Gen AI? The only limits to our predictive abilities will be the data limitations we have, and the limits of our imagination. Data is the new oil, so go get the data you need to power your team.

Productivity Gains

As described before, improved data architecture enables vast improvements in efficiency for people analytics. But as anyone who has studied Lean/Six Sigma knows, vast productivity improvements in one area usually only highlight bottlenecks in other areas. What should be pursued is called *"One Piece Flow"* (Liker, 2004) from manufacturing. One-piece flow occurs when items move through the production process one at a time, without waiting in batches or queues. It aims to minimize waste, reduce lead times, and improve quality by focusing on continuous movement and flow. This approach aligns with the Just-in-Time (JIT) principle, ensuring that each step produces only what is needed for the next step at the right time. What this means for people analytics is that we should be using Gen AI at as many steps in the people analytics value chain as possible to reduce waste and increase efficiency and throughput. Here are some examples of areas where productivity gains will be employed using Gen AI:

- **Workflows**—Workflow automation may be the most exciting topic for the introduction of Gen AI into people analytics. It is the secret weapon for productivity gains. Let Gen AI streamline people analytics workflows by automating repetitive tasks like data cleaning, report generation, and summarization. It can also facilitate seamless integration between systems, enabling smoother data pipelines and faster insights.

- **Products**—Teams spend countless hours generating products to interface with HR and business users. Let Gen AI enhance the development of analytics products by generating tailored dashboards, visualizations, and predictive models with minimal manual intervention. It also enables the rapid prototyping of new tools, helping teams iterate and deliver solutions that better meet stakeholder needs. Let's never build another dashboard again.

- **Research**—Having scientific grounding for our work is critical. Let Gen AI accelerate literature reviews by summarizing large volumes of academic papers and industry reports. It can also assist in hypothesis generation and exploratory analysis by uncovering hidden patterns and trends within datasets. Do research at scale. No more waiting six months to find a result.

- **Project Management and Meetings**—Having a project manager on your people analytics team today can be a secret productivity unlock. Now you can let Gen AI be your project manager, and boost project management efficiency by generating task plans, tracking project milestones, and providing status updates based on real-time data. For meetings, it can transcribe, summarize, and highlight actionable insights, ensuring teams stay aligned and productive.

Focus on asking the right questions and influencing action to be taken. This is the way forward for people analytics. For years, analytics teams have talked about freeing themselves for doing more "strategic" work when the burdens of the repetitive work were automated. Now it is time to pay the piper and see if this wasn't just an excuse for not doing more impactful work. We will have the time—now let's make the requisite "strategic" impact on the business. Let's pay for ourselves.

Quality Work

We should be doing better, more impactful work. Each business is different, and in the first section of this book, *Business Value*, we discussed at length the necessity for doing work that directly impacts the business and creates tangible value. The problem with this is most people analytics teams are looking to address problems within their span of influence (e.g., using HCM data only) and for customers in their direct reporting structure (i.e., HR functions). Everyone knows that most business problems cut across multiple business functions and multiple data sources. Therefore, it is imperative that people analytics functions get out of their shell and start spanning boundaries. We all do turnover prediction because it's within our four walls and relatively easy. We should be doing things because they are hard, not because they are convenient. And not just be copy-cats of the "low hanging fruit" research from other people analytics teams. Gen AI opens this door to do hard things at scale.

Below are examples of high-impact predictive use cases for generative AI in people analytics. I've kept the focus on five use cases that tangibly demonstrate business value, including ROI considerations, and underscore how other business units beyond HR can recognize the power of people analytics. However, there are probably better examples of ideas to pursue at your organization. Pursue those ideas first, and don't be a copy-cat of these ideas just because they are in a book.

1. PREDICTING ORGANIZATIONAL SKILL SHIFTS AND FUTURE ROLE GAPS

Generative AI can analyze industry trends using external data, internal performance data, and employee development behaviors based on learning management systems to forecast which skills and roles will soon be in demand—or become obsolete due to Gen AI for your organization. This really is a business critical analysis at most firms.

Why it's important (business value and ROI):

- **Avoid critical skill shortages:** By proactively identifying emerging skill gaps, organizations can invest in upskilling/reskilling *before* the shortage hurts project deliverables or product launches.

- **Reduce hiring costs:** When HR knows precisely which roles and skills will be needed 6–12 months out, it lowers recruitment costs, shortens time-to-fill, and ensures continuous pipeline health.

- **Enhance revenue and speed to market:** Having the right talent at the right time shortens product development cycles and drives innovation. Business units see direct top-line impact when cutting-edge skills are readily available.

Key ROI Metrics:

- **Cost of vacancy reduction** (unfilled roles cause project delays)
- **Training ROI** (targeting training dollars where they're needed most)
- **Time-to-market gains** (accelerating product innovation)

2. FORECASTING PRODUCTIVITY GAINS AND ROI FROM TARGETED LEARNING AND DEVELOPMENT

Generative AI models examine historical performance data from your performance management system, project outcomes from your PMO tools, and learning engagement from your LMS to predict how specific training programs will—or won't—boost productivity, quality, or revenue.

Why it's important (business value and ROI):

- **Pinpoint high-ROI training:** Instead of blanket training for everyone, AI narrows down the programs that measurably improve individual and team performance—directly linking L and D spend to business outcomes.

- **Cross-functional collaboration:** Finance and operations can see a direct link between an L and D investment (e.g., a new data-science upskilling course) and improved project quality or delivery speed. This solidifies HR's strategic role.

- **Avoid wasted budget:** By predicting which employees (and which skill sets) stand to benefit most, you can focus resources where they'll produce tangible returns.

Key ROI Metrics:

- **Lift in performance indicators** (sales quotas, project completion rates)
- **Employee engagement and retention** (are trained employees less likely to leave?)
- **Cost savings from reduced errors or rework**

3. PROACTIVE MANAGEMENT OF TALENT SURPLUSES OR SHORTFALLS IN PROJECT-BASED ENVIRONMENTS

Generative AI can marry operational project forecasts from tools like Jira with people data to anticipate exactly when certain roles or skill sets will be underutilized or overburdened. For workforce planning purposes, this data can be married with external data to show talent availability for overburdened roles and wage impact for areas of surplus. This will help HR partner with operations to dynamically redeploy talent where it's needed most.

Why it's important (business value and ROI):

- **Optimized staffing costs:** Talent surpluses mean you're paying for idle capacity. Shortfalls mean expensive overtime or missed deadlines. Predicting these scenarios early allows balanced resource allocation.
- **Better resource planning:** Cross-functional teams (like finance and supply chain) can see workforce constraints in advance, adjusting project timelines or budgets.
- **Prevent project overruns:** Workforce constraints can be a silent culprit behind cost overruns. AI-driven predictions help contain costs by aligning the right number of people with the right skill sets to the right projects.

Key ROI Metrics:

- **Reduced overtime/pay premiums** (fewer last-minute hires or contractor fees)
- **Project margin improvements** (avoiding project delays tied to staffing)
- **Improved utilization rates** (keeping employees fully and appropriately engaged)

4. DATA-DRIVEN INTERNAL MOBILITY AND SUCCESSION PATHING

Generative AI pinpoints internal candidates for upcoming leadership or specialized role vacancies using talent management systems by analyzing their career trajectories, performance reviews, the requisite skill requirements and associate job architecture, and aspirations gleaned from feedback platforms or even engagement surveys.

Why it's important (business value and ROI):

- **Retain institutional knowledge:** Instead of constantly hiring externally, organizations can fill critical roles faster and more effectively from within. This reduces talent acquisition costs and ramps up time.

- **Boost morale and engagement:** Employees seeing real internal mobility opportunities are less likely to jump ship, saving on turnover costs.

- **Cross-BU impact:** Business units gain leaders who already understand the culture, have the skills, know the process flows, and have stakeholder networks, reducing onboarding friction and speeding strategic execution.

Key ROI Metrics:

- **Reduced external recruiting costs** (fewer headhunter fees, less churn)

- **Time-to-productivity** (internal hires can often hit the ground running)

- **Improved leadership pipeline readiness** (fewer critical leadership gaps)

5. PREDICTING TEAM-LEVEL BUSINESS OUTCOMES FROM PEOPLE METRICS

By correlating performance metrics (e.g., sales data, project outputs) with people analytics (e.g., team cohesion, skill competencies, burnout indicators), Gen AI can predict which teams are on track to exceed or miss targets—and why.

Why it's important (business value and ROI):

- **Direct impact on revenue and profit:** When teams consistently deliver or miss key performance targets, the bottom line is affected. AI lets you intervene earlier (e.g., extra support, coaching, resource reallocation).

- **Alignment with overall strategy:** Executives in sales, operations, or R and D can see that people analytics directly correlate with—and can forecast—business-critical metrics like revenue, product quality, or customer satisfaction.

- **Measurable interventions:** Instead of guessing what's wrong with a stagnating team, AI insights can point to specific root causes (lack of training, manager–employee mismatch, insufficient staffing).

Key ROI Metrics:

- **Uplift in quarterly revenue or operational KPIs** (by addressing team issues proactively)

- **Reduced project or product delays** (less rework, fewer slowdowns)

- **Lower team turnover** (improved team culture and performance)

The above five applications of using Gen AI to predict business outcomes transcend typical "hype" by providing tangible, cross-functional business value. They show how HR can evolve from a support function to a true strategic driver—delivering data-driven ROI, enhancing collaboration with other departments, and future-proofing the people analytics team to drive value for years to come.

Algorithmic Decision-Making

The introduction of Gen AI in HR has significantly expanded the potential for algorithmic decision-making in people analytics. This fact challenges traditional practices and sparks debates about the ethical and practical implications of these types of decisions, questioning "who is the human in the loop" to make these decisions. Gen AI enables HR professionals to analyze vast datasets, which allows for the ability to automate tasks and decisions at a scale previously unimaginable. However, this surge in AI adoption comes with critical concerns about fairness. Algorithms trained on historical data may inadvertently replicate or even amplify existing imbalances in selection, for instance, potentially leading to discriminatory practices. Legal frameworks, like the New York City AI hiring law, aim to mitigate these risks—although the law as currently consititued may promote procedures that risk being both unfair and legally questionable in their pursuit of equal outcomes.

One of the central debates in algorithmic decision-making within people analytics revolves around the appropriate division of labor between human judgment and machine intelligence, which Jackson Roatch and I covered in our article "Elephant Hunting: Weighing Human vs. Algorithmic Input in Decision Making in People Analytics" (DC News, 2023). While humans bring moral reasoning and contextual understanding, they are also prone to cognitive biases, such as favoritism or stereotyping, that can undermine fairness. Algorithms, on the other hand, excel in consistency, scalability, and the ability to focus on relevant data points, often outperforming humans in predictive accuracy. However, their lack of contextual awareness, sometimes referred to as the "broken-leg problem," highlights the importance of human oversight. The challenge lies in designing systems where humans and AI collaborate effectively, with algorithms augmenting human decision-making rather than replacing it entirely. Your organization must have some mechanism for oversight or auditing by humans to understand what decisions are being made, how they are made, and what factors drove the decision.

Generative AI also redefines the counterfactual in HR decision-making. The value of AI-driven processes should be assessed not in isolation but relative to the current status quo of human-led decision-making, which is often inconsistent and overtly biased itself. For example, hiring processes dominated by "gut instincts" and unstructured interviews are rife with subjectivity and often yield suboptimal results. By integrating AI into these workflows, organizations can introduce structure, transparency, and a level of objectivity that minimizes unfairness. At the same time, mechanisms must be in place to allow humans to override algorithmic recommendations when contextual nuances or critical external information are at play, ensuring a dynamic balance between human and machine input.

The widespread use of Gen AI in HR presents an opportunity to elevate decision-making standards in people analytics, but it requires the bravery to make the change and the scientific rigor to prove the efficacy (or lack thereof). Organizations can move beyond the binary narrative of humans versus machines and explore synergies that harness the strengths of both. This includes leveraging behavioral science and I/O psychology to create systems that account for human psychology, offering mechanisms for contesting or refining AI-driven decisions, and ensuring transparency in how algorithms operate. You should be aware of the *Uniform Guidelines on Employee Selection Procedures* (Uniform Guidelines, 2025) and the SIOP *Recommendations for AI-based Assessments* (SIOP, 2025) when being involved in such kinds of decisions. Let's allow for experimentation to maximize the potential for better talent decisions, while enhancing business outcomes and fostering trust among stakeholders.

REAL-WORLD EXAMPLE

"The Lindy Effect and Algorithmic Decision Making in People Analytics" with Jackson Roatch, People Analytics Leaders at WEX and Author of The Moderating Mediator Blog

(Paraphrased for length from Ep. 66 of "Directionally Correct, A People Analytics Podcast")

The Lindy Effect in People Analytics

Jackson Roatch draws on the Lindy Effect—a statistical phenomenon that suggests the longevity of something is proportional to how long it has already existed—to explore the relationship between employee tenure and turnover. Originally coined in the 1950s in the context of Broadway comedians, the Lindy Effect posits that things that have been around longer are likely to persist. Roatch applies this concept to workplace dynamics, highlighting how longer employee tenure correlates with reduced turnover risk. By connecting this observation to organizational data and theory, Roatch provides a framework for understanding worker retention that resonates across departments and industries.

Algorithmic Decision-Making: Ethical Challenges and Opportunities

Jackson discusses the inflection point AI has reached in high-stakes decisions like personnel selection. While AI offers the potential to screen vast amounts of data (e.g., resumes) quickly and efficiently, it also introduces concerns about bias. Bias, Roatch explains, arises as systematic error—consistent over- or underestimation of a measure—often affecting protected demographic groups such as age, gender, or ethnicity. This scaling of bias is one of the primary ethical challenges of AI in people analytics.

He emphasizes the dual nature of bias in decision-making: While human decision-making, such as unstructured interviews, is inherently biased (favoring traits like charisma or physical appearance), algorithmic bias is at least measurable and auditable. Unlike human biases, which are hidden and often undocumented, biases in AI can be identified and mitigated with the right tools and frameworks, making algorithmic decision-making a potentially more transparent alternative.

Comparing AI to the Status Quo

A key insight from Roatch's discussion is the need to compare algorithmic decision-making to the existing counterfactual—namely, unstructured job interviews. He argues that unstructured interviews, the current norm, are riddled with biases and lack any measurable data. For example, hiring decisions based on personal impressions often privilege the most charismatic or conventionally attractive candidates. In contrast, AI-based decision-making, while imperfect, offers a retraceable path to identify and correct bias.

Jackson underscores the importance of auditing AI models, a growing area in I/O psychology. These audits allow organizations to measure and improve their algorithms systematically. Even if an AI model only explains a small percentage of the variance in hiring outcomes, it can still represent a significant improvement over random chance or unmeasured human biases.

Key Takeaways for Ethical Algorithmic Decision-Making

1 The Lindy Effect and Workforce Dynamics: Employee tenure is a strong predictor of retention, reinforcing the importance of using theory-backed insights to inform workforce planning.

2 Understanding Bias: Systematic errors in AI models, particularly those affecting protected groups, need to be rigorously measured and mitigated to ensure fairness.

3 Comparing AI to Human Decision-Making: While human biases in hiring are pervasive and undocumented, AI biases are measurable and correctable, making algorithmic decision-making a more transparent alternative.

4 Auditing AI Models: Auditing tools and practices are crucial for identifying bias and improving the performance of AI-driven systems in personnel selection.

5 Balancing Innovation with Ethics: AI models may not be perfect, but their ability to provide consistent, measurable insights offers an opportunity for progress compared to traditional, unstructured methods.

Roatch's insights illuminate the complexities and potential of algorithmic decision-making in people analytics. By grounding his approach in the Lindy Effect and emphasizing the need for ethical AI practices, he provides a compelling case for how organizations can responsibly adopt advanced technologies to improve workforce decisions.

People Analytics is Not Data Science

People analytics may employ data scientists, but people analytics is not data science alone. People analytics is often conflated with data science, but in practice, it is significantly more complex and multifaceted—and the introduction of Gen AI only makes this fact more apparent, as many aspects of data science are being automated. While data science thrives within the digital realm, people analytics requires bridging the gap between digital insights and human behavior. This additional layer of complexity makes people analytics both more challenging and, in my opinion, more rewarding. Let's break this down using a comparison of workflows through the lens of the "input-process-output" framework.

The Data Science Workflow: A Digital Loop

Data science operates within a streamlined, digital ecosystem, where inputs, processes, and outputs are all confined to computational systems. A classic example is fraud detection:

- **Input:** Digital data (e.g., credit card transactions)
- **Process:** Digital algorithms (e.g., fraud detection models)

- **Output:** Digital outcome (e.g., flagged fraudulent credit card transactions)

This workflow focuses on optimizing digital systems and processes, remaining entirely within a virtual context.

The People Analytics Workflow: Bridging Digital and Human Realms

People analytics introduces a layer of complexity because its goal is not just to generate insights but to drive behavior change and measurable outcomes in the real world. Let's examine the workflow using turnover prediction as an example:

- **Input:** Qualitative and quantitative data (e.g., HCM data, survey results)
- **Process 1:** Analytical modeling (e.g., turnover prediction models)
- **Process 2:** Human behavior change (e.g., employee retention initiatives informed by insights)
- **Output 1:** Human outcome (e.g., improved retention rates)
- **Output 2:** Business outcome (e.g., increased ROI)

Unlike data science, people analytics doesn't stop at generating outputs. The process extends into the real world, requiring collaboration across HR, business leadership, and other stakeholders to implement and evaluate changes. This book is written as a way of bridging these divides to make human and business impact, while adopting the best practices in prediction and modeling for the age of Gen AI.

Why People Analytics Is More Complex

The key distinction lies in **Process 2:** Transforming analytical insights into meaningful actions that influence human behavior. This step introduces several challenges:

1 **Interdisciplinary Expertise:** Requires collaboration between data scientists, I/O psychologists, data engineers, consultants, other HR functions, and business leaders.

2 **Behavioral Change:** Success depends on effectively influencing human behavior, which is inherently unpredictable and context dependent.

3 **Dual Outputs:** Unlike data science, people analytics aims to deliver both human-centric (e.g., satisfaction, engagement) and business-centric (e.g., cost savings, revenue growth) outcomes.

Visualizing the Difference

To make this comparison more tangible, below is a visual representation of the workflows:

Data Science Workflow:

- Digital Data → Digital Algorithms → Digital Outcome

Example: Credit card transactions → Fraud detection model → Flagged transactions

People Analytics Workflow:

- Qualitative/Quantitative Data → Analytical Modeling → Human Behavior Change → Human Outcome and Business Outcome

Example: HCM/Survey Data → Turnover Prediction Model → Retention Initiatives → Higher Retention and ROI

This expanded workflow illustrates why people analytics extends beyond the boundaries of traditional data science, requiring both technical expertise and a deep understanding of human behavior. By recognizing these differences, we can better appreciate the nuanced and impactful nature of people analytics as a field dedicated to not just understanding people but driving meaningful change in organizations. Now that you know how to make predictions using Gen AI, and how to do people analytics effectively, you are equipped to make a direct business impact today.

Summary

AI has transformed predictive modeling from an experimental exercise into an actionable strategic asset in people analytics. This chapter explores how organizations can move beyond generating insights to taking predictive action that drives tangible business value. By leveraging AI-powered forecasting methods, historical trends, and real-time data, people analytics teams can anticipate workforce challenges and proactively shape the future. The chapter discusses how methodologies from fields like demography, history, and data science can improve predictive accuracy, while also addressing the risks and ethical considerations of AI-driven decision-making.

Key Takeaways

1 **The Power of Prediction in People Analytics**

   o AI enables organizations to forecast workforce trends with greater accuracy, helping HR leaders shift from reactive to proactive decision-making.

   o Predictions must be actionable—insights without intervention offer little business value.

2 **Demographics as a Predictive Tool**

   o Workforce planning can borrow from demographic modeling to anticipate skill gaps, generational shifts, and labor market trends.

   o Simple variables like hiring rates, turnover, and tenure demographics can accurately project future workforce composition.

3 **Learning from History to Improve Prediction**

   o Historians use primary sources, human interactions, and counterfactual analysis to understand past events—similar methods can help predict organizational behavior.

   o Studying historical workplace trends and organizational behavior helps anticipate recurring challenges.

4 **Machine Learning vs. Generative AI for Predictions**

   o Traditional machine learning excels at structured predictive modeling (e.g., attrition forecasts), but Gen AI enhances automation and decision support.

   o Gen AI's key strength is processing unstructured data, such as employee sentiment, to provide contextually rich insights.

5 **The Fallacy of Perfect Prediction**

   o Predictions are never absolute—organizations should embrace probabilistic thinking and scenario planning rather than expecting certainty.

   o Black swan events (e.g., Covid-19) disrupt even the best predictions, highlighting the need for agility in decision-making.

6 **Real-World Applications of AI-Powered Prediction**

   o Companies like AWS and Datavant use AI to forecast turnover risks, workforce planning needs, and employee engagement patterns.

   o Ethical AI in people analytics requires balancing predictive accuracy with employee privacy and fairness.

7 Algorithmic Decision-Making and Ethical Risks

o AI can reduce human bias in hiring and promotions, but poorly designed models risk amplifying existing inequities.

o Transparency and governance frameworks are necessary to ensure fair, interpretable AI-driven decisions.

8 The Role of Causality in AI Predictions

o AI models should incorporate causal reasoning to distinguish correlation from causation in workforce trends.

o Counterfactual simulations can help HR leaders test the impact of interventions before implementing changes.

9 When to Use Predictive Analytics in HR

o Predictive analytics should be applied when organizations need to anticipate outcomes that significantly impact workforce strategy, such as attrition risk, skill shortages, or workforce planning.

o AI-driven forecasting should complement—not replace—human expertise and qualitative insights.

10 AI and the Future of Workforce Decision-Making

o AI-driven insights can enhance workforce planning, internal mobility strategies, and employee experience design.

o The key to success is integrating AI predictions with actionable HR strategies, ensuring that insights translate into measurable business impact.

By understanding AI's predictive capabilities, organizations can build a more agile and future-ready workforce, leveraging data-driven foresight to navigate uncertainty and seize new opportunities.

References

Andrew (2022). "You should always (always) have a Naive model. It's the simplest, cleanest, most intuitive way to explain whether your system is at least treading water. And if it is (that's a big IF), how much better than Naive is it." | Statistical Modeling, Causal Inference, and Social Science. Columbia.edu. statmodeling.stat.columbia.edu/2022/09/08/you-should-always-always-have-a-naive-model-its-the-simplest-cleanest-most-intuitive-way-to-explain-whether-your-system-is-at-least-treading-water-and-if-it-is-thats-a-big-if-how-much-b/ (archived at https://perma.cc/98FY-YBLG).

Box, G. E. P., and Draper, N. R. (1987). *Empirical Model-Building and Response Surfaces*. Wiley.

DC News. (2023a). A Historian, A Demographer, and A Data Scientist Walk Into a Bar… Substack. directionallycorrectnews.substack.com/p/a-historian-demographer-and-data?r=ybtwi&utm_campaign=post&utm_medium=web&triedRedirect=true (archived at https://perma.cc/M2VD-45BB).

Ferguson, N. (2011). *Virtual History: Alternatives and Counterfactuals*. Penguin.

Hastie, T., Tibshirani, R. and Friedman, J. H. (2004). *The Elements of Statistical Learning: Data Mining, Inference, and Prediction*. New York: Springer.

Helms, J. (2017). Plan Ahead. It Wasn't Raining When Noah Built the Ark. Finding Your Way. johnmichaelhelms.com/plan-ahead-it-wasnt-raining-when-noah-built-the-ark/?utm_source=chatgpt.com (archived at https://perma.cc/66VU-HCAY).

Lightcast (2024). Workforce Analytics: Examples and Best Practices. Lightcast. Available at: lightcast.io/resources/blog/what-is-workforce-analytics (archived at https://perma.cc/287Z-EQ7Q).

Liker, J. K. (2004). *The Toyota Way: 14 Management Principles from the World's Greatest Manufacturer*. McGraw-Hill.

Napper, C., Hines, S., Campion, E. and Campion, M. (2023). Revolutionizing Natural Language Processing and Machine Learning in Employee Selection. Directionally Correct. www.podbean.com/eas/pb-gmts5-151f6d3 (archived at https://perma.cc/U2YB-38GJ) Ep. 58.

Napper, C., Hines, S. and Hammond, R. (2024). Turnover Prediction and Machine Learning Ethics in People Analytics. Directionally Correct. www.podbean.com/eas/pb-hujxy-159002d (archived at https://perma.cc/8D6P-EU9D) Ep. 82.

Napper, C., Hines, S. and Roatch, J. (2023). The Lindy Effect and Algorithmic Decision Making in People Analytics. Directionally Correct. www.podbean.com/eas/pb-qxskv-151f6cb (archived at https://perma.cc/R7FH-8CN4) Ep. 66.

Pearl, J. and Mackenzie, D. (2020). *The Book of Why: The New Science of Cause and Effect*. Basic Books.

Society for Industrial and Organizational Psychology. (2025). SIOP Releases Recommendations for AI-Based Assessments. www.siop.org/Research-Publications/Items-of-Interest/ArtMID/19366/ArticleID/7327/SIOP-Releases-Recommendations-for-AI-Based-Assessments (archived at https://perma.cc/6CJW-4LYD).

Starbuck, C. (2023). *The Fundamentals of People Analytics*. Springer.

Taleb, N. N. (2007). *The Black Swan*. Allen Lane.

Uniform Guidelines (2025). Uniform Employee Selection Guidelines on Employee Selection Procedures. www.uniformguidelines.com/ (archived at https://perma.cc/33PH-975G).

Zaillian, S., Sorkin, A., Chervin, S. and Lewis, M. (2011). *Moneyball*. IMDb. www.imdb.com/title/tt1210166/ (archived at https://perma.cc/KL2Z-37KT).

7

The Ethics of AI: Don't Cross the Line

This chapter addresses the ethical use of analytics and Gen AI, establishing a framework for responsible data use that supports sustainable business practices while still helping a business dominate.

"With great power comes great responsibility."—Voltaire.

As a child, the concept of "telling a story" was a euphemism for lying. At the time, storytelling was seen as an act of deception, a way to manipulate facts to serve one's own interests. Fast forward to a career in people analytics, and we hear a very different message constantly: *"Tell a story with the data."* The same behavior that was once chastised as a child is now a professional imperative, albeit with more polished intentions. To be clear, we know HR analysts aren't actually being encouraged to lie when they are coached to use better data storytelling. However, it can't help but be observed that there is a slippery slope between shaping a narrative and distorting the truth.

This could cynically be called "learning to lie with data." Every analyst has had temptation foisted upon them to massage the data, cajole the data, or even "torture the data until it confesses" by a leader who doesn't like what the data says and wants it to say something different, that is likely more politically expedient to their ears. And this is when the analyst gets the feedback: "You need to learn to tell a better story with the data." As we discussed in the first section of the book, *Business Value*, we can try to be a neutral arbiter of information, but the power and politics in an organization have a strong pull of gravity. We must graduate to being decision-makers if we so choose, which is especially relevant now with the introduction of Gen AI.

The ethics of data storytelling are murky enough, but artificial intelligence takes it to an entirely new level. AI systems are not just tools for analysis; they are tools for scale. They can summarize, visualize, and extrapolate from data faster than any human, weaving narratives that feel compelling and authoritative. But here's the catch: If those narratives are built on biased assumptions, cherry-picked data, or skewed datasets, AI doesn't just enable lies or outright incorrect results, it amplifies them. What used to be an individual's lie becomes a systemic distortion, broadcast to potentially thousands of employees and/or leaders without a second thought.

This is where the ethics of AI intersects with the art of storytelling. The power to "tell a story" becomes the power to reshape reality, and if we aren't careful, we risk crossing an invisible line where persuasion becomes deception. The problem isn't just that AI can lie or that actors who use AI can lie; it's that lies can be told at scale, and that scale makes all the difference.

The Role of Virtue in People Analytics

When people analytics began as a discipline, it used to be an exciting place where leaders in the field were constantly sharing new ideas, advanced techniques, and new experimental use cases for how people analytics could make an impact on the business. Then something happened. Over time less and less content was published about the next advanced people analytics use case or the next innovative idea. More and more content was published about words that were somewhat foreign at the time. Words like "privacy," "GDPR," "ethics," and phrases like "*just because you can doesn't mean you should*" and "*with great power comes great responsibility.*" Was the field plateauing, and why so soon? Why couldn't we get back to more advancements in the field again?

Fast forward to this moment, and we have become aware that people analytics practitioners have a responsibility on our hands to be ethical and virtuous actors, especially as increasingly nascent and more invasive data collection procedures proliferate. Also, how AI can be layered on top of software and data infrastructure to create an increasingly dystopian and surveillance state at work for employees. Our responsibility goes as follows: The trust, the privacy, and even the livelihood of employees falls into our hands more and more by the day. I had presupposed that people analytics was a force for good, and used to take a childish view that our field was above reproach due to our sterling reputation and integrity of our inhabitants. C'est la vie, we are all human... and flawed as such.

Governance

"*Quis custodiet ipsos custodes?*" is an ancient Latin phrase for "*Who will watch the watchmen?*" Due to our heightened level of responsibility, many people analytics practitioners have proposed the solution of increased *"governance."* As currently constituted, governance appears to be a "catch-all" term for positive topics like getting stakeholder alignment, determining who owns data and has decision-making rights, and getting investment/resources in people analytics. The term also meant, however, more oversight because of new concepts like data privacy councils, ethics charters, and governance boards of people analytics. Governance was quickly becoming the new instantiation of the institutional review board (IRB) from higher education for protecting human subjects; but instead of focused in the research university context, governance is now the IRB of the workplace.

But has anyone asked the question: *Who will watch the watchman?*

Charlie Munger, the partner of Warren Buffet at Berkshire Hathaway, once famously said *"if you show me the incentives, I'll show you the outcome"* (Munger, 2025). As long as the incentives, whether it be as a people analytics leader or the Governance Committee member, are misaligned with that of employees, the opportunity for misdeeds pervades. It doesn't really matter *why* the incentives are misaligned; only that the misalignment exists.

In people analytics, understanding the various "flavors" of data governance within your organization is crucial for the success and integrity of any project. Each aspect of governance brings unique considerations that shape how data is collected, analyzed, and used. Recognizing and navigating these dimensions of data governance is essential for fostering trust, ensuring compliance, and driving meaningful insights in people analytics. Here are some flavors of data governance:

- **Legal:** Legal governance involves ensuring compliance with laws and regulations, often guided by corporate lawyers who are risk-averse and prioritize avoiding legal infractions.

- **Regulatory:** This flavor focuses on adherence to data protection regulations like GDPR and CPRA, with oversight from Data Protection Officers (DPOs) to maintain compliance.

- **Ethical:** Ethical governance asks whether employees would view the analysis as virtuous or invasive, prompting reflection on the moral implications of data use.

- **Cultural:** Cultural governance examines whether a research question aligns with organizational values and the overall data culture, ensuring that analytics initiatives resonate with company norms.

- **Normative:** Normative governance looks at historical precedents by asking, "Have we done this before?" This helps identify potential risks or reasons why certain analyses may not have been previously conducted.
- **Political:** Political governance considers the influence of internal stakeholders, such as HR data power brokers, assessing whether they have approved the analysis and are supportive of its findings.

THE NEW YORK TIMES TEST

In relation to governance, can your people analytics team pass the "*New York Times Test*"? In short, if the work your team is doing showed up on the front-page of the *New York Times*, would it reflect poorly on you, your team, the organization, or maybe even the entire field of people analytics? There have been few, but notable examples of failing the NYT test by prominent leaders in our field—and it should worry us all.

REAL-WORLD EXAMPLE

"Embedding Employee Data Privacy and People Analytics" with Amy Stevenson, Director of People Insights at HP

(Paraphrased for length from Ep. 7 of "Directionally Correct, A People Analytics Podcast")

The Role of Privacy Expertise in People Analytics

Amy Stevenson, Director of People Insights at HP, highlighted on Directionally Correct the increasing importance of embedding privacy expertise directly within the people analytics function. Traditionally, HR departments have worked with privacy and legal teams, but HP has recognized the value of having a dedicated resource within the analytics team itself. This individual serves as a bridge between HR and legal, ensuring that privacy considerations are deeply integrated into analytics practices and strategy.

This proactive approach allows HP to stay ahead of regulatory developments, such as GDPR, and to plan for emerging technologies by establishing privacy as a cornerstone of ethical analytics. Stevenson emphasizes the need to create "codes of practice" that augment existing employee privacy policies. These charters help HR teams understand the practical implications of data requests and allow analytics teams to push back when certain projects may conflict with ethical or privacy standards.

Privacy as a Competitive Advantage

For Dr. Stevenson, privacy isn't just a compliance issue—it's central to building trust with employees. She argues that employees want agency over how their data is used, likening it to an "Employee Bill of Rights." This trust is critical as advanced modeling and personalization techniques, akin to Netflix-style recommendations, become more common in people analytics. Without transparency and clear boundaries, these initiatives risk alienating employees by crossing ethical lines.

Stevenson's team operates with the principle of "privacy by default," which goes beyond the procedural "privacy by design" by fostering critical conversations about whether a project should proceed at all. Questions like, "Is this ethical?" or "Does this help or harm employees?" guide decision-making, helping HP balance agility with rigor.

Balancing Innovation and Privacy

While she acknowledges the tension between agility and rigor, Amy stresses the importance of ethical decision-making in an ever-evolving technological landscape. The rapid advancements in tools and methods mean that analytics teams need to anticipate future challenges and align their actions with core values, such as "do no harm."

Stevenson also points out that good intentions in analytics can quickly go awry without proper governance. Transparency, disclosure, and the ability to empathize with employees are crucial in avoiding missteps and ensuring that analytics initiatives are seen as enablers, not threats.

Key Takeaways for Ethical People Analytics

1 Dedicated Privacy Expertise: Embedding privacy professionals within analytics teams strengthens governance and future-proofs operations.

2 Transparent Codes of Practice: Establishing clear guidelines helps align HR and analytics teams, ensuring ethical and practical data use.

3 Privacy by Default: Beyond compliance, organizations must embed privacy into their culture and decision-making frameworks.

4 Empathy and Communication: Placing oneself in employees' shoes and maintaining transparency fosters trust and minimizes resistance.

5 Proactive Governance: With emerging technologies on the horizon, organizations must balance agility and rigor to prepare for challenges and maintain ethical standards.

Stevenson's insights illustrate how privacy and governance can be leveraged as strategic assets in people analytics, setting the stage for innovation that respects both organizational goals and employee rights.

As Amy Stevenson states in the real-world example: Employee agency matters. Do employees know what is being done with their data? Do they know why it is being used? Do they stand to benefit or be harmed by the data? It is no wonder that GDPR created an employee data 'bill of rights' due to the imbalance of power between employer and employee. If employers had the right to collect any data on employees and use it however they want, there's no way that wouldn't devolve into an indentured servant-like situation.

And this problem only expands as the robustness and invasiveness of information collected on employees increases. People are already asking their AI chatbots interesting questions about themselves like, "Based on my previous chats, what can you tell me about my personality?" or even more mischievous versions like "Based on my previous chats, would you hire me?" With the digital exhaust "trail of breadcrumbs" that is being left everywhere employees interface with their work environment and the proliferation of software's ability to track workers, and IoT sensors to track the physical movements of employees, means there's literally nowhere to hide.

Are you not at least a little nervous, as an employee yourself, about the data that people analytics teams might be combing over?

Virtue & Character

As a people analytics professional, I argue we must first take our own council. Before the IRB, before governance, before abandoning the advancement of people analytics, we must have and aspire to a value called "*virtue*." But what is virtue and what does it mean to be virtuous? Here's what you might find when you search "virtue" on a search engine:

- "Behavior showing high moral standards."

It is said that "*character is what you do when no one is looking*," and being virtuous means to uphold the highest moral standards as a part of your character. To do the right thing with or without the *watchman* watching. The founders of the United States spoke about the necessity of virtue when creating the United States. Two examples from the founders include: "*Democracy [in the US] will not survive without a virtuous people focused on self-government*" and "*That human rights can only be assured amongst virtuous people*" (DC News, 2022).

An organization by its nature is an example of self-governance, and the "rights" of employees—such as the aforementioned GDPR employee bill of rights, in addition to many hard-fought employee labor laws—are much like human rights. Both will falter without virtuous actors and caretakers in place. The opposite of virtue is not vice, it is disregard. A people analytics leader who is not virtuous will disregard the employee side of the employer–employee balance people analytics teams must strike. We, as people analytics leaders, are the keepers of the private, the secret, and the personal. In a way, we are a priestly class of actors in the shadows and hold the responsibility to act as such in an ethical and virtuous manner. If no one is looking, we could do real harm, and therefore it is incumbent upon us to not let that happen.

Laws, governance, rights, and adjudication are no match for virtue. Name a law that's never been broken. There isn't one. When the incentives are pushing towards doing something that is good for the organization but bad for employees, who will hold the line? My personal virtuous commitment is what I call "*the asymmetry of employee benefit from people analytics.*" If there is fundamentally an imbalance of power between the employer and the employee when it comes to their data, it requires an ethic and commitment to balance the scales to truly be an employee-centric people analytics organization. People analytics should only share insights that are employee-neutral or friendly in an asymmetrical way if they have not previously *opted-in* to their data being shared, and make an overt commitment to steer clear of the creepy and unethical use of data. There are scores of research examples that show when the employee does better, the organization does better too. No one needs to live under the "*eye of Sauron*" to be effective at work (Tolkien, 2018). And no organization needs to create a "*1984*"-like work environment to be profitable (Orwell, 2013).

Counterintuitively, the virtuous person is more unencumbered as a leader because they never have the worry of having guilt on their conscience or second guessing their actions and motives. As Franklin Covey's *Speed of Trust* exercises show (Covey and Merrill, 2006), a culture with low trust pays a price called the *Trust Tax*. Similarly, the unvirtuous people analytics team must pay the governance and oversight tax, much like a trust tax. They need guidance because they cannot first take their own council.

What Does Being Unbiased Mean?

In people analytics, being unbiased is not as simple as removing all forms of subjectivity from data or decisions. The term "bias" itself is fraught with ambiguity, as different perspectives shape its meaning. For some, bias refers to cognitive distortions such as *confirmation bias, availability bias*, or *anchoring* that influence decision-making. With over 100 recognized cognitive biases and distortions (Ackerman, 2017), addressing them requires systematic efforts to identify and mitigate flawed reasoning. However, in other contexts, bias is used as a code word for inequitable outcomes, such as disparate impacts across demographic groups. This dual meaning complicates discussions of fairness and highlights the tension between competing philosophies of "merit," where the best performer is rewarded, and "equity," where fairness is measured by equality of outcomes. As these philosophies clash, what one group might call "unbiased" could be perceived as unjust by another.

The challenge of defining bias is compounded by the fact that fairness itself is multifaceted. Procedural justice, which emphasizes fairness in the processes that lead to decisions, is often contrasted with distributive justice, which focuses on the fairness of outcomes. The formula "talent equals performance minus effort" reminds us that not all talent is created equal; some individuals achieve excellence despite needing significant effort, while others perform well fairly easily due to innate characteristics or predispositions. Recognizing these nuances is crucial to avoiding "language games" that reduce bias to a simplistic concept and hinder sincere efforts to understand and address it. Ultimately, fairness in people analytics requires balancing procedural rigor with an acknowledgment of the complexities of talent and opportunity.

While societal and legal views on bias are evolving, the virtuous path remains constant: A commitment to keeping virtuous behavior central to people analytics and understanding of how data reflects human realities is key. As the legal landscape changes in relation to equity and bias (such as the overturning of affirmative action by the U.S. Supreme Court and recent Executive Orders abolishing DEI), organizations must ensure their practices meet both regulatory standards and ethical imperatives. By striving for fairness, people analytics can be a powerful tool for creating systems where individuals are evaluated based on merit but also holistically.

Machine Learning & AI Bias

Machine learning introduces several new types of bias that can significantly impact fairness and decision-making in people analytics and beyond. These biases often emerge at different stages of the machine learning pipeline and can reinforce unfairness if left unaddressed. Hickman et al. (2024) introduces a new list of biases that come from advents in machine learning being applied to people analytics and are listed as follows:

- **Aggregation Bias:** This occurs when a single model is applied across groups with differing predictor–outcome relationships, failing to account for group-specific nuances.
- **Emergent Bias:** Arises after deployment as real-world predictor–outcome relationships evolve over time, leading to unintended consequences.
- **Historical Bias:** Reflects entrenched societal inequalities embedded in the training data, perpetuating past imbalances.
- **Human Bias:** Introduced through biased human input, such as flawed ground truth labels or subjective ratings, which skew model outputs.
- **Learning Bias:** Happens when a model amplifies pre-existing group disparities in its predictions or scores.
- **Measurement Bias:** Arises when predictor or ground truth variables systematically misrepresent certain groups, leading to distorted outcomes.
- **Representation Bias:** Occurs when certain groups are underrepresented or misrepresented in the training data, reducing model performance and fairness for those groups.
- **Causal Bias:** Happens when demographic variables causally influence predictor variables and outcomes, creating feedback loops that embed inequity.

Understanding and mitigating these biases where appropriate is critical to building machine learning systems that are fair, transparent, and aligned with ethical principles. Recently, under-thought laws such as the NYC AI Law have been passed that have added complexity to how to do people analytics. Thankfully, Guru Sethupathy, the CEO of FairNow AI, discussed how this may impact people analytics in this real-world example.

REAL-WORLD EXAMPLE

"Navigating the NYC AI Law and Fair AI Practices" with Guru Sethupathy, former leader of People Analytics at Capital One and CEO of FairNow AI

(Paraphrased for length from Ep. 56 of "Directionally Correct, A People Analytics Podcast")

The Challenge: Regulation in AI for HR

Dr. Guru Sethupathy's experience at Capital One and his journey founding FairNow AI offer unique insights into the evolving landscape of AI regulation in HR. Observing the sophistication in risk management within financial services, Sethupathy recognized a gap in HR's ability to govern and monitor algorithmic decision-making. The lack of oversight and the increasing reliance on AI tools in HR sparked his mission to address these challenges.

A key catalyst for this work was the New York City AI Law, which went into effect on July 5, 2023. The law imposes requirements on organizations using automated decision tools (ADTs) in HR, demanding public reporting of outcomes and adherence to fairness standards. While well-intentioned, the law presents significant challenges.

Key Issues with the NYC AI Law

1 Ambiguous Definitions: The law defines "substantially assisting decision-making" in vague terms, leading to confusion about what qualifies as an ADT.

2 Mandatory Public Reporting: Organizations must publicly disclose fairness metrics, such as impact ratios. However, Sethupathy argues this can lead to misinterpretation. For instance, a single number (e.g., a 66 percent impact ratio) often lacks the nuance and context required to understand systemic fairness. Such data can be weaponized, reinforcing biases or preconceived notions.

3 Counterproductive Incentives: Sethupathy notes that companies may avoid using AI tools altogether to escape regulatory scrutiny. This could push HR functions back to less reliable, more biased human decision-making, undermining progress.

Balancing Compliance and Progress

Dr. Sethupathy emphasizes the need for HR to adopt rigorous governance practices, akin to those in financial services. He advocates for transparency, fairness, and validation processes to ensure AI tools meet ethical and legal standards. However, he cautions against oversimplified metrics that can harm organizations and obscure true fairness.

The Broader Context: A Patchwork of Regulations

Sethupathy notes that AI regulations in the U.S. are fragmented, with states and cities implementing their own standards. He predicts a future where:

- Federal guidelines (e.g., the White House's Blueprint for Responsible AI) provide overarching principles.

- Organizations align with market standards like SOC 2 compliance for information security, tailored for AI governance.

Takeaways for People Analytics Teams

1   Invest in AI Governance: Companies need to proactively adopt robust systems for monitoring and validating AI tools. This includes fairness audits, risk assessments, and continuous improvement processes.

2   Navigate Regulatory Complexity: Organizations must prepare for a patchwork of local, state, and federal laws, building compliance frameworks flexible enough to accommodate varying requirements.

3   Focus on Counterfactual Thinking: When assessing AI fairness, HR leaders should consider the counterfactual—how human decision-making compares to automated systems—and recognize that eliminating AI often reintroduces greater bias.

4   Advocate for Nuance: Public reporting requirements should include caveats and contextual explanations to prevent oversimplified or misinterpreted metrics from driving negative perceptions.

Building Responsible AI Practices

Guru Sethupathy's work underscores the need for HR to learn from other industries, like finance, to create well-regulated, fair, and effective AI systems. By embracing the complexities of AI governance and anticipating future regulatory trends, organizations can responsibly leverage AI to enhance decision-making while avoiding pitfalls.

Ethical Implications of Using Gen AI in People Analytics

The use of generative AI in people analytics introduces a powerful capability to transform workforce decision-making at a magnitude and scale previously unimaginable. However, with great power comes significant ethical responsibility. As organizations increasingly deploy Gen AI to predict employee behavior, personalize HR strategies and enhance decision-making, they must address some critical ethical questions. These questions go beyond technical implementation, challenging us to consider the broader societal, organizational, and individual implications of this technology.

1. Who Will Watch the Watchman?

As mentioned earlier in the chapter, a central ethical concern with Gen AI in people analytics is oversight: Who will hold the technology and its users accountable? Gen AI systems can make decisions that impact careers, livelihoods, and workplace fairness. Without appropriate checks and balances, there's a risk of delegating too much authority to algorithms that operate as opaque "black boxes." Here are a few components that are needed to know "who will watch the watchman":

- **Accountability Frameworks:** Organizations must establish clear accountability frameworks to govern the use of Gen AI. This involves defining who is responsible for the outcomes of AI-driven decisions and ensuring transparency in how those decisions are made, and people analytics should be in a leadership role for making said decisions. For example, if an AI model incorrectly predicts an employee is likely to quit, leading to them being excluded from promotions, who is accountable—the AI vendor, the HR team, or the broader organization? This is focal variable in the ongoing age discrimination case Mobley vs Workday that is trying to get to the root of how AI was used in decision making by the technology vendor, Workday.
- **Third-Party Audits:** Some laws are encouraging independent audits of AI systems that can help ensure fairness, accuracy, and compliance with ethical guidelines. Regularly reviewing the performance and outputs of Gen AI models reduces the risk of unintended consequences and builds trust among stakeholders. Even without using a third-party, people analytics teams should audit their algorithms as a best practice.
- **Governance Committees:** Establishing AI ethics committees or governance boards can provide ongoing oversight, as long as technical leaders like people analytics are at the helm. These bodies, comprising stakeholders across the business and HR, can evaluate the ethical implications of Gen AI applications, set guardrails for acceptable use and review the alignment of AI practices with organizational values. But they must be filled with virtuous actors for their true intent to be valid.

2. Who Will Be in Charge?

The question of leadership and ownership is pivotal when deploying Gen AI in people analytics. Unlike traditional analytics, where human expertise is a key part of the process, Gen AI introduces a layer of automation that can blur lines of responsibility. People analytics should take ownership and remain accountable for the prescriptions its team makes to HR and the business. While HR leaders understand the workforce context, people analytics teams possess the technical expertise to develop and implement Gen AI models. Successful and ethical deployment requires collaboration between these teams to ensure the technology serves human needs without unintentionally undermining them.

The ethical use of Gen AI will not be relegated solely to people analytics; it must be embedded in HR leadership at every level. HR executives, in particular, have a duty to champion responsible AI use, fostering a culture where decisions are guided by fairness, transparency, and accountability. Employees themselves should have a voice in how Gen AI is used within the organization as well. Creating opportunities for employees to provide input on AI applications and processes ensures that the technology aligns with their interests and values.

3. Is This the Future We Want to Live In?

The deployment of Gen AI in people analytics raises existential questions about the type of workplace, and society, we are creating. While the technology promises increased efficiency, personalization, and predictive power, it also risks dehumanizing aspects of work and creating unfairness. Before we pursue Gen AI guns-a-blazing, here are some components to consider:

- **Balancing Efficiency with Humanity:** Gen AI's ability to optimize processes and predict outcomes is undeniably valuable, but at what cost? If decisions about hiring, promotions, or terminations are entirely driven by AI, there's a risk of creating a permanent class of algorithmically unemployable people. Gen AI cannot be the sole decision-maker because it cannot be held accountable; only humans can be held accountable. Organizations must strive to balance the efficiency of Gen AI with the humanity of HR practices.

- **Mitigating Inaccuracies and Promoting Fairness:** One of the most significant ethical risks of using Gen AI in people analytics is the potential for increasing bias through inaccurate results. If historical data contains imbalances—such as gender or racial disparities—AI models trained on that data may replicate or exacerbate them. Organizations must proactively mitigate these risks by using detection tools, implementing fairness constraints in model training, and continuously monitoring outcomes.

- **Transparency and Trust:** Employees now have a right to know how Gen AI is being used in decisions that affect them. Transparent communication about the role of AI, the data it uses, and the safeguards in place is essential for building trust. For example, if an AI model predicts an employee's likelihood of leaving, the organization should be transparent about how that prediction will (or won't) influence managerial decisions.

- **Future of Work Considerations:** As Gen AI reshapes people analytics, it also reshapes the nature of work itself. Questions about surveillance, privacy, and autonomy come to the forefront. For example, using Gen AI to monitor employee behavior raises concerns about the erosion of privacy and the potential for micromanagement. Organizations must carefully consider how these applications align with their broader vision for the future of work.

4. Practical Steps to Address Ethical Concerns

To navigate the ethical complexities of Gen AI in people analytics, organizations should adopt practices, such as the following, to govern how they conduct themselves. Each organization will likely have their own flavor of these, but here is a start:

- **Develop Ethical AI Guidelines:** Create a set of principles that govern the use of Gen AI in HR, ensuring that these guidelines are aligned with organizational values and legal requirements.

- **Prioritize Explainability:** Invest in AI systems that provide interpretable results, making it easier for decision-makers and employees to understand how predictions are made.

- **Conduct Impact Assessments:** Before deploying Gen AI applications, conduct thorough assessments to evaluate potential risks and unintended consequences, including employee imbalances and privacy concerns.

- **Foster a Culture of Ethics and Accountability:** Train employees and leaders on the ethical implications of Gen AI and encourage open dialogue about its use.

The ethical implications of using Gen AI in people analytics extend far beyond technical challenges—they touch on fundamental questions about fairness, accountability, and the future of work. While Gen AI offers transformative potential, its deployment must be guided by a commitment to ethical principles and a clear understanding of its societal impact. By addressing these questions head-on and prioritizing responsible AI practices, organizations can harness the power of Gen AI while safeguarding the dignity and rights of their workforce.

Synthetic Data—Ethical for Gen AI?

In people analytics, organizations often grapple with the challenge of accessing high-quality data while respecting employee privacy, legal constraints, and ethical concerns. One emerging solution is **synthetic data**—artificially generated data that mimics real datasets. By replicating key statistical properties of real-world data, synthetic data offers a viable alternative when real data is scarce, sensitive, or difficult to obtain.

Unlike random or purely fictional data, synthetic data is created through a structured process that ensures it maintains meaningful relationships and patterns found in actual datasets. This means it can be used to develop AI models and conduct analyses without exposing individual employee records or sensitive HR information. Below is a breakdown of how synthetic data is generated and the key considerations for using it in people analytics.

How Synthetic Data Works

The process of generating synthetic data is not a matter of fabricating numbers at random—it requires a systematic approach to ensure that the synthetic dataset maintains the integrity of the original real-world patterns. Here's how it works:

- **Analyze Real Data:** The process starts by identifying key features, statistical distributions, and relationships in an actual dataset. This step ensures that any synthetic data generated later reflects realistic patterns.

- **Train a Generative Model:** Machine learning models, often based on techniques such as generative adversarial networks (GANs) or large language models (LLMs), are trained to understand the structure of the real data. These models learn the patterns, correlations, and variations present in the dataset.

- **Generate Synthetic Data:** Once trained, the model produces new data points that statistically resemble the real dataset. This includes generating realistic yet uncommon edge cases, which are often critical in predictive analytics.

Benefits of Using Synthetic Data in People Analytics

When used responsibly, synthetic data offers several advantages that can enhance HR analytics while mitigating ethical risks. These include:

- **Enhancing Data Privacy:** In HR, data privacy is paramount. Synthetic data allows organizations to analyze and share insights without exposing individual employee records. For example, when conducting workforce planning or turnover analysis, synthetic datasets can be used instead of real employee data, reducing compliance risks.

- **Addressing Data Scarcity:** Certain HR-related challenges, such as analyzing small employee subgroups or predicting rare events (e.g., executive turnover), suffer from a lack of sufficient real-world data. Synthetic data can help fill these gaps by generating larger, statistically valid datasets for analysis.

- **Facilitating Safe Experimentation:** Testing AI-driven HR applications—such as bias detection models or employee engagement predictors—on real data can introduce risks. Synthetic data provides a safe alternative for evaluating models before deploying them in live HR systems.

Limitations and Ethical Considerations

While synthetic data holds great promise, it is not without its challenges. Organizations must remain mindful of its limitations:

- **Accuracy and Generalization Risks:** The quality of synthetic data depends on the robustness of the model used to generate it. If the underlying real data contains biases or errors, those flaws can be reflected in the synthetic version, leading to misleading insights.

- **Not a Replacement for Real Data:** Synthetic data should *supplement* rather than *replace* real data in people analytics. While it can be useful for early-stage model development, validation with real-world employee data is necessary to ensure accuracy.

Ultimately, synthetic data is a powerful tool, but it must be used with caution. HR leaders and data scientists should ensure that synthetic datasets are high quality, unbiased, and ethically generated. By leveraging synthetic data responsibly, organizations can unlock valuable insights while protecting employee privacy and ensuring compliance with ethical AI practices.

Now You Know

In the rapidly evolving landscape of AI-driven people analytics, ethical considerations must remain at the forefront. As organizations harness synthetic data to enhance privacy, create AI governance councils, try to remain virtuous, and facilitate safe experimentation, they must also recognize its limitations and potential risks. Responsible use of AI for people analytics use requires a commitment to transparency, fairness, and continuous oversight. The line between innovation and ethical compromise can be thin, but it is one that HR leaders and data practitioners must vigilantly uphold. We must keep innovating and fast. But by prioritizing ethical AI practices, organizations can leverage the power of data while safeguarding the trust and well-being of their workforce.

Summary

Artificial intelligence in people analytics presents both groundbreaking opportunities and significant ethical dilemmas. The ability to collect, analyze, and act on employee data at scale has made AI a powerful tool—but with that power comes the responsibility to ensure fairness, privacy, and transparency. This chapter explores the ethical considerations of using AI in HR, the potential risks of misusing data, and how organizations can implement responsible governance frameworks. It emphasizes that while AI can drive business success, it must be guided by virtue, oversight, and a commitment to doing what's right.

Key Takeaways

1 **The Power of AI is in Its Scale—And That's the Problem**

   o AI doesn't just analyze data; it can amplify narratives at scale. If biased assumptions or skewed data are fed into AI systems, those distortions spread exponentially, making ethical safeguards critical.

2 **Ethical Data Storytelling: The Fine Line Between Persuasion and Deception**

   o Analysts are often encouraged to "tell a story with data," but AI introduces a new challenge: How do we ensure that storytelling doesn't become data manipulation? Responsible AI usage demands honesty, transparency, and integrity in how insights are presented.

3 **Governance: Who Will Watch the Watchman?**

   o AI ethics require strong governance frameworks, but even governance structures can be flawed. People analytics teams must consider multiple layers of governance, including legal, regulatory, ethical, cultural, and political factors.

4   The "New York Times Test" for AI Decisions

   o   If your AI-driven HR practices were on the front page of a major newspaper, would they be viewed as ethical or exploitative? This simple test forces organizations to consider reputational risks and ethical lapses before implementing AI-driven people analytics.

5   Employee Privacy is a Competitive Advantage, Not Just a Compliance Issue

   o   Transparency about how employee data is used builds trust. Embedding privacy expertise within people analytics teams ensures that AI-driven insights don't compromise employee rights.

6   Virtue is the Foundation of Ethical AI Use

   o   Compliance is not enough; people analytics professionals must have the character to act ethically even when no one is watching. Virtuous decision-making balances business interests with employee well-being.

7   Understanding Bias in AI: It's More Than Just a Statistical Error

   o   Bias in AI can take many forms—historical bias, measurement bias, representation bias, and emergent bias. Understanding these biases and actively working to mitigate them is essential for fairness in HR decision-making.

8   Regulatory Complexity: Navigating Laws Like the NYC AI Law

   o   Emerging laws, such as New York City's AI hiring regulations, introduce compliance challenges. AI-driven HR tools must be audited for fairness, and organizations need to prepare for a fragmented regulatory landscape.

9   Generative AI Brings New Ethical Risks

   o   Gen AI can predict, prescribe, and personalize HR decisions, but should it? Leaders must ensure that AI augments human decision-making rather than replacing it, keeping fairness and accountability in focus.

10 Synthetic Data: A Potential Solution for Ethical AI?

   o   Synthetic data, which mimics real datasets without exposing sensitive information, offers a promising solution to privacy concerns. However, it must be rigorously tested to ensure it maintains fairness and accuracy.

The ethics of AI in people analytics are not just about compliance; they are about responsibility. Organizations must strike a balance between innovation and virtue, ensuring that AI serves both business needs and employee well-being. The future of AI in HR depends on our ability to stay on the right side of the ethical line.

References

Ackerman, C. (2017). Cognitive Distortions: When Your Brain Lies to You. Positive Psychology. positivepsychology.com/cognitive-distortions/ (archived at https://perma.cc/JBP6-ZMHE).

Covey, S. R. and Merrill, R. R. (2006). *The Speed of Trust: The One Thing That Changes Everything*. Free Press.

DC News. (2022). The Role of Virtue in People Analytics. directionallycorrectnews. substack.com/p/the-role-of-virtue-in-people-analytics-de959fa27f72. (archived at https://perma.cc/3LKJ-STDV)

Hickman, L., Huynh, C., Gass, J., Booth, B. M., Kuruzovich, J. and Tay, L. (2024). Whither Bias Goes, I Will Go: An Integrative, Systematic Review of Algorithmic Bias Mitigation. doi.org/10.31234/osf.io/hcxbn (archived at https://perma.cc/8HAZ-LWY7).

Munger, C. (2025). A quote by Charles T. Munger. www.goodreads.com/quotes/11903426-show-me-the-incentive-and-i-ll-show-you-the-outcome (archived at https://perma.cc/3YXQ-VRU9).

Napper, C., Hines, S. and Sethupathy, G. (2023). Navigating the NYC AI Law and Fair AI Practices. Directionally Correct. www.podbean.com/eas/pb-9rexs-151f6d5 (archived at https://perma.cc/64PH-ZL3W) Ep. 56.

Napper, C., Hines, S. and Stevenson, A. (2022). Embedding Employee Data Privacy and People Analytics. Directionally Correct. www.podbean.com/eas/pb-usipy-151f708 (archived at https://perma.cc/W73F-6Y9M) Ep. 7.

Orwell, G. (2013). *1984*. Houghton Mifflin Harcourt.

Tolkien, J. R. R. (2018). *The Two Towers*. Del Rey/Ballantine Books.

PART THREE

How to Win

8

Analytics at Work: Real Scenarios on Using People Analytics to Win

This chapter features real-world applications and case studies from both large and small innovative companies, showing how strategic deployment of people analytics fosters business leadership and market dominance.

"The future is here, it's just not evenly distributed"—William Gibson (Chatterton and Newmarch, 2016)

This book is meant to help you live in the future of people analytics, even if others are are left behind. In the first section of this book, *Business Value*, we focused on the core principles of people analytics, emphasizing how HR leaders and business professionals can leverage data to drive tangible, strategic value. The goal was to establish a solid foundation—one that ensures people analytics is not just an abstract concept but a practical discipline that influences decision-making, workforce planning, and business outcomes. In the second section, *Gen AI*, we expanded on this by exploring the emerging role of Gen AI in reshaping the field, highlighting both its potential to enhance analytics and the challenges it introduces. We examined how AI can process vast amounts of HR data, generate insights at unprecedented speed, and automate complex tasks that were previously time-consuming or even impossible.

Now, in this third section—*How to Win*—we shift our focus from exploration to execution. Winning with people analytics in the Gen AI era requires more than just understanding technology; it demands a strategic mindset, a clear implementation plan, and the ability to seamlessly integrate AI into existing analytics functions. Traditional analytics methods remain important, but their reach is significantly augmented by Gen AI, allowing organizations to scale their capabilities and ROI to maintain a competitive edge. In these chapters of *How to Win*, we will break down the most critical concepts, demystify AI's role in people analytics to be the leader in HR moving forward, and provide actionable strategies to help you integrate Gen AI-powered people analytics into your organization in a way that is both effective and innovative.

What If We Never Made Another Dashboard Again?

As much as I wish it weren't the case, much of what we call "people analytics" today is the building of dashboards to share with customers. And this is for good reason. Up until now, creating a dashboard was one of the few ways you could scale the democratization of insights. Building a dashboard builds bandwidth for you and your team, and a well-designed dashboard serves as a single source of truth, providing business leaders and HR professionals with critical insights in a digestible format. However, Gen AI is now here, and the calculus of how to build a dashboard is changing. But before we discuss how Gen AI can help, let's discuss what it takes to have a successful dashboard: **Data, Context, and the Story.**

Step 1: Data

Some of the most valuable, insightful, and intellectually stimulating work in people analytics requires advanced techniques—machine learning, NLP, organizational network analysis, survival models, optimization models, and more. However, the most immediate challenge facing any new leader in people analytics is far more fundamental: Your stakeholders don't have, may have never had, and/or aren't accustomed to having the data they need to make decisions. That's why the first step is simply getting the data right. This means integrating data from disparate sources, cleaning it, defining key metrics, and ensuring accessibility across the organization, much of which we have already discussed in prior chapters.

To avoid getting stuck in this step at the data aggregation phase, we must move past fragmented datasets by creating scalable data aggregation and visualization processes. The goal should be continuous improvement—centralizing data, prototyping visualizations, gathering user feedback, identifying business impact, and refining accordingly. Whether you historically have chosen to build a custom dashboard using open-source tools like R Shiny or buy a solution like Tableau or Looker, the key is ensuring that your data tells a story that resonates with decision-makers. Even the best dashboard in the world will fall flat if it lacks context.

Step 2: Context

This bears repeating, but not all people analytics dashboards are created equal. The value of a dashboard isn't determined by the solution architect or data analyst who built it—it's determined by the end user. A visually stunning dashboard means nothing if leaders don't understand how to act on the data presented. Context is what transforms raw numbers into meaningful insights, and it comes in two forms: **Organizational context** and **data context.**

Organizational context means understanding how data aligns with business priorities. People analytics often struggles for funding compared to IT, Finance, or centralized data science teams, even though people costs make up 70 percent of operating expenses in most companies. The best people analytics leaders overcome this setback by making sure their data is tied directly to business objectives, ensuring that leaders see how analytics impacts revenue, efficiency, and strategy. The first section of this book, *Business Value*, is focused squarely on how to make the people analytics team understand organizational context and add value as a consequence.

Data context, on the other hand, ensures that numbers aren't just numbers; they have meaning. Without context, dashboards become confusing and unhelpful, leading to disengagement from stakeholders. To provide meaningful context, data should always be compared against a target, a benchmark, or a historical trend.

- **Target**—A predefined goal or success metric that indicates whether performance is meeting expectations (e.g., "Reduce voluntary turnover to below 10 percent this year").

- **Benchmark**—A comparison against an external standard, such as industry peers or competitors (e.g., "Our turnover rate is 12 percent, while the industry average is 15 percent").

- **Historical Trend**—A comparison of current performance to past data to assess progress over time (e.g., "Turnover was 18 percent last year and has decreased to 12 percent this year").

These comparison points allow leaders to assess whether they are making progress, how they compare to industry standards, and whether their actions are driving measurable change. A dashboard without context is just noise; a dashboard with context becomes a tool for informed decision-making.

Step 3: The Story

Even with the right data and context, a dashboard's ultimate effectiveness depends on its ability to tell a compelling story. Data in dashboards has the potential—not the guarantee—to track, inform, and illuminate the past, present, and future of the organization. A truly great dashboard doesn't just present numbers; it guides decision-makers through a narrative, showing them where they've been, where they are now, and where they are headed. Ideally, as a people analytics function matures, dashboards should evolve from static reports to interactive, self-service tools that allow leaders to explore data dynamically.

Think of a great story—it's never a one-way conversation. The same should be true for dashboards. The best people analytics dashboards create an ongoing dialogue between the data and decision-makers, adapting over time as business needs change. This continuous evolution is what separates a functional dashboard from a transformational one.

The Future: Gen AI Dashboards

Until now, building a great people analytics dashboard required a significant amount of effort—data wrangling, visualization design, stakeholder alignment, and ongoing maintenance. But what if that work disappeared? What if we never had to manually build another dashboard again?

This is where Gen AI is changing the game. Instead of spending weeks or months building a static dashboard, AI-powered analytics platforms can automatically generate interactive dashboards on demand, tailored to specific business questions. Leaders no longer have to sift through pages of reports; instead, they can ask natural language questions and receive real-time, contextualized insights. AI can detect patterns, highlight anomalies, suggest actions, and even predict future trends without human intervention.

Imagine an executive asking, "How is turnover trending for our top-performing employees compared to last year?" and receiving an instant, AI-generated dashboard with context, benchmarks, and key insights—without a single analyst lifting a finger. This exists today if you know where to find it and is only getting better. Your teams should be investing here. With Gen AI, people analytics teams can shift from building dashboards to being *the Inquisitors and the Change Agents* from Chapter 4.

So, what if we never built another dashboard again? The future isn't about creating dashboards—it's about making decisions. And with Gen AI automating the process, we can finally focus on what matters most: Winning with people analytics.

What If Conducting People Analytics Projects Became Automated?

Currently a key skill in people analytics, executing an effective project, is essential for demonstrating the value of our function within the organization. However, the process can be complex, requiring strategic alignment, data analysis, stakeholder management, and organizational change efforts. It can take months. Sometimes the window of opportunity for the research to make a decision has passed before the project is even completed. The more experienced you become, the more you realize that the key to success in people analytics is simplicity, clarity, and structured problem-solving— which is why the scientific method remains the backbone of an effective people analytics project.

Alec Levenson and Alexis Fink have highlighted the importance of integrating organizational development (OD) with analytics (Levenson, Stevenson and Fink 2021), ensuring that insights don't just sit in a report but lead to real business impact. Similarly, it's important to choose the right problem to solve, ensuring that projects align with business priorities. Over time, I've developed a structured **People Analytics Problem-Solving Framework**, based on various methodologies but fundamentally rooted in the scientific method. These steps provide a clear roadmap for tackling business challenges using data:

People Analytics Problem-Solving Steps

1 Identify business problems and research questions
2 Review previous findings
3 Select variables and hypotheses to test
4 Collect data
5 Analyze data and build models
6 Present results and take action
7 Monitor outcomes and adjust as needed

While these steps provide a structured approach, project success also depends on effective scoping. Many projects fail not because the analysis was flawed but because expectations, stakeholders, and outcomes were not properly defined before the project started. That's why a *People Analytics Project Scoping Template* is a critical tool for ensuring clarity, alignment, and impact.

People Analytics Project Scoping Template

1 Aligning on Research Questions
   o What problem are we solving, and why does it matter?
   o What specific hypotheses need to be tested?
   o How will we know if the research questions are definitively answered?

2 Data Collection
   o What data sources and analyses are required?
   o Do we have existing data, or do we need to collect new data?

3 Timeline and Stakeholder Engagement
   o What are the key milestones and deadlines?
   o Who are the decision-makers, and how will we keep them engaged?

4 Action and Impact
   o Are stakeholders willing to take action based on the results?
   o What actions will be taken for different outcomes?
   o How will we measure success and ensure sustained impact?

Historically, the biggest mistake in people analytics projects is waiting until the final step (Presenting Results) to consider how the findings will be used. If stakeholders don't agree up front to take action based on the results of the project, don't do the project. Every research question should have a predefined decision tree outlining potential outcomes and corresponding actions. This ensures that analytics is driving decisions, not just producing reports.

Running a People Analytics Project in the Real World

While frameworks and templates are helpful, executing a project in the real world is often far messier. Here are the real steps that happen when running a project in the real world:

1 **Identify a business problem that truly matters**—Ask around. People will tell you what's broken. Get early commitment from stakeholders to take action before you start working.

2 **Apply the 80/20 rule**—Focus on the 20 percent of issues that drive 80 percent of the business impact.

3 **Check if someone has already tried solving the problem**—Avoid reinventing the wheel; learn from internal and external research that has been conducted before.

4 **Find the best available data**—Use existing data first. Only collect new data if necessary and ensure future projects can leverage it.

5 **Analyze data with the end in mind**—Visualize and craft your story as you analyze the data, not afterward.

6 **Present results with clear recommendations**—Stakeholders don't care about fancy models. They care about what needs to be done and how it impacts the business.

7 **Follow up and drive change**—Most people stop after presenting results to stakeholders. Your real job starts after the meeting—ensuring that insights lead to action. Be the change agent.

8 **Measure whether the intervention worked**—Proving the ROI of people analytics is what separates high-impact teams from cost centers. This happens after the decision is made and implemented. Go back and measure if what you did worked.

The Future: Gen AI to Conduct Projects?

While these steps for executing people analytics projects are fairly standard, Gen AI is fundamentally changing the game on conducting a project. Traditionally, projects required significant effort—formulating hypotheses, gathering data, testing models, visualizing results, and aligning with stakeholders. But what if all of that could be automated? If you get your data infrastructure in order, described in Chapter 5, the answer is yes. With Gen AI, organizations can shift from manually conducting people analytics projects to AI-driven, real-time decision-making. Here's how:

- **Instant Hypothesis Generation**—AI can analyze business performance, detect anomalies, and suggest relevant research questions before you even start a project. This will still require critical thinking and awareness of the business context to execute effectively, but there will be no shortage of hypotheses to test in the future.

- **Automated Data Collection and Cleaning**—No more manual wrangling. AI will ingest, integrate, and clean data from multiple HR, finance, and business systems instantly.

- **AI-Driven Analysis and Modeling**—Advanced statistical models, machine learning algorithms, and predictive analytics will be generated on demand.

- **Real-Time Executive Briefs**—Instead of spending weeks preparing reports, people analytics or business leaders can ask AI a question in natural language and receive immediate, contextualized insights.

- **Automated Impact Measurement**—AI can continuously track and report on whether interventions actually lead to business improvements, eliminating the need for separate impact studies. Automated ROI.

Imagine a world where instead of scoping, executing, and presenting projects manually, leaders simply ask, "What's driving our retention problem?", and Gen AI instantly surfaces root causes, suggested actions, and forecasts outcomes. No more months-long projects—just real-time, automated insights that drive business impact. This can happen today. The future is here, it's just not evenly distributed. So, what if conducting a people analytics project became automated? The future isn't about doing more projects effectively—it's about eliminating the need for laborious projects altogether and letting AI enable real-time, continuous people analytics that empowers leaders to make better decisions, faster.

REAL-WORLD EXAMPLE

"The Man Who Started More People Analytics Functions" with Craig Starbuck, Head of People Data, Analytics, and Technology at Chime, CEO of OrgAcuity

(Paraphrased for length from Ep. 28 of "Directionally Correct, A People Analytics Podcast")

The Challenge of Starting

Establishing an effective people analytics function in organizations at varying stages of maturity requires a nuanced, strategic approach. Dr. Craig Starbuck has built six people analytics functions, including his most recent role at Roku and Chime, offering valuable insights into what works and what doesn't in launching and scaling people analytics.

Key Learnings and Best Practices

1. Align with Business Strategy

- Understand the Business First: In the first 60–90 days, focus on learning the business strategy, markets, and dynamics. Meet stakeholders outside HR to grasp how people analytics can support broader business objectives.
- Tether Analytics to Business Needs: Analytics must address specific business problems. If the work is disconnected from the business, it risks being perceived as academic and less impactful.

2. Start Small: The Power of Minimum Viable Product (MVP)

- Avoid Overengineering: Early in his career, Craig launched an overly complex diversity dashboard that included every possible data point. It was overwhelming, underutilized, and eventually scrapped.

- Focus on Simplicity: Begin with a minimal solution that addresses a core problem and iterate based on user feedback. For example, at Roku, Craig introduced a *Monthly People Insights Report*, which provides concise data points, insights, and narratives to help stakeholders become comfortable using data.

3. Challenge Traditional Maturity Models

- Skip Steps if Necessary: Conventional maturity curves often advocate a linear progression—operational reporting, dashboards, predictive modeling, etc. Craig argues that this model doesn't always align with business needs.

- Solve Immediate Problems First: At Roku, his team prioritized ad hoc analyses to address pressing business questions. These insights then inform which scalable solutions to develop, skipping unnecessary interim steps.

4. Engage Stakeholders Early and Often

- Iterative Feedback Loop: Build solutions with continuous input from stakeholders. Starting small allows for rapid iterations and helps the people team become comfortable consuming and discussing data.

- Narrative Matters: Pair data points with narratives to make insights accessible and actionable for HR leaders and business partners.

5. Learn from Mistakes

- Avoid Perfectionism: Craig emphasizes the importance of resisting stakeholder demands for unnecessary details (e.g., font size, color choices) in early stages. Keep the focus on functionality over aesthetics.

- Adapt Approach for Each Organization: The right strategy depends on the organization's culture, maturity, and immediate needs. There's no universal formula for success.

Takeaways for People Analytics Leaders

1 Prioritize Business Alignment: Analytics should always serve the broader business strategy. Build trust by addressing real business problems early.

2 Adopt an MVP Mindset: Start small, iterate, and grow the function in alignment with stakeholder feedback and business priorities.

3   Challenge Conventional Thinking: Maturity models and rigid frameworks don't work in every context. Be flexible and focus on solving the most pressing challenges first.

4   Balance Innovation with Practicality: Encourage the team to think creatively while maintaining practicality in execution.

5   Focus on Stakeholder Engagement: Success is as much about educating and involving stakeholders as it is about building robust analytics capabilities.

The Journey

Craig's journey highlights that building a people analytics function is more art than science. By aligning with business needs, focusing on simplicity, and engaging stakeholders, leaders can create impactful and scalable analytics capabilities tailored to their organization's unique needs.

How to Build the People Analytics Team of the Future

It's difficult not to notice a recent push to standardize—and likely commoditize—the operating model of the people analytics function. While standardization has its merits, a bespoke, organization-centric approach to building a people analytics team is preferred because it avoids a one-size-fits-all model. No two people analytics functions look the same. The theoretical underpinning for my preference for custom functions comes from principal agent theory (Harvard Law School, 2024). Principal agent theory, which emerged in the 1970s from a number of economists and theorists, describes the pitfalls that often arise when one person or group, the "agent," is misaligned when representing another person or group, known as the "principal." How does a new people analytics leader ensure that a function is aligned with the organization's success rather than wasting resources on pet projects and ineffective technology? The answer is a customized laser focus on delivering tangible value tailored to the specific organization in which people analytics resides.

Before we talk about how Gen AI is going to impact the future structure of people analytics, let's talk about the capabilities that are needed today. The capabilities needed in a people analytics team vary significantly depending on the size, scope, and strategic goals of the organization. Tailor your team to the problems your organization needs to address. However, you may be interested in some of the competencies that are needed to effectively run a people analytics function today in a broad sense. Below, the competencies required for large people analytics teams, small startup teams, integrated people analytics and workforce planning functions, and how Gen AI is reshaping these capabilities altogether, are explored.

Large Organizations (30+ People Analytics Team Members)

Large, multinational companies often have well-established HR structures, sometimes making it challenging for a people analytics team to carve out its niche. The function must operate strategically, aligning with ongoing HR transformation efforts (e.g., digital transformation, future-of-work initiatives, design thinking, etc.). In these environments, people analytics teams tend to be large and specialized, sometimes even exceeding 50 team members. These teams typically include dedicated roles for HR data governance, predictive modeling, survey design and listening, dashboard development, change management, and sometimes workforce planning and talent intelligence. However, without clear strategic alignment, these teams risk inefficiency and redundancy.

KEY COMPETENCIES FOR LARGE TEAMS:

- **Strategic Business Alignment**—Understanding corporate strategy and how analytics can drive meaningful business outcomes.

- **Governance and Compliance**—Managing HR data integrity, privacy, and security at an enterprise scale.

- **Embedded HR Analytics Partnerships**—Aligning people analytics with HR business partners to integrate insights into talent strategies.

- **Center of Excellence (CoE) Model Execution**—Operating a structured CoE approach to standardize methodologies and insights delivery, as well as with functions outside of HR, such as Finance.

- **Data Science and AI/ML Specialization**—Leveraging machine learning, NLP, and organizational network analysis (ONA) to generate advanced insights.

- **Workforce Planning and Talent Intelligence**—Partnering with HR and finance to forecast talent needs and drive long-term workforce strategies.

- **Change Management and Internal Consulting**—Engaging HR and business leaders to translate analytics insights into organizational action.
- **HR Technology and Automation**—Leveraging HR tech platforms (e.g., Workday, SAP, Oracle) and integrating automation into analytics workflows.
- **Data Engineering**—Building and maintaining scalable HR data infrastructure, ensuring data quality, integration, and accessibility for analytics applications.

Startups & Small Organizations

Startups and smaller companies present a different challenge: Limited resources, minimal supporting infrastructure, and a need for rapid experimentation. Unlike in large companies, people analytics functions in smaller companies often double as HR tech experts and workforce planning strategists due to a lack of specialized teams.

KEY COMPETENCIES FOR SMALL TEAMS:

- **HR Tech and Data Engineering**—Managing and integrating HR data systems without a dedicated HRIS team.
- **Hands-on Data Analysis and Insights Delivery**—Executing end-to-end analytics projects from data ingestion to storytelling.
- **Hacking and Rapid Prototyping**—Creating practical solutions using low-code/no-code automation and data tools.
- **First-Principles Thinking**—Rethinking HR processes from the ground up rather than following legacy corporate models.
- **Cross-Functional Collaboration**—Engaging with finance, operations, and product teams to integrate workforce insights.
- **Talent Strategy Design**—Informing talent acquisition, retention, and development strategies using data.
- **Scalability and Productization**—Building reusable analytics solutions to scale insights across the organization.

People Analytics + Workforce Planning & Talent Intelligence

Many companies are integrating people analytics with workforce planning and talent intelligence, creating a more comprehensive function focused on both operational and strategic workforce insights. This integration ensures that analytics doesn't operate in a vacuum but directly informs business-critical decisions about workforce composition, hiring strategies, and succession planning. Remember all three functions are branches from the same "tree of the value of human capital labor data" from Chapter 3.

KEY COMPETENCIES FOR AN INTEGRATED FUNCTION:

- **Labor Market Intelligence**—Utilizing external data labor market data, such as from providers like Lightcast, to benchmark talent supply, demand, and competitive insights.
- **Strategic Workforce Planning**—Forecasting talent needs and skills gaps based on business strategy and external trends.
- **Predictive Talent Insights**—Identifying turnover risk, high-potential talent, and future leadership gaps using AI-driven analytics.
- **Compensation and Skills-Based Workforce Modeling**—Informing pay equity, skills taxonomy, and career pathing decisions with data.
- **HR and Business Strategy Integration**—Partnering with finance and operations to ensure talent strategies support business goals.
- **Technology-Enabled Workforce Planning**—Using AI and scenario modeling to optimize workforce investments and hiring plans.

The Role of Gen AI in Building the People Analytics Team of the Future

As we have discussed at length, Gen AI is transforming the composition of people analytics teams by automating traditionally manual tasks and enabling deeper insights with fewer resources. Rather than requiring large teams to manage complex HR data ecosystems, Gen AI allows for highly automated, AI-powered analytics functions that can be operated with lean, specialized teams.

HOW GEN AI IS CHANGING PEOPLE ANALYTICS:

- **Automation of Data Management**—AI-driven ETL (Extract, Transform, Load) pipelines reduce the need for manual data engineering.
- **Self-Service AI Chatbots**—Employees and HR leaders can interact with AI-powered insights platforms to get real-time answers to workforce questions.

- **AI-Augmented Decision-Making**—Advanced generative AI models enable HR leaders to simulate workforce scenarios and optimize strategies.

- **Predictive and Prescriptive Analytics at Scale**—AI enhances forecasting capabilities, providing deeper insights with minimal human intervention.

- **Increased Focus on Strategic Thinking and Business Impact**—Analysts can shift focus from technical execution to influencing and driving business decisions.

Why You May Never Need a 50+ Person People Analytics Team Again

Historically, scaling a people analytics function meant hiring more analysts, data engineers, and visualization specialists. With the rise of Gen AI and automation, the need for massive people analytics teams is diminishing. Instead, companies can build lean, high-impact teams with expertise in:

- **Better Business Consultation**—Embedding people analytics into business strategy with a consultative approach to maximize impact.

- **Critical and Analytical Thinking**—Enhancing decision-making with structured, evidence-based approaches to complex workforce challenges.

- **Change Management**—Ensuring analytics-driven insights lead to actual organizational change through structured adoption strategies.

- **Operational Execution and ROI**—Demonstrating clear value by linking people analytics initiatives directly to business outcomes and financial performance.

The future of people analytics isn't about growing teams; it's about leveraging technology to create greater impact with fewer resources. The companies that successfully integrate AI into their people analytics functions will be the ones that remain agile, forward-thinking, and capable of delivering meaningful business insights with a fraction of the traditional headcount. This will allow people analytics teams to spend more time on measuring tricky topics, like organizational culture, which they may not have had time to do effectively in the past.

How to Measure Culture

Historically, measuring organizational culture has been a challenge in people analytics. Culture is an abstract concept, often defined as the shared values, norms, and behaviors within a workplace. Traditionally, organizations have relied on employee surveys to assess culture, using Likert-type items, open-ended responses, and periodic engagement surveys, while more recently pivoting to the use of shorter pulse surveys. Beyond surveys, qualitative assessments such as focus groups, exit interviews, and ethnographic studies have been used to gain deeper insights into workplace culture. These methods provide rich context but are difficult to scale. Some organizations have also turned to organizational network analysis (ONA), examining collaboration patterns in email/calendar metadata or "active" ONA employee surveys to understand informal influence structures. However, these approaches often require specialized expertise and many organizations have not adopted it as common practice.

Despite their widespread use, traditional methods have struggled with real-time culture monitoring. They often rely on self-reported data, which can be influenced by social desirability bias, making it difficult to get an objective measure of what's happening inside an organization. Additionally, because culture is fluid and continuously evolving, external shocks can change a culture quite rapidly. This is where digital exhaust and AI-powered methods are transforming the way we measure culture.

The Rise of Digital Exhaust

The shift from static, survey-based assessments to real-time culture meas-urement has been accelerated by the use of digital exhaust—the vast amounts of behavioral data employees generate through their daily interactions with workplace systems. Digital communication platforms (Slack, Microsoft Teams, email), collaboration tools (Google Docs, Jira, Asana), and even metadata from HRIS and performance management systems now offer a passive, unobtrusive way to measure culture based on actual behaviors rather than self-reports.

By applying natural language processing (NLP) and machine learning, organizations analyze patterns in communication, sentiment, and collabora-tion to detect cultural trends. ONA has also become more dynamic due to the broad use of off-the-shelf products, using real-time interactions to map who actually holds influence within an organization, rather than relying solely on hierarchical structures.

Culture Measurement with Gen AI

Gen AI takes measurement using digital exhaust a step further by providing real-time interpretation and predictive insights about cultural trends. Rather than relying on software to measure digital exhaust, AI models can synthesize data from multiple sources and identify emerging culture patterns before they become a problem. For example, Gen AI can simulate future cultural shifts based on intervention strategies, allowing HR leaders to test the impact of policy changes in a virtual environment before implementing them.

Perhaps the biggest advantage of Gen AI is its ability to provide personalized, real-time feedback to leaders. Instead of waiting for an annual culture survey, managers will receive ongoing insights about how their team is feeling and functioning, allowing them to make data-driven adjustments on the fly. As Gen AI becomes more deeply integrated into people analytics, measuring culture will move from being a retrospective, survey-based exercise to an ongoing, proactive process that continuously tracks and improves workplace culture in real time. Organizations that embrace these advancements will not only understand their culture more accurately but also shape it more effectively.

REAL-WORLD EXAMPLE

"How is Culture Measured in People Analytics?" with Sue Lam, VP of People Analytics, Strategy, and Culture at Coca-Cola

(Paraphrased for length from Ep. 26 of "Directionally Correct, A People Analytics Podcast")

Defining Culture in the Workplace

Dr. Sue Lam, VP of People Analytics, Strategy, and Culture at Coca-Cola, defines culture as "everything we do in order to get work done inside the company." This broad definition encompasses narratives, processes, symbols, and behaviors. While academics debate the nuances of "culture" versus "climate," Lam highlights that culture is difficult to measure and even harder to act upon, particularly from an analytics perspective. Despite these challenges, culture can be understood through three measurable behavioral components: symbols, character, and policies.

Culture as Symbols

Symbols are the visible, tangible representations of an organization's culture. These include the actions, behaviors, and artifacts that signal cultural values. Lam provides an example from Coca-Cola: when James Quincey became CEO, he adopted informal behaviors such as wearing jeans, eating in the cafeteria, and interacting casually with employees. These symbolic actions communicated a cultural message of accessibility and inclusivity, reshaping employees' perception of leadership.

Culture as Character

Character reflects what individuals and the organization do when no one is watching. This component delves into ethical behaviors, power dynamics, and trust. It examines whether individuals uphold values such as honesty and fairness when unobserved. Lam emphasizes that character sets the tone for workplace behaviors and reflects the organization's underlying ethical standards.

Culture as Policies and Tolerances

The third pillar of culture pertains to the policies, procedures, and tolerances within an organization. Lam describes this as the question of "what are you willing to tolerate?" and "what can you get away with?" This involves examining whether senior leaders' actions align with their words. If executives fail to model the cultural values they espouse, it creates confusion and undermines cultural change initiatives. Employees are left to decide whether to follow what leaders say or what leaders actually do, highlighting the importance of consistency in driving meaningful cultural change.

Key Takeaways

1 Culture Is Broad and Complex: It encompasses everything from symbols and narratives to processes and behaviors.
2 Symbols Matter: Leadership actions, like those of Coca-Cola's CEO, can send powerful cultural messages that influence employees' perceptions.
3 Character Sets the Ethical Tone: Culture is reflected in how employees and leaders behave when unobserved, shaping trust and integrity within the organization.
4 Policies Define Tolerance: What leaders tolerate or demonstrate directly impacts how employees interpret and embody cultural values.

Sue Lam's insights demonstrate that while measuring culture is challenging, it is possible to analyze its behavioral components—symbols, character, and policies. By examining these aspects, organizations can better understand their cultural dynamics and align leadership actions with desired values. Coca-Cola's focus on these elements offers a blueprint for leveraging people analytics to foster a culture that aligns with strategic goals and employee expectations.

Will We Need Surveys in the Future?

For decades, surveys have been one of the foundations of collecting people analytics sentiment and experiences of employees, providing insights into key areas such as employee engagement, lifetime value, experience, and the overall employee lifecycle. Traditional engagement surveys, often conducted annually or bi-annually, aimed to capture broad sentiments around workplace satisfaction, leadership effectiveness, and organizational culture. However, these surveys came with significant limitations—they provide point-in-time snapshots rather than continuous insights, and their effectiveness heavily depends on response rates and honest feedback.

To address these shortcomings, organizations introduced pulse surveys, which aimed to provide more frequent, real-time insights by asking employees a limited set of questions at regular intervals. Pulse surveys became popular because they allowed HR teams to detect engagement fluctuations over time. However, they still fell short of providing context, leaving organizations to speculate about why engagement levels were changing. Additionally, survey fatigue became a major challenge—employees, required to answer the same repetitive questions, often disengaged from the process, leading to lower response rates and unreliable data.

Recognizing these gaps, some companies shifted toward employee lifecycle surveys, which attempted to gather feedback based on specific moments in the employee lifecycle—onboarding, promotions, offboarding, or major organizational changes. These surveys improved relevance and actionability, but they still suffered from the same fundamental weakness as pulse and engagement surveys: They relied on self-reported data that could be biased, delayed, or influenced by factors unrelated to actual workplace experience.

Employee Voice

Employee surveys have often served as the primary method for organizations to gauge engagement, experience, and key aspects of the employee lifecycle. More than just a data collection tool, surveys have been a proxy for "employee voice"—a way for companies to hear directly from their workforce, understand their concerns, and make informed decisions based on employee feedback. In this sense, employee surveys have functioned much like an intelligence-gathering mechanism, similar to what intelligence agencies use to understand environments, predict trends, and make strategic decisions.

Organizations have long relied on surveys to gather intelligence on their workforce, capturing data on:

- **Employee engagement**—How connected and committed employees feel toward their work and organization.

- **Employee experience**—The sum of interactions employees have with their organization across the entire employee lifecycle.

- **Employee lifetime value**—The total value an employee contributes to the company over their tenure.

- **The employee lifecycle**—Key touchpoints such as onboarding, promotion, performance reviews, and exit experiences.

By systematically collecting and analyzing these responses, this process mirrors how intelligence organizations gather and analyze information to assess threats, predict future scenarios, and drive strategic decision-making. Surveys have been the HR equivalent of reconnaissance missions—extracting insights from employees to inform policies and interventions.

REAL-WORLD EXAMPLE

"Employee Voice as Intelligence at Google" with Kristin Saboe, Head of Employee Voice at Google, and Lecturer at Georgetown

(Paraphrased for length from Ep. 67 of "Directionally Correct, A People Analytics Podcast")

Defining Employee Voice and Listening

Dr. Kristin Saboe, Head of Employee Voice at Google, describes employee voice as the process of gathering and leveraging insights from employees to guide strategy and decision-making. Historically associated with annual surveys, the function has evolved into a sophisticated, data-driven discipline. Employee voice is unique because it captures privileged data—what employees choose to share about their thoughts and experiences—distinct from traditional administrative metrics. This makes it a strategic multiplier, enabling organizations to measure, nudge, and align behaviors with strategic goals.

The Evolution of Listening Functions

Employee listening functions are maturing rapidly and becoming central to organizational decision-making. Once seen as a post hoc feedback mechanism, these functions now influence strategies from inception. Saboe advocates for integrating listening teams at the earliest stages of program and policy development to ensure precise measurement and alignment with organizational goals. She highlights how early involvement strengthens outcomes and ensures alignment with both employee needs and long-term strategic objectives.

Bridging Military and Corporate Approaches to Intelligence

Dr. Saboe draws parallels between employee voice functions and military intelligence practices. Her military background influences her emphasis on triangulating data, maintaining trust, and handling employee data securely. Similar to military operations, where secure and accurate information drives decisions, effective employee listening requires discernment and trust to ensure data is both actionable and ethical.

Cross-Sector Lessons: Innovation and Resilience

Saboe highlights lessons from her cross-sector experience, particularly how government and military research can inform corporate strategies. She points to organizations like DARPA, whose mission is to advance foundational research for widespread benefit. For instance, military research on performance optimization, grit, and resilience—concepts critical for soldiers in challenging environments—later trickled into the corporate world. These foundational investments laid the groundwork for widespread adoption during the Covid-19 pandemic, demonstrating the value of proactive, long-term research.

Key Takeaways

1 Employee Voice as Strategic Intelligence: Employee voice is a unique, privileged source of data that can drive strategy, policy, and culture when integrated early in decision-making processes.

2 Active Listening: Moving beyond passive data collection to active engagement with employee insights strengthens trust and improves outcomes.

3 Cross-Sector Insights: Innovations in public and military sectors, such as resilience and performance optimization research, offer valuable lessons for corporate strategy and employee well-being.

4 Trust and Ethics in Data Handling: The ethical handling of employee data is critical to maintaining trust and ensuring actionable insights.

Kristin Saboe's work at Google highlights the transformative potential of employee voice as a central intelligence function. By integrating listening practices into strategic planning, organizations can align their goals with employee needs, fostering a culture of trust and innovation. Furthermore, cross-sector lessons reveal the importance of foundational investments in research and innovation to address emerging challenges. For companies aiming to harness the power of employee voice, this case study underscores the importance of early integration, active listening, and ethical data practices.

A Future Without Surveys: How Gen AI Will Transform People Analytics

With generative AI and advanced analytics, organizations will no longer need to rely on surveys to understand the employee experience. Instead, AI models will continuously analyze "digital exhaust"—the passive, organic data generated through employees' interactions in workplace tools, collaboration platforms, and HR systems—to provide real-time, unbiased, and context-rich insights into engagement, productivity, and well-being. Gen AI can process data from sources such as:

- **Communication tools** (Slack, Teams, email sentiment analysis) to assess employee sentiment and psychological safety.
- **Project management systems** (Asana, Jira, Trello) to track workload, collaboration patterns, and signs of burnout.
- **HRIS and performance management systems** to detect trends in turnover risk, promotion equity, and career progression.

Unlike surveys, which require employees to explicitly share their feelings and experiences, Gen AI passively observes and interprets behavior patterns, eliminating survey fatigue and ensuring continuous, real-time insights. It can even predict future engagement risks, alerting the HR team as well as leaders before issues escalate.

Additionally, AI-powered feedback systems will personalize insights at the individual level. Rather than treating all employees as a homogenous group, Gen AI will tailor its analysis based on role, department, tenure, and past behavioral patterns—ensuring that interventions are targeted and meaningful rather than based on aggregate survey averages.

Will Surveys Ever Fully Disappear?

While surveys may not disappear entirely, they will no longer be the primary tool for measuring employee engagement, experience, or lifecycle trends. Some people just *like* taking surveys. It makes them feel "heard." In a Gen AI-powered world, surveys will likely be reserved for specific use cases where direct input is required, such as when employees need to voice personal concerns outside of digital channels.

However, for most people analytics applications, the future will be defined by passive, real-time, and predictive AI-driven insights, making surveys an outdated and unnecessary burden for employees. Organizations that embrace this shift will gain a significant competitive advantage, fostering a more dynamic, responsive, and engaging workplace without requiring employees to constantly answer the same old questions. The future is here, it's just not evenly distributed.

Leadership & Leadership Analytics

Leadership and management as terms are often used interchangeably, but they are distinct concepts that require different skill sets and impact organizations in different ways. Management is the operational side of leading a team—hiring, developing, and retaining talent, overseeing execution, and ensuring productivity. Leadership, on the other hand, is about influence, motivation, vision, and communication. A manager can ensure that tasks get done, but a leader inspires people to want to do the tasks. The best organizations recognize that not all good managers are good leaders, and that not all great leaders are good managers. This distinction is critical to understanding how leadership effectiveness is measured, how it impacts performance, and how the future of leadership will be shaped by Gen AI.

The "L" Factor: One Universal Form of Leadership Effectiveness

Recent research suggests that rather than there being different "types" of effective leadership, there is a single underlying construct—often referred to as the "L" factor—that determines whether someone is truly effective as a leader (Eva et al., 2024). This means that whether a leader is authoritative or democratic, strategic or tactical, visionary or operational, what ultimately matters is how well they lead people toward achieving organizational goals.

The "Peter Principle" (Peter and Hull, 1994)—which suggests that people are promoted to their highest level of incompetence—helps explain why many organizations struggle with leadership quality. High performers are often promoted into leadership roles based on their individual contributions, not their leadership potential. But the skills that make someone a great performer don't necessarily make them a great leader. In fact, some of the very traits that get people promoted—like being overly dutiful and conscientious—can lead to poor leadership behaviors such as micromanagement, lack of delegation, and an inability to advocate for their teams. Organizations must rethink how they identify and develop leaders, focusing on traits that predict the "L" factor rather than simply rewarding past performance.

Measuring Leadership and Managerial Effectiveness

To develop better leaders and managers, organizations must first be able to measure leadership effectiveness. Traditional approaches, such as 360-degree feedback and engagement surveys, provide some insight, but more sophisticated leadership analytics models now incorporate data on:

- **Retention and Turnover:** Great managers retain top talent; poor managers drive people away.

- **Team Performance:** Effective leadership can be measured through team-level productivity, goal achievement, and innovation.

- **Manager Quality Index (MQI):** A composite score including factors like team engagement, hiring success, communication effectiveness, and upward feedback scores.

- **Psychological Safety:** The ability of employees to express ideas and concerns without fear of retribution is a key indicator of leadership effectiveness.

Organizations that take a data-driven approach to leadership development can better identify which managers need coaching, which employees have high leadership potential, and which leadership behaviors correlate with long-term business success.

How Gen AI Will Improve Leadership & Management

The future of leadership will not be about replacing leaders with AI but rather augmenting their decision-making and improving managerial effectiveness at scale through AI-driven insights. Many of the operational responsibilities of managers—such as performance tracking, coaching recommendations, and workforce planning—can now be automated or enhanced with AI. This shift will free up managers to focus on what matters most—leading, inspiring, and developing people. Some key areas where AI will transform leadership and management include:

- **AI-Driven Coaching:** Gen AI can provide real-time feedback to managers on their communication, decision-making, and team interactions, offering suggestions for improvement based on best leadership practices.

- **Enhanced Manager Decision-Making:** AI can analyze past decisions, compare them with organizational outcomes, and recommend better decision-making strategies.

- **Personalized Leadership Development:** AI can assess a leader's strengths and weaknesses and create customized development plans, including recommended readings, training, and coaching sessions tailored to their leadership style.

- **Automated Employee Feedback Analysis:** AI can process thousands of survey responses, Slack messages, and performance reviews, identifying trends and insights about team morale, engagement, and leadership effectiveness.

- **Predictive Talent Management:** AI will enable early identification of leadership potential, recommending employees for leadership development programs before they are even considered for promotion.

The Future of Leadership in an AI-Driven World

While many roles in business may be automated by AI in the coming years or decades, senior leaders and executives will be among the last roles to be fully replaced, if such replacement occurs at all. This is because leadership involves complex human judgment, strategic vision, and interpersonal influence—skills that AI struggles to replicate. However, even though leadership will remain human-driven, their decision-making will be drastically augmented by AI. Imagine a future where every leadership decision is supported by AI-driven insights—from hiring decisions to merger strategies to culture-building initiatives. AI will act as an executive-level assistant, analyzing millions of data points in real time and providing recommendations based on best practices, historical trends, and predictive analytics. Leaders who embrace this technology will outperform those who rely solely on intuition, making smarter, faster, and more strategic decisions—enabling them to achieve their peak performance.

Peak Performance & The New Hyperscaling World

For decades, organizations have focused on managing for typical performance—ensuring employees meet consistent, sustainable productivity levels over time. In contrast, elite athletes and high performers strive for maximal performance, pushing their limits in pursuit of peak excellence. The workplace has long accepted that employees exist somewhere in between these two extremes—productive, but not pushing their absolute limits every day. But what if Gen AI changes that equation? What if AI removes cognitive bottlenecks, automates repetitive tasks, and scales human capability exponentially?

Instead of an incremental increase in efficiency, what happens when every employee suddenly becomes 10 times (10x) more effective? This isn't a theoretical question—it's happening before our eyes in disciplines like coding and software creation. AI is no longer just optimizing workflows; it is fundamentally reshaping what peak performance means in knowledge work.

The Shift from Typical Performance to Hyperscaling

In the corporate world, performance distribution follows a power law, not a normal distribution (O'Boyle and Aguinis, 2012); meaning a small percentage of employees produce a disproportionate amount of value—these are the "10x" performers, the knowledge work equivalent of elite athletes. However, if AI enables every employee to reach peak performance more frequently, the implications are massive:

- Will companies become 10x more productive with the same workforce?
- Or will they need 10x fewer employees to produce the same output?
- If peak performance becomes the norm, how will companies differentiate true excellence from AI-augmented performance? Or will the previous 10x performers become the new 100x performers?

These are not just questions of efficiency but of organizational structure, workforce planning, and competitive advantage. The hyperscaling of individual productivity could lead to the macro-level hyperscaling of entire organizations, shifting industries in ways we have never seen before.

Measuring and Achieving Peak Performance in an AI World

Historically, measuring peak performance has been difficult. Performance metrics favor sustained excellence over isolated brilliance, and most traditional measurement tools focus on central tendencies rather than outliers. However, peak performance—by its very nature—is an outlier. The best athletes don't set records every day; they do it once in a lifetime under the perfect conditions. In an AI-driven world, we must redefine how we measure and optimize performance:

- **AI as a Performance Multiplier:** AI allows employees to reach their peak more frequently by removing cognitive and administrative burdens. Knowledge workers will no longer have to wait for "flow states" to emerge naturally—AI will structure their work to maximize deep focus and minimize distractions.

- **Real-Time Peak Performance Measurement:** Instead of measuring performance retrospectively, AI can dynamically track and predict peak performance states, offering real-time nudges to optimize focus and output.

- **New Forms of Excellence:** If everyone's typical performance increases dramatically, organizations must rethink how they define "elite performers" in an AI-powered workplace. Is peak performance still about individual skill, or does it become about how well employees integrate AI into their workflows?

The Unintended Consequences of Hyperscaling Performance

While hyperscaling productivity sounds ideal, it raises significant societal and structural questions:

- Will AI make certain roles obsolete? If one AI-augmented employee can do the work of 10, organizations may drastically reduce headcount, leading to economic and societal shifts in employment.

- Will the nature of work change? If employees no longer struggle with mundane tasks, will problem-solving, creativity, and interpersonal skills become the new differentiators?

- Will burnout be eliminated—or intensified? If AI enables continuous peak performance, will organizations expect it from employees all the time? Will workers feel pressured to push beyond sustainable limits, despite AI's assistance?

These shifts could create new hierarchies of value in organizations, where the best employees are not just those who work hard, but those who can integrate AI seamlessly into their cognitive processes.

The AI-Driven Future of Organizations

As we close this chapter on the future of HR and business analytics, one thing is clear: We are entering an era of radical transformation. AI is not just changing workflows—it is redefining the very nature of work itself. Peak performance, leadership analytics, culture, surveys, and every other component of people analytics are about to be hyper-scaled by AI. Leaders will make better decisions, organizations will measure human capital more accurately, and employees will have access to unprecedented levels of cognitive augmentation. But with these advancements come new challenges—rethinking how we define leadership, performance, and even what it means to be employed. This is not just about making work more efficient—it's about redefining what work is. Those who embrace AI as a performance amplifier will thrive. Those who ignore it will be left behind. The future of people analytics isn't just data-driven—it's AI-powered, and it's already here.

Summary

This chapter delves into real-world applications of people analytics, demonstrating how companies—both large and small—leverage data-driven decision-making to gain a competitive edge. By integrating AI and analytics into workforce strategy, organizations can optimize performance, streamline decision-making, and enhance leadership effectiveness. The chapter explores best practices, case studies, and forward-looking insights on how analytics can be transformed from a reporting function into a powerful driver of business success.

Key Takeaways

1 **Winning with People Analytics Requires Execution, Not Just Exploration**

   o While understanding people analytics is important, real impact comes from integrating it into business strategy with a clear implementation plan. Execution separates high-performing companies from those stuck in theory.

2 **Gen AI is Transforming How We Use Dashboards**

   o Traditional dashboards required extensive effort to build, maintain, and interpret. With Gen AI, organizations can generate insights dynamically—eliminating the need for static dashboards and enabling real-time, AI-driven decision-making.

3 **Data Without Context is Just Noise**

   o Effective analytics requires more than numbers—it demands context. The best insights compare data against targets, benchmarks, or historical trends to guide business leaders toward actionable decisions.

4 Gen AI is Automating People Analytics Projects

o Traditionally, people analytics projects followed structured steps: scoping, data collection, analysis, and presentation. Gen AI now automates much of this process, enabling real-time analysis and decision-making without months-long research cycles.

5 People Analytics is Most Effective When Aligned with Business Strategy

o Successful analytics functions don't just produce reports—they solve pressing business problems. Organizations that tie their analytics efforts directly to business objectives see the highest impact.

6 Building a People Analytics Team is No Longer a One-Size-Fits-All Approach

o The capabilities needed for a successful people analytics function vary by organization size and maturity. With Gen AI automating many technical tasks, future teams will focus more on strategy, decision-making, and business consulting.

7 The Future of Culture Measurement Lies in AI and Digital Exhaust

o Traditional employee surveys provide limited insights into workplace culture. AI-driven analysis of digital communication patterns, collaboration behaviors, and real-time feedback is revolutionizing how companies measure and shape their culture.

8 Employee Voice is Shifting from Surveys to AI-Driven Intelligence

o Companies have historically relied on surveys to gauge employee sentiment, but AI-powered listening tools can now analyze engagement, productivity, and well-being in real-time without requiring constant employee input.

9 AI is Reshaping Leadership and Managerial Effectiveness

o Leadership success is being redefined with AI-driven coaching, decision-making assistance, and predictive insights. The best leaders will be those who embrace AI as a tool to enhance their effectiveness, not replace human judgment.

10 The Future of Work is About Hyperscaling Performance

o AI is enabling employees to achieve peak performance by removing cognitive bottlenecks and automating repetitive tasks. This shift will redefine how organizations measure productivity, differentiate top performers, and structure their workforce.

The future of people analytics is not about more reports or dashboards—it's about making faster, smarter, and more impactful decisions using AI and data. Companies that integrate AI-driven people analytics into their core business strategy will gain a significant competitive advantage, shaping the future of work in the process.

References

Chatterton, T. and Newmarch, G. (2016). "The Future is Already Here—It's Just Not Very Evenly Distributed." In *Everyday Futures*, edited by N. Spurling and L. Kuijer. Institute for Social Futures. wp.lancs.ac.uk/everydayfutures/essay-collection/ (archived at https://perma.cc/76RS-5FG7).

Eva, N., Howard, J. L., Liden, R. C., Morin, A. J. S. and Schwarz, G. (2024). An Inconvenient Truth: A Comprehensive Examination of the Added Value (or Lack Thereof) of Leadership Measures. *Journal of Management Studies.* doi.org/10.1111/joms.13156 (archived at https://perma.cc/5FXE-C5JT).

Harvard Law School (2024). Principal Agent Theory. PON—Program on Negotiation at Harvard Law School. www.pon.harvard.edu/tag/principal-agent-theory/ (archived at https://perma.cc/E2GX-HZE3).

Levenson, A., Stevenson, M. and Fink, A. (2021), Are OD and Analytics Twins Separated at Birth? Toward an Integrated Framework. In *Research in Organizational Change and Development* (Research in Organizational Change and Development, Vol. 29), edited by A. B. (Rami) Shani and D. A. Noumair. Emerald Publishing Limited.

Napper, C., Hines, S. and Saboe, K. (2023). Employee Voice as Intelligence at Google. Directionally Correct. www.podbean.com/eas/pb-uen7m-151f6ca (archived at https://perma.cc/E3PU-GCK5) Ep. 67.

Napper, C., Hines, S. and Starbuck, C. (2022). The Man Who Started More People Analytics Functions. Directionally Correct. www.podbean.com/eas/pb-fqtpi-151f6f2 (archived at https://perma.cc/ZG72-9Y87) Ep. 28.

Napper, C. and Lam, S. (2022). How is Culture Measured in People Analytics? Directionally Correct. www.podbean.com/eas/pb-abg85-151f6f4 (archived at https://perma.cc/9QTF-WATQ) Ep. 26.

O'Boyle, E. and Aguinis, H. (2012). The Best and the Rest: Revisiting the Norm of Normality of Individual Performance. www.hermanaguinis.com/pdf/PPsych2012.pdf (archived at https://perma.cc/5FXE-C5JT).

Peter, L. J. and Hull, R. (1994). *The Peter Principle*. Souvenir Press.

9

Innovative HR Technologies and Future Trends in HR

This chapter will investigate cutting-edge HR technologies and emerging trends, discussing how staying ahead of technological advances can serve as a key differentiator in a competitive business landscape.

"Our future success is directly proportional to our ability to understand, adopt and integrate new technology into our work."—Toba Beta (2010)

The future of HR isn't just about adopting new technologies, it's about rethinking how we solve problems from the ground up. Toba Beta's quote serves as a fitting prelude to this chapter, because success in HR today isn't just about keeping pace with innovation; it's about integrating technology in a way that fundamentally transforms how we understand and manage people. Our impact will only be proportional to our ability to adopt cutting - edge technologies again, like AI agents, to reshape how we do people analytics, workforce planning, and talent intelligence. AI-driven agents will reshape everything from talent acquisition to employee experience, while organizational network analysis will uncover hidden dynamics that drive collaboration and performance. Workforce planning, once a reactive exercise, will now be powered by predictive models that anticipate talent needs before they arise. Also talent intelligence, leveraging vast amounts of data to make sharper hiring, retention, and development decisions, will become a competitive advantage rather than a luxury.

However, adopting these innovations without a clear problem-solving framework is like buying the fastest car without knowing where you're going. That's where first-principles thinking comes in. Instead of layering new tools onto old processes, leading organizations are reimagining HR challenges at their core: What are we really trying to optimize? How do we measure success? How do we know what we're doing is working? Which assumptions need to be questioned? By approaching HR technology from this foundational perspective, organizations can ensure they're not just chasing trends but implementing solutions that create lasting impact. In this chapter, we'll explore how AI and people analytics are reshaping HR, the future trends driving innovation, and how to navigate these changes with clarity and purpose.

The Exponential Curve of People Analytics

Humans are wired to understand linear change. If something increases at a steady rate—one step at a time—we intuitively grasp it. But exponentials? Those break our mental models. At first, an exponential curve appears to progress slowly, almost imperceptibly. Then, at an inflection point, it rockets upward, defying expectations. That's exactly what has been happening in people analytics. For much of its history, HR operated with little to no data. Decisions were made based on intuition, experience, and anecdotal evidence. Then, computers emerged—first with punch cards, enabling the earliest tabulations of employee data. As computing power advanced, organizations began digitizing records, moving data from paper forms to spreadsheets in the first wave of digital transformation. Analytics software followed, allowing companies to analyze trends and make projections. Then came data visualization tools, purpose-built people analytics platforms, and eventually, machine learning applications. Each stage accelerated the field, and yet, many still assume that progress from here will be linear. **It won't be.**

The curve is bending sharply upward. Entire areas of people analytics that once required massive teams, expensive software, and years of experience will soon be scalable, automated, and accessible to anyone. What once seemed labor-intensive, impractical, or outright impossible will soon be routine. The next phase isn't just about improving analytics—it's about democratizing it, making once-unthinkable insights available at scale with minimal effort. No longer will you need to prioritize one analytics project over another. Do them all. Do them at once. Scale the results to everyone. Nothing will stop you. The final two chapters of the book serve two purposes: First, to show what's possible in people analytics today; and second, to illustrate how nearly everything we discuss will soon be available at levels of ease that will surprise even the experts with the use of Gen AI. The era of robust, scalable, and automated people analytics is here. Buckle up—the ride is only getting started.

An HR Future with Autonomous Agents

AI agents are rapidly redefining how work gets done in HR, automating repetitive tasks, providing real-time insights, and making data-driven decisions at scale. These agents are software programs powered by machine learning and natural language processing that can execute tasks, analyze data, and interact with employees in a conversational manner. In people analytics, AI agents are already being deployed to generate reports, summarize employee feedback, and detect patterns in workforce data that might otherwise go unnoticed. However, their effectiveness hinges on one key factor: Accuracy. Unlike traditional automation tools, AI agents don't just follow pre-programmed rules—they learn and adapt. This means that even small inaccuracies can compound across multiple tasks, leading to flawed recommendations or misguided actions. As seen in Figure 9.1, if an AI agent is 99 percent accurate on a particular task, as the agent performs 10 tasks, the accuracy of the overall objective will be 90 percent. However, if the AI agent is only 90 percent accurate on one task (which is considered an optimistic assessment of AI agent accuracy in 2025 terms) as the agent performs 10 tasks the accuracy of the overall objective of the agent will be only 35 percent. This level of accuracy is not within the acceptable bounds of organizational decision-making, or societal decision-making for that matter.

FIGURE 9.1 Why AI Agent Accuracy Matters

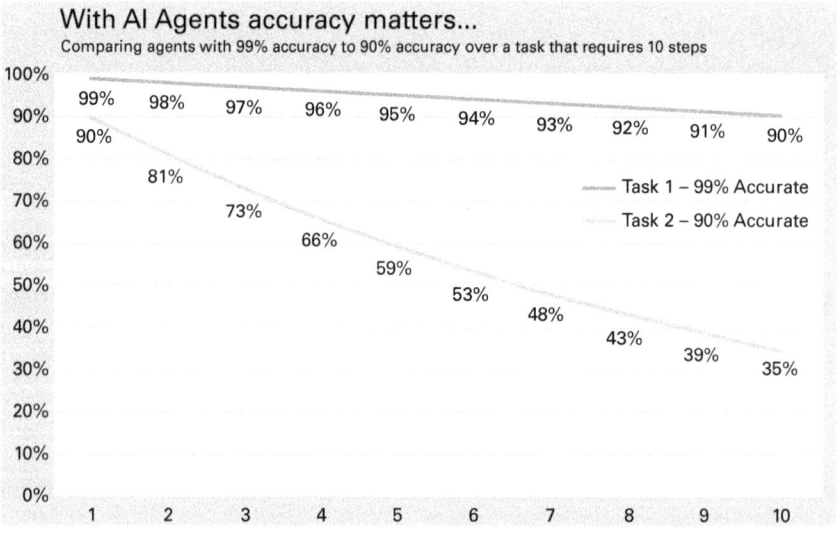

The accuracy of AI agents must improve for levels equating to 99 percent accuracy and above for them to be reliable tools in HR. Because these agents won't just be completing 10 tasks; the agents could be completing hundreds or even thousands of independent functions to perform an objective, as well as communicating with other agents to complete the task. For HR leaders, ensuring AI outputs are precise and trustworthy is critical before handing off decision-making authority to these systems. We are not there yet, but we should be getting close in the coming years.

The next evolution beyond AI agents is the rise of fully autonomous agents, self-directed AI systems that can not only process information but also take action based on it with minimal human intervention. While today's AI agents can assist HR teams by generating insights or recommending actions, autonomous agents will go further, executing complex workflows across multiple HR functions in real time. Imagine an AI agent that doesn't just analyze engagement survey results but autonomously drafts targeted employee communications to address morale issues, updates workforce planning models to anticipate turnover risks, and even initiates personalized learning recommendations based on detected skill gaps. These agents will operate across HR disciplines simultaneously, making decisions and refining their approaches based on continuous feedback from organizational data.

The most immediate and high-impact use cases for autonomous agents in HR will revolve around knowledge management, employee support, and decision augmentation. HR teams spend significant time answering repetitive policy questions, managing compliance documentation, and surfacing best practices—all of which will be handled more efficiently by autonomous AI systems. A well-trained agent could serve as an always-available HR knowledge assistant, instantly retrieving policies, providing guidance on benefits and compliance, and escalating complex issues to the right human expert. In people analytics, these agents will automate workforce reporting, detect emerging trends in employee sentiment, and even suggest interventions before issues escalate. Other game-changing applications will include AI-driven talent matching, automated onboarding experiences, and real-time coaching for managers. As organizations continue to adopt these technologies, HR's role will shift from executing routine tasks to designing and overseeing intelligent systems that optimize the employee experience and drive business outcomes.

REAL-WORLD EXAMPLE

"Autonomous AI Agents in HR and People Analytics" with Anthony Onesto, the Chief People Officer at Suzy, author of *AI in HR Today* newsletter

(Paraphrased for length from Ep. 72 of "Directionally Correct, A People Analytics Podcast")

The Rise of Autonomous AI Agents

Anthony Onesto, Chief People Officer at Suzy, describes his excitement about the potential of autonomous AI agents in HR and people analytics. These agents could revolutionize tasks such as recruiting by automating the search, engagement, and initial assessment processes. Onesto envisions a future where an AI agent can analyze a job description, scrape databases like LinkedIn or GitHub, and identify qualified candidates faster and more effectively than human recruiters. While the technology isn't fully realized, its transformative potential is already clear.

Revolutionizing Recruitment with AI

Recruitment is a prime example of how autonomous AI agents could streamline HR functions. Currently, recruiters manually search, network, and pitch roles to candidates, often constrained by time and resources. An AI agent could handle these tasks autonomously, finding, engaging, and even pre-screening candidates before handing them off to a human recruiter. This approach could significantly reduce manual workload, speed up hiring, and improve efficiency. However, as Onesto notes, the widespread adoption of such agents could create a competitive arms race where AI systems interact with one another, leading to an entirely new recruiting landscape.

Challenges and Ethical Considerations

While the possibilities are exciting, Onesto emphasizes the need for ethical considerations and guardrails. For example, AI-driven systems can unintentionally reinforce biases if not properly monitored. Tools that optimize for certain outcomes, such as hiring trends, could perpetuate inequalities if left unchecked. Laws like New York's requirement to disclose the use of AI in hiring decisions are steps in the right direction, but companies must remain vigilant to ensure their systems are fair and inclusive.

Applications Beyond Recruitment

Autonomous agents have potential applications far beyond recruiting. Onesto envisions these tools taking over repetitive, manual HR tasks, freeing HR professionals to focus on strategic initiatives. From grading resumes to managing high-volume jobs, these systems could transform traditional HR operations. Moreover, AI agents trained to mimic executive decision-making could offer 24/7 support, handling urgent decisions with high accuracy, especially in global organizations.

The Human–AI Partnership

Despite the promise of autonomous AI, Onesto stresses the importance of a "human in the loop" approach. AI systems may excel at optimizing processes, but they require human oversight to address biases, refine algorithms, and ensure outputs align with organizational values. For example, recruiters and HR leaders must remain engaged to evaluate whether AI-driven decisions reflect the diversity and inclusivity goals of the organization.

Key Takeaways

1   Autonomous AI Agents in Recruitment: These agents could automate the end-to-end recruitment process, improving efficiency and speed.

2   Ethical Considerations: Guardrails are essential to prevent AI systems from perpetuating biases, ensuring fair and equitable outcomes.

3   Beyond Recruitment: Autonomous agents have the potential to transform many HR functions, taking over repetitive tasks and enabling a more strategic HR focus.

4   The Human–AI Partnership: Human oversight is critical to refining AI systems, addressing biases, and maintaining organizational values.

Anthony Onesto's insights highlight the transformative potential of autonomous AI agents in HR and people analytics. These agents could revolutionize recruitment and other HR functions, improving efficiency and creating new opportunities for strategic focus. However, organizations must balance this innovation with ethical considerations and maintain a strong human–AI partnership to ensure fairness, inclusivity, and alignment with company values. The future of HR lies in leveraging AI as a powerful tool while retaining human oversight to guide its evolution responsibly.

Build vs. Buy & Open Source vs. Closed Source

The classic "build vs. buy" debate has long shaped how HR and people analytics teams adopt new technologies, and with the rise of Gen AI, this question remains as relevant as ever. However, there's a new dimension to consider: While no HR function is realistically going to develop its own large language models (LLMs) from scratch, they do have a choice in how they deploy AI agents. Should they leverage open-source models like Meta's Llama, Hugging Face's repositories, or even emerging models from China like DeepSeek? Or should they stick with the tried-and-true closed-source options like OpenAI, Anthropic, and Google's Gemini—likely at a higher cost structure? Each path has its advantages. Open-source models offer greater flexibility, customization, and cost efficiency, but they also require more in-house expertise to fine-tune and maintain. Closed-source models, on the other hand, provide reliability, enterprise-grade security, and seamless integrations but may come with limitations in transparency and customization. Or should they just wait for their HR technology providers to create the AI agents that will tackle their specific use cases and business problems?

For people analytics, the decision isn't just about choosing an AI model—it's about determining how these AI agents will access and process data. AI agents are only as powerful as the information they can leverage, as we discussed in Chapter 5. Traditional HR analytics tools pull from structured internal systems like HCM (Human Capital Management), ATS (Applicant Tracking Systems), and LMS (Learning Management Systems). Yet to truly unlock the power of Gen AI, organizations must integrate external labor market data, skills taxonomies and ontologies, and economic trend sources such as Lightcast data, to give themselves a comprehensive internal and external perspective on the business problems they face and the environment in which they operate. Workforce planning, talent intelligence, and predictive analytics will require AI agents to ingest and synthesize vast amounts of structured and unstructured data across internal and external sources. The quality of insights—and ultimately, the competitive advantage—will depend on how well an organization can structure, enrich, and govern its own proprietary data layer.

This proprietary data layer will be the heart of an organization's AI strategy. While foundation models provide the underlying intelligence, it's the company-specific data that makes AI truly useful in the HR context. This means organizations must invest in robust data pipelines, governance frameworks, and API infrastructures that allow AI agents to access real-time, high-quality data. Additionally, security and compliance will be critical factors, as AI agents will handle sensitive HR data. Choosing between open-source and closed-source models isn't just about cost or performance—it's about who controls the data, how well it aligns with the company's HR strategy, and how effectively it can scale across the enterprise.

The right approach will likely be a hybrid one. Some organizations will opt for open-source models to fine-tune AI agents for proprietary use cases while still leveraging closed-source solutions for general-purpose AI capabilities. Others may wait for HR tech vendors to integrate Gen AI into their platforms and simply adopt best-in-class solutions as they emerge. Regardless of the path chosen, one thing is certain: The future of AI in HR isn't just about picking the right model—it's about crafting an intelligent ecosystem where AI agents can harness proprietary data to deliver meaningful, high-value insights. This is how you can win.

REAL-WORLD EXAMPLE

"Using Autonomous Agents to Drive Value with People Analytics" with James Gallman, VP of HR Shared Services and former People Analytics leader at Disney, Allstate, and Boeing

(Paraphrased for length from Ep. 99 of "Directionally Correct, A People Analytics Podcast")

Democratizing People Analytics for Employees

James Gallman, VP of HR Shared Services and former People Analytics leader at Disney, Allstate, and Boeing, emphasizes the need to make people analytics insights accessible to employees, not just HR or senior leaders. While analytics has traditionally focused on providing insights to management, James argues that organizations have a responsibility to share actionable insights directly with employees. For example, employees could benefit from personalized recommendations about improving their engagement, participation in development opportunities, or achieving career growth within the organization.

Personalized Nudges in the Flow of Work

Gallman advocates for delivering personalized, actionable insights through virtual agents integrated into the flow of work, such as within Microsoft Teams. These agents could provide "nudges" tailored to individual employees, encouraging specific actions like scheduling one-on-one meetings with managers or pursuing learning and development opportunities. However, Gallman emphasizes the importance of maintaining a high signal-to-noise ratio. Nudges should be specific, relevant, and actionable to avoid becoming the HR equivalent of spam.

Scaling Insights Locally Through Autonomous Agents

Gallman highlights the potential of autonomous agents to scale people analytics insights while keeping them locally relevant. These agents could act as intermediaries, delivering insights to individual employees or frontline managers based on localized data. For example, an agent might alert a manager to potential burnout risks within their team or suggest career development pathways tailored to an individual's skills and goals. Through leveraging generative AI and large language models (LLMs), organizations can democratize insights while maintaining the local focus critical to engagement and change management.

Challenges in Integrating Autonomous Agents

The adoption of autonomous agents is not without challenges. Organizations often operate within fragmented technology ecosystems, with separate platforms for HR management, learning, ticketing, and performance management. Each system may develop its own agent, creating isolated "walled gardens" that fail to communicate effectively. Gallman envisions a future where agents can "call" other agents, enabling seamless integration across platforms. This would allow employees to navigate complex systems effortlessly, with their personal agent acting as a bridge across disparate technologies.

Balancing Organizational and Employee Needs

Gallman stresses the need for balance in people analytics. While organizations must use analytics to achieve business objectives, they also have a responsibility to enhance employee experiences. He likens this to a multiplier effect: If organizations could make every manager just 5 percent better, the positive impact on employees and their families would be astronomical. By focusing on both organizational goals and individual employee well-being, people analytics can drive holistic value.

Key Takeaways

1 Democratizing Insights: People analytics should empower employees with actionable insights, not just inform HR and leadership.

2 High-Impact Nudges: Personalized nudges delivered through virtual agents can encourage meaningful actions, provided they remain relevant and actionable.

3 Scaling Locally: Autonomous agents can scale insights organization-wide while maintaining local relevance for individuals and teams.

4 Integration Challenges: Overcoming fragmented technology ecosystems requires agents that can communicate across platforms.

5 Dual Value Creation: Analytics must balance organizational priorities with enhancing employee experiences to maximize impact.

James Gallman's insights demonstrate the transformative potential of autonomous agents in people analytics. By democratizing insights, integrating nudges into the flow of work, and addressing technological fragmentation, organizations can unlock new value for both employees and the business. Achieving this balance will require thoughtful implementation, a commitment to ethical practices, and a focus on enhancing the employee experience. Ultimately, autonomous agents represent a powerful tool for scaling localized, actionable insights and driving meaningful change.

Organizational Networks: Mapping New Insights

"Imagine how much harder physics would be if electrons had feelings"—
Richard Feynman (Labh, 2022)

Understanding how work gets done within organizations has always been a challenge, and org charts have never really been that helpful at understanding the real flow of information, power, and influence in organizations. Traditionally, HR data has focused on static, one-to-one relationships—who reports to whom, who is hired, and who gets promoted. While useful, these models fail to capture the full complexity of how organizations function in practice. Organizational network analysis (ONA) changed that by introducing a "many-to-many" framework, allowing HR and people analytics teams to uncover how employees interact, collaborate, and influence one another in ways that traditional org charts and survey data do not reflect.

But ONA is more than just a method for producing visually compelling network maps. Its real power lies in its ability to *quantify qualitative insights*, revealing hidden patterns of communication, collaboration bottlenecks, informal influence structures, and early warning signals for disengagement and attrition. The challenge, however, has been scaling ONA beyond small pilots or one-off studies. Data collection, whether through surveys (active ONA) or passive sources like email and meeting metadata (passive ONA), has historically been slow, resource-intensive, and difficult to integrate into decision-making at scale, or extremely expensive from gatekeeping vendors. That is changing. With Gen AI advancing both analytics and data infrastructure, ONA can now scale in ways that were previously unattainable.

Organizations will not only be able to map networks in real time but also receive automated insights and prescriptive recommendations targeted at the right individuals. Instead of simply identifying that a team is siloed or that a leader is influential, AI will be able to suggest interventions—who should be connected, where collaboration should be improved, and how knowledge transfer can be optimized.

Beyond Visualization: The Real Power of ONA

For ONA to become a core part of people analytics, it must move beyond novelty. Too often, ONA has been seen as an academic exercise or a novelty tool used primarily for leadership identification. It must be more than pretty charts to be helpful. In reality, its value comes from answering fundamental questions about how work happens, where friction exists, and how organizations can become more agile and effective.

Traditional people analytics has relied on linear models:

- **One-to-One Relationships:** How does an individual's engagement level predict their likelihood of leaving?
- **Many-to-One Relationships:** How do many variables related to a manager's leadership style, behaviors, experiences, and skills impact their team's productivity?

ONA shifts this approach by analyzing **many-to-many relationships**, such as:

- How do employees or entire teams form knowledge-sharing networks?
- Who are the informal leaders that drive company culture and decision-making?
- Where are the communication bottlenecks that slow down innovation and how does information flow through an organization?
- How do teams naturally organize themselves, and where do silos emerge?

By embracing network-based thinking, organizations can move from static, siloed insights to dynamic, system-wide understanding. This is the qualitative insight that comes from quantitative ONA data.

Scaling ONA with Gen AI

Historically, ONA has struggled with scalability. Even when leveraging digital metadata, analyzing networks across thousands of employees required manual effort, expert interpretation, and long processing times. No one can make decisions based on a giant ONA blob that shows thousands upon thousands of interconnections. It needs context to be helpful and scale. With Gen AI, that barrier is disappearing.

AI-powered ONA will:

- Automate data collection and analysis in real time, removing the need for labor-intensive surveys.
- Surface insights immediately, rather than waiting weeks for reports. An executive summary of insights will be a breeze.
- Generate prescriptive recommendations, directing specific actions to improve collaboration and efficiency to exactly who needs to see those actions.

This shift transforms ONA from a diagnostic tool into a real-time decision-making engine. Instead of merely identifying that knowledge silos exist, AI-driven ONA will suggest how to break them down, who needs to be introduced, and where workflow improvements can have the greatest impact.

Key Use Cases for ONA in HR and People Analytics

BREAKING DOWN SILOS

One of the most persistent organizational challenges is functional silos—teams that work well internally but rarely communicate across departments. This lack of cross-functional collaboration leads to inefficiencies, duplicated efforts, and slower innovation. ONA can identify which teams are isolated, the degree of their disconnection, and where intervention is needed. AI-driven recommendations can then facilitate better collaboration, ensuring that teams are not just connected on paper but actually working together in meaningful ways.

IDENTIFYING HIDDEN INFLUENCERS

Formal hierarchies do not always reflect the true power dynamics within an organization. Some employees, regardless of their title, act as critical connectors, influencing decision-making, innovation, and cultural norms. ONA allows organizations to find these key individuals who may be overlooked in traditional talent reviews. Once identified, these influencers can be integrated into leadership development programs, change management initiatives, and retention strategies. With AI, these insights can be updated dynamically, ensuring that organizations always know who their real culture carriers and knowledge hubs are.

OPTIMIZING TEAM PRODUCTIVITY

Team effectiveness is not just about individual skills—it is about how people work together. ONA can assess the optimal team size and structure for different types of projects, identifying patterns of collaboration that lead to high performance. For remote and hybrid teams, ONA can highlight gaps in informal interactions, helping leaders take proactive steps to strengthen virtual collaboration and maintain engagement.

PREDICTING AND PREVENTING TURNOVER

Attrition rarely happens in isolation. Employees who leave often influence others in their network, creating ripple effects throughout an organization. ONA can detect early signs of disengagement by tracking changes in collaboration patterns, such as:

- Employees becoming disconnected from their usual work networks.
- Reduced collaboration between key influencers and their peers.
- A leader's departure triggers a cascade of resignations in their team.

AI-driven ONA can generate retention strategies in real time, providing HR teams with early warning systems and data-backed intervention plans.

REAL-WORLD EXAMPLE

"Organizational Network Analytics and The Future of the Office" with Michael Arena, Dean at Biola University, former senior HR leader at Amazon Web Services and General Motors

(Paraphrased for length from Ep. 33 of "Directionally Correct, A People Analytics Podcast")

Balancing the Remote vs. In-Office Debate

Dr. Michael Arena, Dean at Biola University and former senior HR leader at Amazon Web Services and General Motors, highlights the polarization in the remote vs. in-office debate. While leaders often advocate for in-office work to foster connections and collaboration, employees may resist, citing personal preferences and perceived productivity. Arena emphasizes the need for evidence-based approaches to avoid biases and align workplace strategies with organizational and employee needs.

The Role of Proximity in Collaboration

Dr. Arena explains that proximity, long thought to drive productivity, is actually a proxy for cohesion. While remote environments have shown that cohesion can be maintained among existing connections, forming new relationships remains a significant challenge. The loss of chance encounters, such as hallway conversations or water cooler moments, limits opportunities for generating new ideas. Arena underscores the importance of intentional design to enable proximity-based interactions, particularly for bridging connections between teams and fostering innovation.

Intentional Social Architectures

To navigate the hybrid workplace effectively, Arena introduces the concept of "social lottery" and intentional interaction design. Random, unstructured encounters were never optimally managed in traditional office environments. In hybrid setups, merely mandating in-office days is insufficient. For example, requiring employees to come in two days a week only marginally increases the likelihood of meaningful interactions. Instead, organizations must design interventions to place teams or individuals in close proximity at key moments, such as the discovery phase of a project or during periods of cross-team collaboration.

Adaptive Teaming and Functional Frameworks

Arena proposes an adaptive teaming model to guide hybrid work strategies. Teams should first determine their current state—discovery, development, or diffusion—and align their collaboration methods accordingly. For example, discovery phases may require in-person brainstorming sessions, while heads-down work can be conducted remotely. This "form follows function" approach ensures teams use the appropriate social and physical architectures to maximize outcomes. Arena envisions a future where real estate designs, scheduling tools, and digital platforms complement each other to create environments tailored to the specific needs of teams.

The Importance of New Connections

Arena stresses that creativity and innovation often stem from weak ties— connections with people outside immediate networks. While existing relationships can be nurtured in remote settings, establishing new connections is far more difficult without intentional planning. Organizations can facilitate this by rotating team interactions or creating opportunities for cross-functional collaboration, ensuring that employees continue to build and maintain diverse networks.

Key Takeaways

1   Cohesion, Not Proximity: Proximity is a proxy for cohesion, and while remote work can maintain existing connections, forming new relationships requires intentional in-person interactions.

2   Intentional Design: Random in-office schedules are ineffective. Organizations must design targeted interventions to place the right teams and individuals together at the right time.

3   Adaptive Teaming: Teams should align their collaboration methods with their functional state—discovery, development, or diffusion—to maximize efficiency and outcomes.

4   The Value of Weak Ties: New connections drive creativity and innovation, necessitating intentional strategies to foster cross-team and cross-functional relationships.

5   Frameworks Over Chaos: A structured approach to hybrid work, guided by organizational network analytics, can bring order and effectiveness to workplace interactions.

Michael Arena's insights underscore the importance of intentionality in designing hybrid workplaces. By leveraging organizational network analytics and adaptive teaming, organizations can overcome the limitations of remote work and maximize the potential of in-person interactions. Proactive strategies to foster weak ties and align social architectures with functional needs will shape the future of collaboration. As organizations refine their frameworks and tools, they can create environments that drive innovation, cohesion, and long-term success.

Embedding ONA into Business Strategy

For ONA to have lasting impact, it cannot remain an isolated HR initiative. It must be integrated into broader business decision-making. This means:

- **Aligning ONA with workforce planning** to predict skill gaps and future hiring needs.
- **Using ONA to enhance customer success** by mapping how internal collaboration affects external client outcomes.
- **Building real-time ONA dashboards** that provide business leaders with live insights into collaboration patterns and organizational health.

ONA represents a fundamental shift in how we understand organizations' inner workings. Traditional hierarchical models assume that work flows through chains of command, but ONA reveals that the real drivers of collaboration, innovation, and decision-making exist within networks that are often invisible in conventional HR data. With Gen AI addressing ONA's biggest barriers—scalability and real-time insight generation—organizations can finally move beyond theoretical discussions and make network-based analytics a core part of their people strategy. Those who embrace this shift will gain a deeper, more dynamic understanding of their workforce, leading to more agile, connected, and high-performing organizations.

Workforce Planning: The Newest Old Trend

Workforce planning is not a new concept. In fact, it has existed in some form for decades, evolving from "manpower planning" in industrial and military settings to the strategic workforce planning initiatives seen in large enterprises today (Ackoff, 1970). Yet, for all its longevity, workforce planning remains one of the most underutilized and inconsistently executed disciplines within HR and is a relatively new part of the people analytics umbrella. Its potential impact has always been clear—ensuring that an organization has the right people, with the right skills, at the right time, at the right cost, in the right location. But despite its importance, it has only been mastered by a few organizations and at great cost and effort.

The renewed focus on workforce planning today is not just a reaction to shifting labor market risks (e.g., demographic changes, labor shortages, mismatched skills and jobs, immigration changes, dropping birth rates, etc.) and inflation's impact on wages (Lightcast, 2025); it's an acknowledgment that traditional headcount planning methods have fallen short. Organizations still struggle with talent shortages, inefficient hiring, and an inability to anticipate future skill needs. But what if we could finally break through these challenges? With advancements in people analytics, talent intelligence, organizational network analysis (ONA) and now Gen AI, workforce planning has a real opportunity to fulfill its promise. The ability to integrate external labor market data, real-time organizational network insights, and AI-powered forecasting means workforce planning can become a continuous, dynamic process rather than a static, once-a-year exercise. And more importantly, it can be accurate enough to be trusted, real-time enough to be dynamic, and operational enough to make real decisions based on its conclusions.

Why Workforce Planning Has Never Truly Scaled

One of the biggest reasons workforce planning has remained inconsistent is that no two companies do it the same way. Unlike other HR functions, such as payroll or benefits administration, workforce planning is highly contextual. Each company has its own structure, strategy, and talent needs, making it difficult to implement standardized solutions at scale.

Additionally, workforce planning has often been treated as an isolated function rather than a core part of business strategy. Many organizations engage in workforce planning reactively—when hiring freezes, layoffs, or labor shortages force them to assess their workforce. Few treat it as an ongoing strategic capability embedded into decision-making processes. This lack of continuity has prevented workforce planning from becoming a well-developed competency in most HR teams. Workforce planning practitioners in HR are expected to be highly skilled at doing workforce planning and have well-developed workforce planning operating procedures when workforce planning insights are only considered "business critical" in leaders' eyes only a few times a decade, during times of crisis. That is an unrealistic expectation at most organizations.

Technology has also been a limiting factor. Most workforce planning efforts rely on spreadsheets, disconnected headcount forecasts, or standalone software that struggles to integrate with other HR and business systems. Without the ability to connect internal talent data, external labor market intelligence, financial planning and analysis data, talent acquisition hiring planning, real estate footprint forecasts and constraints, and predictive internal analytics in a seamless way, workforce planning has often been more guesswork than science.

REAL-WORLD EXAMPLE

"Workforce Planning and Strategy at Walmart People Analytics" with Jocelyn Caldwell, VP of People at Pilot Company, former VP of Workforce Strategy at Walmart

(Paraphrased for length from Ep. 76 of "Directionally Correct, A People Analytics Podcast")

The Role of Training and Reskilling

Dr. Jocelyn Caldwell, VP of People at Pilot Company and former VP of Workforce Strategy at Walmart, emphasizes that effective training and reskilling programs require proactive planning and anticipation of future skills needs. Successful reskilling occurs when organizations identify evolving skill requirements well in advance. However, it fails when ambiguity exists about job roles, existing skills, or the trajectory of future needs. Organizations must develop a deep understanding of their workforce and job evolution to create targeted, impactful reskilling programs.

Hiring for Fundamental Skills

Caldwell advocates for identifying and hiring candidates with fundamental, transferable skills that will remain relevant over time. For example, data acumen is increasingly seen as a baseline competency for most roles. However, the lack of a standardized "skills taxonomy" across industries makes it challenging to evaluate and transition employees effectively. Developing a common language for skills is critical to enabling workforce mobility and reskilling.

Predicting Future Skills Needs

Organizations face challenges in forecasting the skills required for future roles. Caldwell suggests a three-to-five-year prediction horizon as the most realistic, acknowledging that workforce planning is more accurate when focused on specific roles likely to evolve quickly, such as those in technology and knowledge work. Efforts to predict skills needs are hindered by the rapid pace of change in some industries, such as AI and software engineering and the difficulty of pinpointing evolving job requirements.

The Impact of AI on Roles

Caldwell highlights that AI is expected to impact knowledge workers more than frontline workers. For example, roles like legal assistants, data analysts, and recruiters, which involve repetitive and manual tasks, are more likely to be augmented by AI. In contrast, roles requiring physical, hands-on work, such as HVAC technicians or electricians, will remain less affected. AI will enable knowledge workers to shift from routine tasks to more strategic, value-added activities, enhancing productivity and job satisfaction.

Segmenting the Workforce for AI Strategy

At Walmart, a segmentation approach is used to manage a massive, diverse workforce of over two million associates. By segmenting roles into those that can be augmented by AI and those that cannot, Walmart is better able to focus its innovation and workforce planning efforts. For example, the majority of Walmart's workforce comprises frontline associates whose roles are less likely to be impacted by AI, whereas knowledge-worker roles are a key focus for experimentation with AI-driven augmentation.

Key Takeaways

1 Proactive Reskilling: Organizations must anticipate future skill needs and develop targeted reskilling programs to ensure employees are ready for evolving roles.

2 Hire for Fundamental Skills: Data acumen and other transferable skills are essential for workforce adaptability in a rapidly changing environment.

3 AI's Impact on Knowledge Work: AI will primarily augment knowledge-worker roles, enabling employees to focus on strategic tasks while automating repetitive ones.

4 Segmenting for Success: A segmentation approach allows organizations to prioritize AI innovations for roles most likely to be impacted, creating tailored strategies for different segments of the workforce.

5 Standardizing Skills Taxonomies: Developing a common language for skills will improve workforce mobility, reskilling, and strategic workforce planning.

Jocelyn Caldwell's experience at Walmart illustrates the importance of proactive workforce planning and strategic use of AI to augment roles. By focusing on fundamental skills, leveraging workforce segmentation, and aligning training with anticipated job evolution, organizations can better prepare for the future. Walmart's approach highlights the value of balancing innovation with a clear understanding of workforce diversity, ensuring that AI complements human capabilities while enabling employees to thrive in an ever-changing workplace.

The Impact of Gen AI on Workforce Planning

Gen AI represents a fundamental shift in how workforce planning can be done. Rather than relying on manual, fragmented processes, AI can automate the data gathering, analysis, and even forecasting required to make workforce planning both scalable and actionable.

- **Real-time integration of talent intelligence**—AI can pull live labor market data, competitor hiring trends, and skills demand fluctuations from tools like Lightcast to adjust workforce plans dynamically.

- **Predictive modeling for future workforce needs**—Instead of static headcount projections, AI can simulate different economic conditions, business strategies, and technological advancements to model future scenarios.

- **Customized workforce planning for each organization**—With AI, companies can create tailored workforce planning models that fit their specific business strategy, rather than forcing a one-size-fits-all framework.

- **Automated scenario planning**—AI can instantly generate and compare different workforce strategies, helping HR leaders make better decisions about where to hire, reskill, or optimize their talent strategy.

These capabilities mean that workforce planning is no longer limited to an annual or quarterly exercise. AI enables it to function as a real-time, continuously evolving process that adapts to changes in business conditions, labor markets, and organizational needs.

Integrating Workforce Planning with ONA

One of the most promising applications of AI-powered workforce planning is its integration with organizational network analysis. Traditional workforce planning has largely focused on roles and headcount, assuming that employees operate in a structured hierarchy. But in reality, organizations function as networks of relationships, not just reporting lines.

By incorporating ONA into workforce planning, companies can:

- **Identify critical knowledge hubs and informal leaders**—Workforce planning typically focuses on formal job roles, but ONA can reveal who actually drives decision-making and collaboration.
- **Ensure talent continuity in key network positions**—Instead of just tracking turnover, ONA-enhanced workforce planning can predict how the departure of a key influencer will affect the organization and preemptively plan for knowledge transfer.
- **Map collaboration trends to workforce needs**—Workforce planning often fails to account for how work actually gets done. By analyzing collaboration patterns, companies can better allocate resources to where work naturally flows rather than relying on static org charts.

This integration shifts workforce planning from being a theoretical headcount exercise to a real-world talent optimization strategy.

The Role of Talent Intelligence in Workforce Planning

Another game-changer in workforce planning is talent intelligence—the ability to integrate external labor market insights into workforce planning models. Historically, workforce planning has been mostly limited to internal data—employee demographics, hiring trends, attrition rates—but this provides only half the picture.

By incorporating real-time external talent intelligence, companies can:

- Benchmark salaries and hiring trends against competitors.
- Identify skill shortages before they impact hiring.
- Optimize workforce location strategies based on talent availability.
- Predict industry-wide shifts in skill demand and adjust workforce plans accordingly.

Talent intelligence tools powered by AI make it possible to automate these insights and integrate them directly into workforce planning platforms. Rather than relying on outdated benchmarking studies or intuition, HR leaders can make data-driven workforce decisions with real-time labor market insights.

Workforce Planning for Both Short-Term and Long-Term Impact

One of the biggest struggles in workforce planning has been balancing immediate business needs with long-term workforce strategy. Wall Street and executive leadership teams often focus on short-term headcount costs, while HR wants to build a sustainable, future-ready workforce. AI can help bridge this gap by aligning Operational Workforce Planning (OWFP) with Strategic Workforce Planning (SWFP):

- **OWFP focuses on near-term needs**—hiring, attrition management, short-term resourcing. AI-driven workforce planning can optimize hiring and retention efforts based on real-time data.
- **SWFP takes a multi-year view,** identifying future skill gaps and planning reskilling efforts. AI can forecast how automation, AI, and economic trends will impact workforce needs over the next 5–10 years.

By integrating these two levels, HR can balance immediate business demands while still positioning the company for long-term talent success.

The Future of Workforce Planning

The resurgence of workforce planning is not just another corporate trend— it's a recognition that talent strategy is now a critical part of business success regardless of the external economic conditions. With AI-powered workforce planning, ONA, and real-time talent intelligence, organizations can move beyond outdated, static planning models and develop a dynamic, continuously updated workforce strategy.

For the first time, HR has the tools to make workforce planning proactive rather than reactive, strategic rather than transactional. The question is no longer whether workforce planning will become a core function of HR, but how quickly companies will adopt and scale these new capabilities.

Differentiating Your Workforce Through Talent

Talent has always been the key differentiator for organizations, but in an era where many skills will become commoditized by Gen AI, the premium on truly differentiated talent will only increase. The organizations that understand this shift—and act on it—will be the ones that drive outsized business outcomes in the years to come.

For decades, businesses have debated whether success comes from great processes and operating systems or great talent. Do great organizations create great employees, or do great employees make an organization exceptional? While strong systems and cultures provide a foundation, history shows that the best companies disproportionately benefit from extreme talent—outliers, power-law performers (O'Boyle and Aguinis, 2012), and 10× engineers (i.e., engineers who perform at a level that is 10 times that of their peers) who operate on a completely different level than others (Ravichandran, 2023).

With Gen AI automating routine work and making baseline performance more accessible, the true source of competitive advantage will shift to the differentiated talent that organizations can attract, develop, and retain. This means HR and people analytics must rethink talent strategies—from hiring and development to workforce planning and leadership pipelines—to maximize the impact of these elite contributors.

The First Principles of Talent: Why Differentiated Talent Matters More Than Ever

Talent is not evenly distributed. A small percentage of individuals drive a disproportionate share of value (O'Boyle and Aguinis, 2012). If you know this to be true, it is important to have a foundational understanding of why your organization succeeds through talent, who the talent is, and what constitutes the parameters for great talent to operate. The "First Principles of Talent" I have created provide a six-step framework for understanding why differentiated talent is so critical in modern organizations:

1 **The worker is the appropriate unit of analysis**—While teams matter, organizations execute business strategies through individuals.

2 **Workers are free agents in the talent marketplace**—Top talent has options. Companies must create environments where these individuals choose to stay.

3 **Talent exists and is scarce**—Not all skills are equal. Some people achieve exponentially greater impact with the same resources.

4 **Organizations have finite resources to acquire and develop talent**—Companies cannot invest equally in all employees; they must prioritize critical roles and individuals.

5 **Different mixes of talent are needed to execute business strategy**—Not every job requires a 10× performer, but some absolutely do to execute strategy.

6 **Competitors with similar business strategies will value the same talent**—This creates talent arms races for high-value skill sets where some win and some lose.

Historically, these principles have always mattered in business success, but Gen AI is amplifying their importance. As AI democratizes access to baseline skills and automation, the gap between ordinary and exceptional talent will widen, not shrink. Organizations that understand this shift will structure their workforce strategies around differentiated talent rather than just general hiring trends.

Why Differentiated Talent Becomes More Valuable in an AI-Driven World

In a world where AI handles routine tasks, the true competitive advantage comes from human creativity, critical thinking, and problem-solving. While AI will enhance productivity, it cannot replace insight, leadership, and deep expertise in high-stakes decision-making. As AI advances, organizations will need to rethink talent through three key shifts:

1 **From Credential-Based Hiring to Skill-Based Hiring**

   o AI will make many credentials commoditized, making traditional hiring less effective.

   o Companies will need to focus on hiring individuals who can operate at the frontier of problem-solving, innovation, and execution and have the requisite skills to do so. They will need to have an extremely detailed inventory of this skilled talent, as it will be their source of competitive advantage.

2 From Process-Driven Organizations to Talent-Driven Organizations

o Many existing business processes will become automated.

o The value will shift to the talent that can navigate complexity and ambiguity.

3 From Linear Talent Investments to Power-Law Talent Investments

o Organizations must move away from spreading resources evenly across all employees equally. There are not equal outcomes to equal investments.

o Instead, they should identify and disproportionately invest in top skills in the top performers who drive the highest impact.

Companies that fail to recognize this shift will find themselves outcompeted by organizations that design their talent strategies around high-impact individuals. It will continue to be important for people analytics teams to innovate during this period. One way to innovate is to learn from other disciplines.

Applying Universal Models to People Analytics: The Missing Piece

For people analytics to fully capitalize on the value of differentiated talent, the field needs to expand beyond HR paradigms and incorporate models from other disciplines. In the past, the best insights in science and business have come from applying "universal models" across different fields. For example, much of the forecasting methodologies in workforce planning don't come from HR, but rather Finance. In people analytics, this means taking concepts from physics, economics, biology, and mathematics and applying them to workforce strategy.

EXAMPLES OF UNIVERSAL MODELS APPLIED TO TALENT STRATEGY:

1 Pareto Distribution (Power Laws in Economics and Nature):

o **Reality:** Not all employees contribute equally—a small number drives a majority of outcomes.

o **Application to Talent:** Workforce planning should prioritize investment in the top 10–20 percent of skills of top performers rather than treating all employees as equal.

2   **Thermodynamics (Energy and Efficiency in Physics):**

- o **Reality:** Energy is neither created nor destroyed—it is optimized or wasted.

- o **Application to Talent:** Inefficient use of top talent wastes organizational potential. High performers should be deployed on the most complex and impactful work.

3   **Natural Selection (Survival and Adaptation in Biology):**

- o **Reality:** The environment dictates survival, favoring adaptable traits.

- o **Application to Talent:** Organizations that build an adaptive, differentiated talent pool will outcompete those that rely on static hiring models and don't adjust to their market landscape.

4   **Marginal Utility (Diminishing Returns in Economics):**

- o **Reality:** The value of additional resources diminishes over time.

- o **Application to Talent:** Companies should invest heavily in developing top talent but there is a point at which the marginal return of investing in top talent versus other employees may flip; therefore, not *all* investments should be made in only top skills and talent.

By incorporating these models into people analytics, organizations can move beyond traditional workforce planning and develop truly differentiated talent strategies.

The Future of Talent Strategy is Differentiation

As Gen AI continues to reshape the workforce, the importance of differentiated talent will only grow. Organizations that treat all employees as equal will struggle to compete with those that prioritize high-impact individuals. Gen AI will improve the lower and average performers to a higher ability, but it will amplify the top performers to levels never seen before (Brynjolfsson et al., 2023). To stay ahead, companies must:

- Adopt a power-law approach to workforce planning.

- Leverage universal models from other disciplines to rethink talent strategy.

- Use Gen AI to enhance, not replace, human creativity and problem-solving.

The future of workforce differentiation belongs to the organizations that recognize talent is not evenly distributed—and act accordingly.

How Will Gen AI Impact People Analytics in the Next Few Years?

Niels Bohr famously said *"it's hard to make predictions, especially about the future"* (World, 2019). Predicting the evolution of people analytics over the next few years involves considering both technological advances—most notably in generative AI—and the broader strategic and cultural shifts in how organizations manage their workforces, as well as some pontification. While no forecast is set in stone, here's a structured look at what might unfold in the late 2020s, along with the "chain of evolution" that could define the field's trajectory. Beyond this point is anyone's guess as to what the world will look like.

Simply put, currently the groundwork will be laid as organizations focus on building strong data pipelines and real-time analytics capabilities, experimenting with Gen AI applications and data infrastructure. Then, the shift to prescriptive analytics will be in full swing. Organizations will move beyond static reports, using AI-powered simulations and real-time recommendations to proactively shape workforce outcomes. People analytics will become the strategic function of HR, helping companies make faster, smarter decisions that tie workforce dynamics to overall business success.

If we do the right things, by this point people analytics will reach full maturity, seamlessly embedded into everyday management. AI-driven insights will be an integral part of leadership decision-making, ensuring that every workforce strategy is aligned with broader business goals. At this stage, organizations that have embraced the evolution of people analytics will be positioned for long-term success, while those that have resisted will face an uphill battle in catching up.

Laying the Foundation and Early Gen AI Integration in People Analytics

The next phase of people analytics will begin in earnest with a focus on building a foundation: Integrating data sources, enhancing real-time analytics capabilities, and experimenting with generative AI, leading organizations will consolidate workforce data from a wide array of systems—HR platforms, collaboration tools, and performance management software, etc.—along with less conventional sources, such as internal communications and interconnectivity in preparation for using AI systems to link the information to gain valued insights. The days of relying on periodic reports are numbered (thank goodness). Instead, real-time dashboards will become the norm if they weren't already, enabling leaders to react more quickly to workforce trends.

Generative AI will make its first meaningful impact in the space, not by replacing human analysts but by starting to automate the heavy lifting of data interpretation in companies who make investments in the space. Leading companies will begin deploying Gen AI to summarize trends, generate reports in natural language, and highlight key insights without requiring HR professionals to sift through massive datasets manually. However, as data usage expands, so too will concerns about the accuracy of results. Explainability will be a key challenge—leaders will need to build trust by ensuring AI-driven insights are not just accurate but also understandable and reliable.

Companies that take this period seriously—investing in strong data infrastructure, reliable AI practices, and real-time analytics—will set themselves up for a cascade of success, with a greater and greater divide between teams who make the right investments, and those who are stuck in the past. Those that wait too long risk being left behind. Although advanced people analytics may have been seen as a luxury in the last few years, it will now be the functions that don't make the investments in advancing Gen AI who will be left behind; they will start to seem like esoteric luxury items, like riding horses or blowing glass. While Gen AI's role in people analytics will still be largely experimental at this stage, the groundwork will be laid for its deeper, more transformative applications in the years ahead. It's time to get onboard.

What Comes Next: The Shift to Prescriptive Analytics

In the next stage, organizations that embraced early AI adoption will move beyond simply analyzing workforce data to actively shaping future outcomes. This will be the period of **prescriptive analytics**, where people analytics shifts from describing what has happened to recommending what should happen next. Gen AI will evolve from a passive tool that summarizes insights to an active assistant that can model "what-if" scenarios. HR leaders will be able to simulate workforce changes—such as the impact of adjusting remote work policies, restructuring teams, or modifying the employee value proposition—and receive data-driven recommendations tailored to their specific business environment. These capabilities will mark a significant departure from traditional people analytics, turning decision-making into a far more dynamic and strategic function.

With better AI models, organizations will also gain real-time actionability. Instead of static dashboards that only report on engagement scores or attrition numbers, leaders will receive immediate, AI-generated recommendations on how to address emerging issues. Furthermore, analytics will become more contextual to the organization and holistic in its breadth, integrating workforce data with financial, operational, and customer data to provide a more complete picture of how workforce decisions impact business outcomes. However, that will only happen once organizations make the right investments in combining their data infrastructure.

Another critical shift will be the growing emphasis on employee well-being and behavioral insights that traditionally fall within the I/O psychology and behavioral science domain. Natural language applications will allow companies to assess internal communication patterns, identifying signs of burnout, disengagement, or even hostile workplace dynamics before they become widespread problems. Advanced AI models will go beyond predicting performance outcomes—they will help HR teams proactively intervene, offering personalized recommendations to boost morale, productivity, and retention. These will be opt-in tools, of course. There is no need to create a *one-world totalitarian state* within our organizations.

People analytics will no longer be a passive reporting function; it will be an essential tool for guiding leadership decisions across analytics, workforce planning, and talent intelligence. It will become time now for people analytics to move from a decision support function and move into the decision-making capacity. No one knows these models and tools, and their limitations, as well as the people analytics team does. We should be in the driver's seat at this point. Companies that embrace these advancements and embrace people analytics leading the change will gain a competitive edge, using data not just to reflect on the past but to shape the future of their workforce. Those that fail to do so risk falling so far behind that it will have material impacts on their business and their organizations will begin to suffer a competitive disadvantage.

The Full Maturation: Strategic Embedding of People Analytics

At this point, the companies that have fully committed to people analytics will see it embedded at the very core of their workforce strategy. AI-driven analytics will no longer be a separate HR function, but a deeply integrated part of day-to-day decision-making and people analytics leaders will start to displace the traditional HR leadership who will not be accustomed to keeping up with this level of technical complexity and change. AI tools will be deployed and accessible so that managers at every level—from frontline supervisors to C-suite executives—will have real-time insights at their fingertips. AI-powered dashboards will be spun up on command to provide tailored recommendations for improving team performance, managing employee development, and even forecasting workforce needs based on broader business trends. No one will need to build them.

Organizations that use these tools effectively will be able to personalize employee career journeys in ways never before possible, offering data-driven insights on learning opportunities, promotions, and performance improvement. Combining internal workforce data with external market data on skills and labor intelligence, the creation of skills-based organizations at scale will be attainable, and employees will be the beneficiaries. However, trust must be paramount—employees will need clear communication about how analytics-driven decisions are made, and organizations will have to maintain high ethical standards and make employee-friendly decisions.

At this stage, people analytics will be fully strategic rather than operational. Changes in workforce dynamics—whether related to hiring trends, engagement scores, or leadership effectiveness—will influence broader business planning in real time. While some routine workforce decisions may be automated, human oversight will remain critical, particularly for high-stakes or sensitive choices. Companies that have successfully integrated AI-driven people analytics will see clear business benefits: stronger employee engagement, better workforce productivity, and a direct correlation between HR strategy and financial performance. This is the employee and employer-friendly future we have all been striving for.

In the End...

While the exact details of the Gen AI evolution in people analytics will depend on technological evolutions, HR tech investments, and shifts in HR and organizational culture, the overarching trend points toward a deepening integration of Gen AI and advanced analytics into every facet of workforce planning and people analytics. People analytics is unlikely to "wither" if it continues to demonstrate clear strategic value, evolves ethically, and adapts to both technological and cultural changes.

Organizations that lead the way in this evolution—investing in data integration, adopting advanced AI, and linking analytics directly to business outcomes—will not only be set for greatness but could redefine how workforces are managed globally. Conversely, those that resist these changes or fail to innovate risk their people analytics capabilities becoming obsolete or irrelevant in a rapidly evolving landscape. Be the former, not the latter.

Summary

The future of HR is not just about adopting new technologies—it's about fundamentally rethinking how we approach workforce management, talent intelligence, and people analytics. As HR technologies evolve exponentially, the field is shifting from a reactive, administrative function to a strategic powerhouse that leverages AI, automation, and advanced analytics to drive business outcomes. This chapter explores the most transformative HR technologies, emerging trends, and how organizations can navigate this rapidly changing landscape to maintain a competitive edge.

Key Takeaways

1 **AI-Driven People Analytics is Scaling Exponentially**

   o The evolution of people analytics has moved from basic reporting to AI-powered insights that automate decision-making. Organizations that leverage AI for real-time analytics and workforce planning will gain a significant competitive advantage.

2 **Autonomous AI Agents Will Redefine HR Workflows**

   o AI-powered agents can already generate reports, summarize feedback, and analyze workforce data. Future autonomous agents will take action on insights, automating HR functions such as talent acquisition, workforce planning, and employee experience management.

3 **First-Principles Thinking is Essential for HR Innovation**

   o Rather than layering new technology onto outdated processes, leading organizations are reimagining HR from the ground up. This involves questioning assumptions, redefining success metrics, and optimizing HR technology with a problem-first approach.

4 **Workforce Planning is Becoming Predictive and Continuous**

   o Traditional workforce planning was reactive and static. AI-powered models now allow for real-time, predictive workforce planning that integrates internal data with external labor market trends, enabling companies to anticipate and adapt to talent needs before they arise.

5 Organizational Network Analysis (ONA) is Unlocking Hidden Workforce Insights

o Traditional org charts fail to capture how work actually happens. ONA helps identify key influencers, collaboration bottlenecks, and hidden networks within an organization, leading to smarter workforce strategies.

6 Talent Intelligence is the New Competitive Advantage

o AI is enabling HR to analyze vast amounts of data to improve hiring, retention, and employee development decisions. Companies that harness talent intelligence will be able to attract and retain top talent more effectively.

7 The Future of HR Will be Defined by Open vs. Closed AI Systems

o Organizations must decide whether to leverage open-source AI models for customization or closed-source models for enterprise security. The right choice will depend on the company's data governance strategy and long-term AI adoption plans.

8 Democratization of People Analytics is the Next Big Shift

o People analytics should not be limited to HR and executives. AI-driven systems will provide employees with real-time, personalized insights, helping them make career decisions and improve engagement autonomously.

9 Hybrid Work Strategies Must be Intentional, Not Arbitrary

o Simply mandating in-office days is ineffective. Data-driven hybrid work strategies, informed by ONA and behavioral analytics, will optimize collaboration while balancing employee flexibility and productivity.

10 The HR Function of the Future Will Be Defined by Differentiated Talent

o As AI automates routine tasks, the organizations that focus on acquiring, developing, and retaining high-impact talent will outperform their competitors. Workforce differentiation—identifying and investing in top performers—will be a critical business strategy.

HR is undergoing an unprecedented transformation, moving beyond administrative functions to become a data-driven, AI-powered strategic force. The organizations that embrace these innovations will lead the future of work, while those that resist will struggle to keep up. By leveraging AI, automation, and real-time analytics, HR can shift from a cost center to a key driver of business success.

References

Ackoff, R. (1970). A Concept of Corporate Planning. *Long Range Planning*, 3 (1), 2–8. doi.org/10.1016/0024-6301(70)90031-2 (archived at https://perma.cc/V4BK-HJC5).

Beta, T. (2010). *Master of Stupidity*. Gramedia Pustaka Utama.

Brynjolfsson, E., Li, D. and Raymond, L. (2023). Generative AI at Work. *arXiv.org*. arxiv.org/abs/2304.11771?utm_source=chatgpt.com (archived at https://perma.cc/3UQF-G9E3).

Labh, S. (2022). What if Electrons had Feelings—Cantor's Paradise. Medium. www.cantorsparadise.com/what-if-electrons-had-feelings-68e7d42f34c1 (archived at https://perma.cc/4BEP-CAEC).

Lightcast (2025). Lightcast's Workforce Risk Outlook Reveals Impending Global Impact of Talent Shortfalls. Lightcast. lightcast.io/resources/blog/workforce-risk-outlook-press-release (archived at https://perma.cc/8XP6-2W8R).

Lucas, M. (2019). How Consumers Embrace Smart Assistants. Researchworld.com. archive.researchworld.com/how-consumers-embrace-smart-assistants/ (archived at https://perma.cc/RG4D-FPRH).

Napper, C., Hines, S. and Arena, M. (2023). Organizational Network Analytics and The Future of the Office. Directionally Correct. www.podbean.com/eas/pb-vp7p7-151f6ed (archived at https://perma.cc/RG4D-FPRH) Ep. 33.

Napper, C., Hines, S. and Caldwell, J. (2024). Workforce Planning and Strategy at Walmart People Analytics. Directionally Correct. www.podbean.com/eas/pb-fmz94-15479c9 (archived at https://perma.cc/7MCM-9DUG) Ep. 76.

Napper, C., Hines, S. and Gallman, J. (2024). Using Autonomous Agents to Drive Value with People Analytics. Directionally Correct. www.podbean.com/eas/pb-bc7w7-1678ffd (archived at https://perma.cc/UV78-ZNUW) Ep. 99.

Napper, C., Hines, S. and Onesto, A. (2023). Autonomous AI Agents in HR and People Analytics. Directionally Correct. www.podbean.com/eas/pb-i3wqc-151f6c5 (archived at https://perma.cc/S2C6-QLRH) Ep. 72.

O'Boyle, E. and Aguinis, H. (2012). The Best and the Rest: Revisiting the Norm of Normality of Individual Performance. www.hermanaguinis.com/pdf/PPsych2012.pdf (archived at https://perma.cc/3SLE-DWST).

Ravichandran, A. (2023). Who is a 10x Engineer? Medium. adhithiravi.medium.com/who-is-a-10x-engineer-a3dd4b6f8007 (archived at https://perma.cc/C4FG-7ZKB).

10

The Future of HR & Business is Analytical

This chapter wraps up by reinforcing the strategic importance of business value while maintaining data-driven approaches and forecasting how the continuous evolution of AI and analytics will be central to future business success and leadership in the market.

> *"The reasonable man adapts himself to the world: The unreasonable one persists in trying to adapt the world to himself. Therefore, all progress depends on the unreasonable man."*—George Bernard Shaw, *Man and Superman* (1903)

George Bernard Shaw's (1903) observation about progress depending on the "unreasonable man" is an apt lens through which to view the future of people analytics. For years, HR has been expected to adapt to the constraints of available data, limited budgets, and organizational inertia. People analytics, although we have shown it can have undeniable value, has often been treated as a luxury—something pursued only when resources allow. Earlier in Chapter 1, we addressed that concern head-on: People analytics isn't a luxury if it delivers the ROI to justify its existence. And now, thanks to advances in Gen AI, the cost of improving analytics is plummeting, while productivity is skyrocketing. This formula allows for the biggest swing in productivity and value of people analytics to occur in the history of business. The shift is clear—HR and people analytics no longer need to passively work within our limitations. Instead, we must take a more "unreasonable" approach, leveraging the exponential power of AI to push into the areas that once seemed too complex, too expensive, or too time-consuming to solve.

This changing landscape is more than just an efficiency gain—it's a fundamental shift in the art of the possible. In the past, people analytics was often forced to focus on what was most urgent: Reports, metrics KPIs and basic data clean up. The harder, more nuanced problems—like measuring quality of hire, quantifying the employee value proposition, or understanding the future of work—were often sidelined, not because they weren't important, but because they required too much time, data, or the immediate business value wasn't clear. But when productivity is no longer constrained by manual effort, and when AI-driven analytics can process vast amounts of data at near-zero marginal cost, people analytics is free to explore these deeper, more strategic business problems.

This chapter is about what happens when HR and people analytics escape their historical resource constraints. When analytics teams have a surplus of productivity, they can move beyond the tactical and start solving the problems that organizations have always wanted to address but never had the bandwidth for. Workforce planning can move from reactive adjustments to proactive, scenario-based forecasting. Leadership analytics can go beyond performance ratings to quantify the actual impact of great leaders on business outcomes. Forensic people analytics can uncover hidden patterns of the "organization within the organization" that previously would have gone unnoticed. And the long-standing question I have had—*"Does everyone really get paid the same?"*—can finally be answered with precision and transparency.

This is the future of HR and business: A function that is not just analytical, but productive, fast, and deeply strategic. It's a future where people analytics doesn't just respond to business needs—it anticipates them, driving the next wave of competitive advantage. Your competitors who don't adopt these methodologies will be at a competitive disadvantage. With the tools now available, it's time for HR leaders to stop adapting to constraints and start shaping the future with data. In the pages ahead, we'll explore the cutting edge of what's now possible, and how organizations can harness this new power to drive real, measurable impact. The future of HR and the business is analytical.

The Future of Work

The future of work is not a singular trajectory, but a rapidly evolving landscape shaped by technological advancements, economic shifts, and societal expectations. While Covid-19 accelerated discussions about remote and hybrid work models, the emergence of generative AI profoundly shifted the conversation to an even more fundamental level. The work of Jesuthasan and Boudreau in *Work Without Jobs: How to Reboot Your Organization's Operating System* (2023) highlights a radical rethinking of employment structures—where work is deconstructed into tasks, skills, and automation rather than traditional job roles. This vision challenges long-standing notions of stability, identity, and career progression, raising critical questions about the future of employment. Will you have a job in the future if the concept of jobs doesn't exist?

The Acceleration of Change

The past five years have demonstrated that the future of work is arriving faster than anticipated. Many transformations once predicted for decades ahead—such as automation of cognitive tasks, remote-first organizations, and fluid workforce structures—are now shaping our realities at work. Gen AI is poised to amplify this acceleration, reshaping work at an unprecedented scale by automating knowledge-based tasks, augmenting decision-making, and fundamentally altering how organizations deploy human talent.

Deconstructing Jobs: A Plausible Future?

Jesuthasan and Boudreau's (2023) argument that jobs will be deconstructed into skills and tasks rather than fixed roles is both provocative and divisive. While this model aligns with automation trends and the gig economy, it raises fundamental concerns:

- **Human Identity and Work:** Jobs have historically provided structure, purpose, and social identity. Will a task-based future erode these intrinsic values?

- **Worker Resistance:** Employees and employers alike may resist radical job deconstruction due to organizational inertia, cultural norms, and the legal frameworks built around employment contracts.

- **Skill Fragmentation:** If work becomes a series of fragmented gigs or projects, how will individuals maintain career progression and financial stability?

A hybrid reality is more likely—where automation deconstructs some roles while human-centric work continues to be organized into stable structures. The organizations that master this balance will lead the future of work. And one must suspect that a slew of HR technology providers are going to fill the gap on creating this hybrid approach, as there are already many who claim to provide gig work opportunities of the future.

Beyond Remote vs. In-Person: The Real Future of Work

The pandemic-era debate of remote vs. in-person work is a narrow framing of a much broader shift. The future of work encompasses fundamental changes in workforce composition, technology integration, and economic models. To understand the complexity of the future of work, we must consider multiple dimensions beyond location:

1. WORKFORCE COMPOSITION

- **Full-Time Employment:** Traditional roles will persist but may be redefined around adaptability and cross-functional skills.

- **Gig and Task-Based Work:** Platforms like Upwork and TaskRabbit may become mainstream for knowledge workers, not just freelancers.

- **AI-Augmented Roles:** Many employees will work alongside AI copilots and AI agents,requiring a blend of technical fluency and strategic oversight.

2. WORK EXECUTION AND DECISION-MAKING

- **Synchronous vs. Asynchronous Work:** The shift toward global, distributed teams necessitates a blend of real-time collaboration (Zoom, Slack) and async workflows (Notion, Jira, recorded meetings).

- **Human–Machine Integration:** AI and robotic process automation (RPA) will handle repetitive knowledge tasks, enabling humans to focus on decision-making and executing tasks in force.

3. THE RISE OF THE ALGORITHMIC BOSS

- AI-driven performance tracking and decision-making tools (e.g., algorithmic scheduling, automated performance evaluations) introduce opportunities for leadership personalization at levels previously unseen. However, ethical considerations persist about losing the human in the loop of management. Remember, *don't create the future you don't want to live in.*

- Workers will increasingly need to manage their personal AI brand and work in harmony with their employers as the balance between their employer, algorithmic boss, and their needs for ongoing career progression may have conflicting priorities.

Gen AI's Role in Shaping the Future of Work

The introduction of Gen AI is not just about automation; it's about augmentation, acceleration, and disruption. Here's how Gen AI is likely to reshape work:

1. WORK WITHOUT TRADITIONAL BOUNDARIES

- **Knowledge Work Automation:** AI will take on tasks such as writing reports, generating insights, and conducting basic data analysis, reducing the need for large administrative teams.

- **AI-Powered Hiring and Workforce Planning:** Gen AI will enable predictive hiring models, assessing skills dynamically and matching talent to tasks in real time.

- **Personal AI Assistants:** Employees may have individualized AI agents that summarize meetings, draft emails, and optimize workflows based on their working style.

2. THE EVOLUTION OF SKILLS AND LEARNING

- **AI as the New Manager and Coach:** Instead of static learning programs, AI-driven career advisors could provide personalized skill development recommendations, ensuring workers stay competitive in a rapidly changing job market.

- **Human–AI Collaboration:** The most valuable employees will not be those who replace AI but those who work seamlessly with it—knowing when to trust AI-generated recommendations and when to override them with human judgment.

3. ECONOMIC POLARIZATION: A NEW ELITE CLASS?

One major risk of AI-driven work deconstruction is the potential for extreme economic bifurcation:

- **Super-Elite AI-Enabled Workers:** A small group of highly skilled, AI-augmented professionals (e.g., AI engineers, strategic analysts) commanding premium compensation.

- **Automated and Task-Based Workforce:** Many mid-tier jobs may be eroded, leaving a workforce reliant on gig-based employment with fluctuating income and limited security.

- **Policy and Ethical Considerations:** Governments and businesses will need to address the risk of AI-induced job displacement and potential mass underemployment.

The Future is What We Shape It to Be

While predictions about the future of work vary, one thing is clear: The conversation is no longer just about where people work, but how work itself is structured, executed, and valued. The future of work is not just an inevitable outcome of technology; it is a series of decisions made by business leaders, policymakers, and workers themselves. Gen AI presents both a challenge and an opportunity. If harnessed thoughtfully, it can enhance productivity, unlock human potential, and create more equitable economic structures. However, if left unchecked, it could widen economic disparities and erode the traditional structures that have provided stability for generations. The organizations and individuals that embrace adaptability, continuous learning, and ethical AI integration will be the ones that thrive in the new world of work.

Revisiting People Analytics Staples with Gen AI

Now that we know the future of work will be different from the past, how does people analytics play a role in shaping it? The traditional pillars of people analytics—ranging from hiring and workforce planning to leadership assessment and talent intelligence—have long relied on structured data, statistical models, and dashboards to guide decision-making. Yet, the rise of Gen AI is fundamentally reshaping these staples, and those who are proactive stand to benefit the most. No longer limited to descriptive or even predictive insights, people analytics infused with Gen AI introduces new capabilities for automation, personalization, and real-time adaptation. This shift means that HR is no longer just data-informed—it is becoming dynamically data-driven, with AI acting as both a disruptor and an enabler.

Gen AI enhances our traditional approaches and even unlocks the ability to do at scale what was once challenging to do in people analytics. Take quality of hire, for instance—AI can provide new scalable methods for data collection to provide a more holistic view of candidate potential. Leadership analytics, once reliant on surveys and competency models, can now leverage AI-driven assessment and understanding to predict leadership effectiveness. Even data visualization, a cornerstone of people analytics, is evolving as AI generates adaptive, interactive dashboards that surface insights tailored to individual users.

If the future of HR and business will be deeply analytical it is incumbent on people analytics professionals to embrace using Gen AI to accelerate our transformation by pushing the boundaries of what people analytics can achieve. Workforce planning, once guided by static models, will become dynamic and scenario-based, enabling organizations to proactively adjust to economic shifts. Talent intelligence, forensic people analytics, and the future of employee selection will all be reimagined. This is not just an iteration of traditional methods—it is a fundamental rethinking of how we understand, measure, and optimize human capital.

Data Visualization: Insights & Dynamic Exploration

Data visualization has been one of the cornerstones of people analytics, serving as a bridge between raw data and actionable insights. Traditionally, it has been used in two primary ways: First, to tell a compelling story through charts, dashboards, and infographics, and second, to facilitate deeper data exploration. While much of the conversation around visualization has focused on storytelling, the true power of data visualization lies in its ability to enable rapid hypothesis generation, uncover patterns, and conduct exploratory analysis. In the Gen AI era, this second purpose is set to evolve dramatically. With AI-powered tools transforming how we interact with data, we are no longer constrained by manual processes or predefined dashboards. Instead, we are entering a world where analysts can test hypotheses at unprecedented speed, visualize complex relationships in real time, and dynamically adjust analyses based on AI-generated insights.

Smart Data Visualization of Today

Today's best practices in data visualization for people analytics revolve around clarity, efficiency, and exploratory rigor. Analysts use histograms to understand distributions, box plots to compare groups, and scatter plots to identify relationships and outliers. Box plots, histograms, and scatter plots are particularly powerful for understanding multivariate statistics:

- **Box Plots:** Can be used to visualize differences between multiple groups, providing insight into variance, distribution, and statistical significance in group differences. By incorporating confidence intervals, analysts can approximate T-tests and ANOVA results without running formal statistical models.

- **Histograms:** These are essential for assessing the normality of the distribution of multiple variables at once. Analysts can overlay distributions for different employee groups (e.g., tenure vs. performance ratings) and detect skewness, kurtosis, and normality assumptions that impact more complex statistical tests.

- **Scatter Plots:** When enhanced with regression lines and color-coded groupings, scatter plots allow analysts to visually inspect correlation, linear and non-linear relationships, and potential interaction effects before running multivariate models. They also help in outlier detection, ensuring data quality before proceeding with more advanced analytics.

Tools like Spotfire, Tableau, and Power BI have enabled analysts to rapidly iterate through visuals, adjusting filters and binning options to uncover hidden insights. A well-structured data analysis plan ensures that analysts approach data exploration systematically, leveraging both deductive and inductive reasoning to refine research questions and test hypotheses. However, even with these tools and frameworks, the process remains constrained by human bandwidth, requiring time-consuming iterations to surface meaningful insights. Additionally, while dashboards have become commonplace, they are often static, requiring manual updates and human intervention to interpret trends and anomalies.

The Future: Gen AI-Driven Visualization & Hypothesis Testing

The next frontier of data visualization will be defined by AI-driven exploration and real-time hypothesis testing. Instead of manually building visuals and iterating through different chart types, Gen AI will automatically generate the most relevant visualizations—creating hundreds or thousands in the background and surfacing only the most relevant to the user—based on the underlying data, continuously refining them as new insights emerge. Imagine an AI assistant that doesn't just create dashboards but proactively suggests alternative visual representations, runs thousands of statistical tests in the background, and flags unexpected correlations that warrant further investigation. The shift will make data exploration more interactive, allowing analysts to simply ask, "What patterns am I missing?" and receive AI-curated visualizations highlighting potential insights.

Additionally, Gen AI will move beyond traditional charts, introducing novel ways to visualize high-dimensional data, such as dynamic network graphs for organizational relationships or interactive simulations for workforce planning. Instead of merely visualizing historical data, AI-powered visualization will incorporate predictive and prescriptive analytics, showing not just what happened, but what's likely to happen next. With this evolution, people analytics will no longer be limited by the speed of manual analysis; instead, HR and business leaders will have an always-on, AI-augmented exploration engine, making this the most exciting time in history to visualize and interact with data.

What About Employee Selection? How Will AI Play a Role?

For over a century, industrial-organizational (I/O) psychologists have refined personnel selection methods to help organizations hire the most qualified candidates at scale. These selection systems, particularly for high-volume, multi-incumbent roles, typically begin with a job analysis—a rigorous assessment of the tasks, knowledge, skills, abilities, and other characteristics (KSAOs) required and validated for success. From there, selection tools such as structured interviews, formal assessments (e.g., cognitive ability, situational judgment, and personality tests), minimum qualifications, and work samples are developed and validated. The underlying goal is to ensure that these methods are both reliable (consistent in their measurement) and valid (predictive of job performance) while also meeting legal defensibility standards set by policy practices and law. However, this process—especially for large organizations—can take months or even years to complete, requiring extensive documentation and statistical validation.

The advent of Gen AI offers a significant acceleration of this process, enhancing selection in two fundamental ways. First, Gen AI will help expedite job analysis, validation, and process for obtaining legal defensibility evidence, allowing organizations to create and refine selection assessments in a fraction of the time. AI-powered tools can process large amounts of workforce data, synthesizing job requirements and automating validation studies to ensure compliance with employment laws. Second, AI introduces new paradigms for assessment that go beyond traditional structured interviews and tests. By incorporating passive data collection, NLP-driven KSAO estimation, and real-time skill analysis, AI-driven selection tools can provide deeper insights into candidate potential. While these advancements promise unprecedented efficiency and predictive accuracy, they also introduce new risks, particularly in terms of fairness and transparency implications of automated decision-making.

The Opportunities and Risks of AI-Driven Selection

AI-driven selection systems have the potential to vastly improve hiring efficiency, reducing time-to-hire while improving the accuracy of selection decisions. Instead of waiting months for validation studies to be completed, AI can analyze historical hiring and performance data in real time, identifying the traits and experiences that best predict success. This means organizations can refine their hiring models continuously, rather than relying on static, infrequently updated assessments. AI can also enhance objectivity by mitigating common human biases in selection, such as interviewers overvaluing personal rapport or misinterpreting candidate responses. However, these advantages hinge on AI's ability to remain fair, transparent, and accountable.

One of the greatest risks AI poses in selection is its ability to create a permanent underclass of unemployable individuals based on opaque and overly deterministic selection criteria. Unlike traditional selection tools, which allow for human discretion in evaluating candidates, AI-driven systems could hard-code certain character flaws, skill gaps, or missing credentials as unemployable, rejecting candidates based on job-related characteristics that correlate with lower historical success rates but in effect making them unemployable if all employers adopt such selection mechanisms. What are we to do in this scenario? Don't create the future you don't want to live in.

REAL-WORLD EXAMPLE

"Gen AI and The Future of Selection with I-O Psychology" with Fred Oswald, Professor, Industrial-Organizational Psychology at Rice University

(Paraphrased for length from Ep. 53 of "Directionally Correct, A People Analytics Podcast")

The Intersection of AI and I/O Psychology

Dr. Fred Oswald, Professor of Industrial-Organizational (I/O) Psychology at Rice University, plays a key role in shaping the future of AI in workforce applications. As a member of the National Artificial Intelligence Advisory Committee (NAIAC), he advises federal leadership on AI's implications for workforce issues, ethical considerations, and policy. Oswald emphasizes that trustworthy AI must balance innovation with preserving individual rights, civil liberties, and fairness, particularly in selection and workforce planning.

AI in Personnel Selection

Dr. Oswald notes that AI holds great potential in personnel selection by automating processes such as job analysis and candidate evaluation. AI-based tools, particularly natural language processing (NLP) systems, could estimate knowledge, skills, and abilities (KSAs) and streamline job analysis. However, maintaining scientific rigor, validity, and fairness in these applications is critical. AI-based selection tools must adhere to established I/O principles, such as reliability and fairness, while addressing new challenges like algorithmic opacity and bias.

The Role of Standards and Principles in AI-Based Selection

Oswald stresses the importance of adhering to foundational I/O psychology principles, such as reliability, validity, and fairness, in the era of AI. A recent committee report he contributed to revisits these principles and introduces new considerations for AI-based tools. For instance, the concept of differential prediction examines whether a measure is more valid for one demographic group than another, highlighting the need for fairness in AI-driven decision-making. Maintaining transparency in algorithmic processes and mitigating bias are key to ensuring ethical and scientifically sound outcomes.

Challenges in Using AI for Workforce Applications

One of the primary challenges with AI-based tools is their opacity. Algorithms are often "black boxes," making it difficult for organizations to understand how decisions are made. Additionally, messy or incomplete data can exacerbate issues of fairness and validity. Oswald emphasizes the importance of organizations acting as discerning consumers when adopting AI tools, ensuring alignment with both ethical guidelines and business objectives.

The Future of Job Analysis and Validation

Oswald envisions a future where job analysis and validation processes are increasingly automated using AI. These systems could provide real-time insights into job requirements and applicant qualifications, reducing the burden on HR professionals. However, questions remain about how to maintain the scientific rigor and fairness of traditional approaches while incorporating these technologies.

Key Takeaways

1   Trustworthy AI in Selection: AI-based tools must balance innovation with fairness, transparency, and scientific rigor, adhering to principles of reliability and validity.

2   Differential Prediction and Bias: Addressing differential prediction is critical to ensuring that AI-based assessments are valid and fair across diverse groups.

3 Algorithmic Opacity: Organizations must navigate the challenge of opaque algorithms by demanding transparency and aligning AI tools with ethical standards.

4 Automation in Job Analysis: AI has the potential to automate job analysis and validation, streamlining processes while maintaining scientific rigor.

5 Role of I/O Psychology: I/O psychologists must act as stewards of fairness and rigor, guiding the ethical use of AI in selection and workforce planning.

Fred Oswald's work highlights the transformative potential of AI in workforce selection while underscoring the importance of ethical and scientific considerations. By adhering to foundational I/O psychology principles and addressing challenges like bias and algorithmic opacity, organizations can harness AI responsibly. The future of job analysis and personnel selection lies in leveraging AI's capabilities while maintaining fairness, transparency, and rigor—ensuring a more equitable and effective workforce.

The Path Forward: Balanced Selection

To responsibly harness AI in selection, organizations must demand transparency from AI vendors and ensure that both advanced technology documentation and legal standards are being fully met. AI tools should not be treated as "black boxes" but rather as auditable decision-making systems where the rationale behind each hiring decision is clear and defensible. This means:

- **Ensuring AI-based assessments are valid and fair:** I/O psychology principles, such as validity, reliability, and fairness, should guide the development of AI-powered hiring tools.

- **Combining AI with human judgment:** AI should augment rather than replace human decision-makers. While AI can handle large-scale pattern recognition, final hiring decisions should involve human oversight to account for nuances that AI may overlook.

- **Establishing legal and ethical safeguards:** AI-driven hiring systems must comply with regulations such as the *Uniform Guidelines on Employee Selection Procedures* (Uniform Guidelines, 2025) and the SIOP *Recommendations for AI-based Assessments* (SIOP, 2025), ensuring that AI-driven hiring processes are fair.

The future of selection will likely be a hybrid approach, where AI augments the efficiency of traditional selection processes while I/O psychologists and HR professionals ensure scientific rigor and ethical responsibility. If leveraged correctly, AI has the potential to make hiring more predictive, efficient, and fair—but only if organizations commit to rigorous testing and validation. If ignored, AI could entrench bad decisions at an unprecedented scale, raising fundamental questions about who gets to work and who is left behind in an AI-driven labor market.

Talent Intelligence, Workforce Planning, and Layoffs

Workforce planning and talent intelligence are upstream levers for effective hiring and selection. When executed well, these practices ensure that organizations not only hire the right people but also avoid the costly missteps of over-hiring, misallocating talent, and ultimately resorting to widespread layoffs. In an ideal world, companies would forecast labor supply and demand months or even years in advance, proactively identifying where new skills will emerge, how demographic shifts will impact hiring pools, and which talent pipelines will be most critical for the future. Yet, in recent years, many companies—particularly in the tech sector—have failed at workforce planning, talent intelligence, and, by extension, people analytics and selection. The result? Mass layoffs, talent shortages, and inefficient cost structures that disrupt both organizations and employees' lives.

Now, with Gen AI and Data-as-a-Service (DaaS) providers like Lightcast, workforce planning and talent intelligence are about to undergo a fundamental transformation. AI-driven systems can now scan global labor markets in real time, providing companies with unprecedented insights into talent supply, emerging skill trends, and competitive dynamics. Instead of relying on annual headcount forecasts, organizations will soon receive real-time alerts when they are over-hiring in one function, underinvesting in another, or missing skill hubs that are growing in emerging markets and developing countries. These capabilities will finally enable organizations to move from reactive workforce management to proactive workforce strategy, reducing their reliance on disruptive layoffs while improving hiring efficiency and long-term planning.

The Role of Talent Intelligence in Workforce Planning

Talent intelligence is the process of analyzing labor market data—including competitor hiring trends, geographic skill availability, and university pipelines—to make informed talent decisions. Traditionally, organizations relied on historical data and internal HR insights to build hiring plans, but this approach is inherently flawed. The modern labor market is too dynamic to be captured by static reports. Instead, AI-driven talent intelligence systems will now continuously monitor workforce trends, identifying where the next wave of critical talent will emerge and when competitors are making strategic talent moves.

For instance, Always-on Intelligence (AoI) programs will allow organizations to track competitors in real time, identifying hiring spikes that indicate new market entries, R and D expansions, or strategic pivots. If a competitor is suddenly hiring cloud engineers in a new city, an AI-powered system can detect this pattern and alert leadership before it becomes a competitive disadvantage for the organization. Similarly, organizations can analyze net talent gain—a metric that compares how many employees a company is poaching from competitors versus how many they are losing—to assess their hiring strategy's effectiveness. These insights not only inform recruiting efforts but also guide strategic decision-making at the highest levels.

The Workforce Planning Crisis and the Future of Layoffs

The last few years have exposed the fundamental failures of workforce planning in major industries, especially tech and now more recently in the federal government. Many companies aggressively over-hired during periods of rapid growth, misjudging the sustainability of their expansion (DC News, 2023). Instead of using talent intelligence and scenario planning to build resilient, cost-effective hiring strategies, they scaled up headcounts without considering the long-term financial implications. When economic conditions shifted, these same companies were forced into mass layoffs, cutting thousands of employees in waves of reactive downsizing. Better workforce planning could have prevented this crisis. Effective workforce planning requires:

1 **Scenario Planning:** Simply put, no one grows forever. Organizations should model multiple workforce scenarios, accounting for revenue fluctuations, automation adoption, and market shifts. The best workforce plans are not rigid but rather adaptable to different business conditions.

2 **Cost Modeling:** Instead of only looking at headcount growth, companies should align talent investment with revenue growth, ensuring that revenue-per-employee metrics remain stable.

3 **Hiring Attribution Analysis:** Understanding which recruiters, hiring managers, and selection methods are leading to high-quality hires allows organizations to double down on effective hiring channels and avoid misallocated talent investments. Keep reading for more on *Quality of Hire* later in the chapter.

The rise of AI-powered workforce planning tools will make these practices scalable and real-time. Soon, organizations will have AI tools that constantly analyze hiring trends, internal workforce shifts, and labor market dynamics—allowing them to course-correct before over-hiring or skills gaps become a crisis.

The Future of Workforce Planning in an AI-Driven World

Workforce planning is evolving from an annual, static exercise into a real-time, dynamic strategy. Instead of making hiring decisions based on outdated forecasting models, organizations will increasingly rely on AI-driven workforce planning engines that continuously update based on market trends, competitor intelligence, and internal workforce data. Some of the key shifts we will see in the near future include:

- **AI-Generated Talent Market Research:** Instead of manual market research, AI will generate instant insights on skill availability, wage trends, and labor movement, helping organizations make smarter hiring decisions.

- **Predictive Layoff Prevention:** AI will proactively flag departments at risk of over-hiring or facing talent shortages, allowing HR leaders to adjust workforce plans before layoffs become necessary.

- **Automated Talent Mapping:** Organizations will have real-time maps of where critical skills are emerging, whether in universities, competitors, or new geographic hubs, helping them prioritize strategic hiring efforts.

For too long, workforce planning has been treated as an afterthought—only becoming a focus during economic down times—leading to misalignment between hiring, business needs, and long-term talent strategy. But with AI-driven insights, the excuses for poor workforce planning are disappearing. Companies that fail to embrace AI-powered talent intelligence and workforce planning tools will continue to suffer from reactive layoffs and inefficient hiring. Those that do embrace it will gain a sustainable competitive advantage, ensuring that their workforce strategy is not only resilient but also predictive and adaptable to an ever-changing labor market.

Quality of Hire: The Next Evolution

Now that we've discussed workforce planning, talent intelligence, and selection, the next logical step is measuring quality and performance on the job. Measuring Quality of Hire (QoH) has long been a challenge in the field of people analytics. While it's widely accepted that hiring better talent leads to better business outcomes, defining and measuring what makes a "high-quality" hire has sparked ongoing debate. The hesitation often stems from concerns about subjectivity, lack of standardization, and lack of accountability in decision-making. However, the rise of Gen AI is transforming how organizations can assess QoH—offering scalable, data-driven methods that are both efficient and reliable. With Gen AI, organizations no longer need to rely solely on traditional methods of evaluating new hires. Instead, they can leverage multiple traits, multiple methods, and continuous data flows to create a dynamic, low-touch, high-impact approach to measuring hiring success.

The Debate Around Quality of Hire

For years, organizations have debated whether QoH is even measurable in a meaningful way. Many HR leaders are comfortable reporting on hiring volume (e.g., "we hired 500 people this quarter") but struggle with measuring hiring effectiveness ("are those hires actually performing well?"). Part of this hesitation stems from:

- **Definitional Challenges**—What exactly defines a quality hire? Is it performance, retention, cultural fit, engagement, or all (or none) of the above?
- **Accountability Concerns**—Who "owns" QoH? The recruiter, hiring manager, or the business unit that employs the new hire?
- **Data Limitations**—Traditionally, collecting robust QoH data required surveys, subjective ratings, and performance reviews, which were often inconsistent and biased.

Despite these challenges, organizations that embrace QoH measurement can make smarter hiring decisions, optimize recruiter performance, and ultimately tie talent acquisition to business outcomes.

How Gen AI Unlocks a Scalable Approach to QoH

With Gen AI, measuring QoH no longer requires extensive manual surveys, rigid performance review cycles, or subjective hiring manager ratings. Instead, AI-powered models can extract meaningful hiring insights by continuously analyzing multiple data points across time once a hire is made. This enables organizations to triangulate QoH using a combination of behavioral signals, productivity markers, and contextual insights.

1. A MULTI-TRAIT, MULTI-METHOD APPROACH

Gen AI can assess QoH by integrating both qualitative and quantitative indicators from different sources, including:

- **Pre-hire data** (e.g., candidate assessments, interview performance, skills tests)
- **Post-hire data** (e.g., performance metrics, engagement levels, promotion rates)
- **Behavioral analytics** (e.g., collaboration patterns, communication trends, digital footprint analysis)

By blending structured (e.g., sales quotas, performance scores) and unstructured (e.g., feedback, engagement surveys) data, organizations can develop a more holistic and adaptive QoH model.

2. LOW-TOUCH, HIGH-IMPACT MEASUREMENT

One of the biggest breakthroughs of Gen AI is its ability to automate insights with minimal human intervention. Instead of relying on self-reported surveys or infrequent evaluations, AI can passively collect and analyze data in real-time. For example:

- AI can analyze email sentiment, collaboration patterns, and meeting behaviors to assess engagement and job fit.
- Machine learning models can predict performance likelihood based on pre-hire assessments and career trajectory data.
- Gen AI can evaluate hiring manager satisfaction trends without requiring direct surveys.

This low-touch approach ensures organizations can measure QoH continuously and at scale without overwhelming HR teams, hiring managers, or new hires themselves.

3. MOVING BEYOND TRADITIONAL QOH MODELS

Most traditional QoH frameworks focus on short-term retention and performance ratings. Gen AI enables organizations to go further by:

- **Predicting long-term success** by analyzing behavioral data and role alignment.

- **Keeping fairness in hiring decisions** by standardizing performance bench-marks across different roles.

- **Personalizing career paths** based on skill development and internal mobility trends.

By expanding beyond basic QoH measures, organizations can make more informed talent decisions while creating a hiring process that is more predictive and business-aligned. As Gen AI continues to evolve, QoH will become even more precise, scalable, and actionable. Organizations that embrace AI-driven approaches will be able to continuously refine hiring models based on real-world performance data, proactively identify high-potential candidates and optimize talent pipelines, and connect hiring decisions to business impact with real-time analytics. QoH is no longer an abstract, debatable concept—it is a measurable, scalable, and business-critical function. Organizations that leverage Gen AI-driven QoH insights will have a strategic advantage in hiring, retaining, and developing top talent.

REAL-WORLD EXAMPLE

"Gen AI for Talent Assessment vs Traditional Methods" with Charles Handler, President and Founder of Rocket Hire

(Paraphrased for length from Ep. 65 of "Directionally Correct, A People Analytics Podcast")

The Evolution of Talent Assessment

Dr. Charles Handler, President and Founder of Rocket Hire, emphasizes the enduring importance of job-relatedness in talent assessment. Traditional methods like work samples, structured interviews, and simulations have proven effective by replicating job tasks and evaluating candidates' ability to perform them. While these approaches remain valuable, advancements in generative AI (Gen AI) present new opportunities to enhance and streamline these methods.

AI-Generated Assessment Tools

Handler discusses the growing use of AI to create assessment tools such as situational judgment tests (SJTs), behavioral scenarios, and multiple-choice questions. These AI-generated items can be high-quality and save significant time in test development. However, Handler stresses that while AI provides a strong foundation, human oversight is critical to refining and validating these tools. Left unchecked, AI can generate questions that are inaccurate or misaligned with organizational needs.

The Role of Simulations and Work Samples

Charles highlights the power of simulations and work samples in providing the most direct measurement of job performance. Technology, including AI, now makes it easier to design high-fidelity simulations that mimic real-world tasks. For example, AI can generate scenarios where candidates must solve problems under time constraints, handle challenging customer interactions, or adapt to high-pressure environments. These simulations not only assess technical skills but also evaluate problem-solving, adaptability, and interpersonal abilities.

Efficiency Gains with AI

Gen AI's ability to create extensive pools of assessment items on demand is a significant advantage. For example, in high-volume roles like call center jobs, AI can generate tailored knowledge items for specific technical competencies. This ensures tests remain fresh and reduces the risk of item exposure or cheating in online, remotely proctored environments. However, Handler reiterates the need for ongoing validation and human review to maintain accuracy, fairness, and relevance.

Ethical Considerations in AI-Driven Assessments

Dr. Handler points to the need for vigilance in addressing bias and fairness when using AI for talent assessment. AI-generated tools must align with scientific standards like reliability and validity while avoiding perpetuating biases. Ensuring ethical practices requires a collaborative effort between I/O psychologists, AI experts, and HR leaders.

Key Takeaways

1   AI Enhances Traditional Methods: Gen AI can significantly improve efficiency in creating job-related assessments, such as SJTs and multiple-choice questions, but human oversight remains essential.

2   Simulations Drive Job-Relatedness: High-fidelity simulations, now easier to design with AI, offer direct measurements of job performance and key soft skills.

3   Dynamic Test Creation: AI enables the rapid generation of new assessment items, ensuring tests remain fresh and reducing risks of item exposure.

4   Ethical Vigilance: Bias and fairness must be carefully monitored when using AI-generated assessments, aligning with scientific standards of reliability and validity.

5   AI as a Collaborative Tool: AI should be seen as a partner in assessment development, enhancing human expertise rather than replacing it.

Charles Handler's insights illustrate how Gen AI is reshaping talent assessment, providing new ways to enhance traditional methods while improving efficiency. By leveraging AI for simulations and item generation, organizations can create high-quality assessments that are job-related and scalable. However, Handler emphasizes the continued importance of human involvement to refine, validate, and ensure the ethical use of AI-driven tools. The future of talent assessment lies in a collaborative approach where AI amplifies the impact of evidence-based practices in I/O psychology.

Quantifying the Employee Value Proposition

In today's competitive talent landscape, quantifying a well-defined Employee Value Proposition (EVP) is essential for attracting and retaining top talent. The Society for Industrial and Organizational Psychology (SIOP) recently published a white paper titled "Deciphering the Employee Value Proposition (EVP): A Conjoint Analysis Approach to Strategic EVP Development" (SIOP, 2024), which offers valuable insights into measuring and enhancing an organization's EVP. The paper advocates for the use of conjoint analysis—a technique traditionally employed in market research (Adrian, 2019)—to discern which job attributes employees value most and the trade-offs they are willing to make among different job factors, usually via survey responses that are forced-choice between two options to ultimately rank the results as trade-offs. By presenting employees with various work scenarios that differ across key factors such as workload, compensation, flexibility, career growth, sense of belonging, and organizational benefits package components, organizations can quantitatively assess the relative importance of each attribute. This method enables a data-driven approach to EVP development, ensuring that the offerings align with employee preferences and regional differences.

Building upon these findings, the integration of Gen AI offers a transformative approach to EVP assessment. Gen AI can analyze vast amounts of internal and external labor market data in real-time, providing continuous insights into competitive employment and market trends, employee sentiment and brand, and candidate preferences without the need for repetitive surveys. By monitoring communication channels, feedback platforms, and social media, AI-driven tools can detect emerging trends and potential issues, enabling organizations to proactively adjust their EVP to meet evolving employee expectations. This dynamic analysis mirrors the outcomes of conjoint analysis by identifying which aspects of the EVP are most valued by employees, but with the added advantage of immediacy and ongoing assessment.

Moreover, Gen AI facilitates the fusion of internal workforce data with external market trends via data, offering a comprehensive view of the competitive landscape. This holistic perspective allows organizations to benchmark their EVP against industry standards and identify areas for differentiation. For instance, if real-time data indicates a growing employee preference for flexible work arrangements, and market analysis shows competitors are adopting such practices, an organization can swiftly adapt its policies to remain attractive to current and prospective talent. This agility not only enhances the organization's appeal in the talent marketplace but also fosters a culture of responsiveness and innovation.

In essence, while traditional conjoint analysis provides a robust foundation for understanding employee preferences, the advent of Gen AI enables a more dynamic and continuous evaluation of the EVP. By leveraging AI-driven insights, organizations can create a responsive and competitive EVP that resonates with their workforce's evolving needs, thereby strengthening their position in the talent market.

Does Everyone Get Paid the Same?

For years, EVP and compensation debates have centered around pay transparency, pay equity, and benchmarking against market rates. But now, with the productivity explosion fueled by Gen AI in people analytics, we have an unprecedented opportunity: To finally answer a fundamental and often controversial question that I have had for years—**Does everyone get paid the same?** And no, I don't mean like in a socialist system where everyone literally gets paid the same.

This question isn't just rhetorical, it has profound implications for workers, employers, and society at large. Historically, answering this question with precision has been impossible due to fragmented and siloed data. However, as Gen AI dramatically lowers the cost and time required for data analysis, people analytics teams can go beyond surface-level salary comparisons and dive into the *true* market mechanics of compensation. Organizations can create entire synthetic organizations with synthetic workers to model the real market impacts of supply and demand and wage pressures, to combine with internal organizational cultural and job dynamics to model these scenarios. By integrating internal data from HCM, ATS, LMS, and payroll systems with external labor market intelligence, we can quantify the *"miscellaneous heartache"* that determines why some jobs pay more than others—not just in terms of supply and demand, but also by measuring the trade-offs in effort, stress, flexibility, and risk associated with different roles.

The Theory: Everyone Gets Paid the Same

It's an idea that sounds both provocative and counterintuitive and there is research to support it (Truglia, 2022). Surely, a surgeon makes more than a barista, and a software engineer earns more than a retail worker—so how can we say everyone gets paid the same? The answer lies in the concept that compensation is not just about the absolute dollar amount—it's about the trade-offs that come with the job.

Here's the fundamental hypothesis:

- *Everyone (who is not an executive or owner) gets paid the same in capitalistic systems. Those who command greater wages only do so by adding "facets of pay"—or compensable trade-offs—to their role that go beyond the minimum allowable wage dictated by market conditions.*

In simpler terms: Pay is proportional to the combination of labor market demand and job-related "miscellaneous heartache." The more of these facets of pay accumulate in a role, the higher the pay—but the job typically becomes harder, more stressful, or more demanding in return for the higher pay. But how do you measure "miscellaneous heartache"?

To move beyond theory and into practical people analytics, we need a framework for what contributes to pay differences. These dimensions, or *facets of pay*, represent the "social cost" a worker must endure to receive higher wages. With Gen AI-enabled analytics, we can begin quantifying these trade-offs with actual data.

The Facets of Pay: What Determines Compensation Differences?

1 **Physical Demands**—Harder physical labor often commands higher wages than less taxing physical labor. The more physically taxing the work, the higher the pay needs to be to compensate.

2 **Market Supply and Demand**—If demand exceeds supply, wages rise. However, careers with extreme demand (e.g., like AI engineers right now) often see supply eventually catch up, normalizing wages over time.

3 **Required Credentials and Skills**—Barriers to entry to get hired such as degrees, certifications, or technical skills increase wages. But these also require upfront costs (time, education, licensing). These have a time-value of money cost to the person who acquires the skills and the employer must account for that in their pay.

4 **Experience and Tenure**—More experience sometimes leads to higher wages, but only when it correlates with higher productivity. Many industries cap pay bands to prevent diminishing returns due to experience not leading to more productivity.

5 **Job Performance and Productivity**—Higher performance can justify higher pay, but it often comes with increased stress, expectations, and accountability within a role.

6 **Decision-Making Rights and Accountability**—The more responsibility of a role, the higher the potential pay. CEOs and managers earn more because they carry the risk of failure. With this risk comes the ability to be fired and also the emotional stress of accountability for others.

7 **Psychological Stress and Emotional Labor**—Roles that require emotional labor (customer service, teaching, nursing) should command higher wages—but often don't. AI can now quantify these stressors to push for better pay models that account for this stress.

8 **Hours Worked and Flexibility**—The more hours required (and the less flexibility allowed), the higher the pay—historically, remote work was penalized, and this trend seems to be reemerging with post-pandemic wages for remote roles starting to drop.

9 **Competitive vs. Cooperative Environments**—Competitive work cultures (e.g., investment banking, law) pay more due to cutthroat dynamics. Conversely, collaborative workplaces often pay less but provide intrinsic job satisfaction.

10 **Job Enjoyment and Intrinsic Motivation**—People will accept lower pay for meaningful work (e.g., nonprofits, social work). The inverse is also true—boring or stressful jobs sometimes require more compensation to attract talent.

Using Gen AI to Operationalize the Theory

Historically, quantifying all the "facets of pay" and their interrelationships was nearly impossible due to fragmented, qualitative, or anecdotal data. However, with AI-powered people analytics, we can now analyze compensation trade-offs at an individual level, across industries, and even across geographies if you have the right internal and external, qualitative and quantitative data capabilities.

Here's how AI can answer *"Does everyone get paid the same?"* in measurable ways:

- **Modeling compensation trade-offs**—Using AI, we can construct models that estimate how much each facet of pay contributes to wage differences.

- **Predicting career trajectories**—AI can determine the "true cost" of a promotion—does a 20 percent raise mean a 20 percent increase in workload and stress?

- **Pay fairness audits**—AI can analyze whether employees are being compensated appropriately for their job trade-offs, for example: Are aspects of emotional labor compensated fairly?

- **Longitudinal pay studies**—AI can track pay progression over time to see how supply, demand, and job complexity affect wages, even through cohort analysis and even modeling entire careers and lifetimes.

REAL-WORLD EXAMPLE

"Labor Economics and Does Everyone Get Paid the Same?" with Jay Denton, Chief Economist at Radix, former Chief Analytics Officer at LaborIQ

(Paraphrased for length from Ep. 32 of "Directionally Correct, A People Analytics Podcast")

The Complexity of Compensation

Jay Denton, Chief Economist at Radix and former Chief Analytics Officer at LaborIQ, provides insights into the factors that influence compensation. At its core, pay is influenced by supply and demand, the difficulty of acquiring the skills required for the role, and the responsibilities associated with the job. While there is no uniform rule for pay, certain patterns emerge when considering factors like job complexity, responsibility, and decision-making authority.

The "Miscellaneous Heartache" Hypothesis

Denton discusses a hypothesis that pay is proportional to the difficulty of a job, encompassing factors like the hours worked, skills required, and decisions made. While the hypothesis is not literally true in every case, it aligns with general trends in labor economics: roles that demand higher effort, responsibility, or future-oriented planning tend to command higher compensation. This principle is reflected in tools like ONET's job zones, which categorize jobs based on the training and skills required, revealing a general correlation between job difficulty and pay.

Decision Rights and Compensation

Compensation often reflects the autonomy, decision-making authority, and risk of failure associated with a role. Denton references a concept introduced by Tom Foster, which suggests that the further into the future an employee must plan and operate independently, the higher their compensation. For example, frontline workers may focus solely on daily tasks, while managers think months ahead, and executives consider years of strategy. This temporal scope of responsibility helps explain the pay hierarchy within organizations.

Exceptions to the Rule

While the hypothesis generally holds true, there are notable exceptions. For example, CEOs' pay varies significantly depending on factors like equity, ownership, and organizational scale. A CEO of a small startup may earn far less in cash compensation than one leading a Fortune 500 company, as startup leaders often rely on equity as a primary form of pay. Nonlinear gains from ownership and stock options can skew compensation comparisons, making these roles outliers in the broader pattern.

Aggregating Pay Across Industries

When examining pay across industries, Denton notes that compensation normalizes over time as roles and responsibilities align with economic and organizational factors. Larger, more profitable companies tend to pay more, reflecting their ability to offer competitive salaries. Similarly, a company's lifecycle influences pay, with startups often constrained by limited resources compared to market leaders with established profitability.

Key Takeaways

1 Compensation Reflects Job Complexity: Roles requiring more skills, responsibility, and long-term planning tend to pay more.

2 Decision-Making Authority Matters: Compensation increases with the autonomy, decision rights, and risk of failure associated with a role.

3 Job Training and Pay Correlate: ONET job zones demonstrate a general relationship between training/skill requirements and compensation.

4 Outliers Exist: Nonlinear pay structures, like equity-based compensation for CEOs, create exceptions to the hypothesis.

5 Lifecycle and Scale Impact Pay: Companies' ability to pay is influenced by their stage in the business lifecycle and organizational scale.

Jay Denton's insights shed light on the economic principles that underlie compensation patterns. While not everyone is literally paid the same, there is a broad correlation between job difficulty, responsibility, and pay. Factors like decision-making autonomy and organizational lifecycle further shape compensation trends. Understanding these dynamics provides organizations with a framework to make equitable and market-driven pay decisions, aligning with both employee expectations and business realities.

The Pay Transparency Paradox

Pay transparency has been a hot trend in the HR zeitgeist and in local and state legislation in the last few years. This sounds good in theory, but does it always work out as a benefit to employees in practice? As companies embrace pay transparency, in the research we're seeing two major trends (Hawkins, 2025):

- **Pay gaps across demographics (gender, race) shrink**—Good news!
- **However, wages overall flatten or decrease as well**—Not-so-good news...

Why? Because once compensation becomes an open marketplace, companies optimize costs downward. Compensation professionals are *not* incentivized to pay people more than is necessary to get them in the door or retain them. If AI tells compensation functions that two employees with different job titles are performing similar work, expect salaries to regress toward the "everyone gets paid the same" baseline.

THE FUTURE OF PAY IN AN AI-DRIVEN WORLD

So, where does this leave workers? If pay is increasingly standardized, wages are compressed, and AI puts a strain on their upward mobility, how can someone break out of the cycle and earn beyond their "miscellaneous heartache" threshold?

1 **Ownership is the only true escape**—If you want outsized earnings, the only way is to own assets (equity, investments, or your own business).

2 **Work in non-standardized fields**—The fastest-growing, least-commoditized industries (e.g., AI, biotech) offer the best short-term opportunities.

3 **Negotiate relentlessly**—AI is increasingly being used to manage wages; workers must become equally skilled in using AI to take a more data-driven approach to salary negotiations.

4 **Leverage skills arbitrage**—The best way to increase earnings is to possess in-demand skills that are still scarce.

The Hard Truth About Pay

The data-driven reality is this: If you are paid in money, the everyone gets paid the same theory applies to you and will dictate your current and future earning potential. The compensation game is designed to keep wages within a tightly controlled range (e.g., pay band, comparison ratios, grade levels, etc.), and as AI makes these calculations more precise, the theory of "everyone gets paid the same" will become even more true. You will be able to model it for your organization if you so choose, and perhaps that is when people analytics will truly assume the most powerful role in HR from compensation.

However, if you are paid in equity or assets, this theory does not apply to you. In that case, you're playing a different game altogether. Well done. As AI reshapes HR and people analytics, the question isn't just *"What are you paid?"* but *"What are you really being paid for?"* And more importantly—are you OK with that answer?

Experimental Note: Forensic People Analytics

People analytics has long been about understanding the workforce through data, often borrowing techniques from fields such as history and demography, like we discussed in Chapter 6, to enhance predictive modeling. However, diagnosing the past can often be a more effective tool than attempting to predict the future with imperfect forecasting models as we discussed earlier in the book. But what if people analytics expanded its reach beyond traditional methods and borrowed from disciplines such as investigative journalism and criminal forensics? This is where *forensic people analytics* comes into play—a method of organizational diagnosis aimed at uncovering hidden structures, behaviors, and potential risks within a company.

Beyond Descriptive Statistics: The Investigative Lens

We mastered descriptive statistics quite some time ago in people analytics to map out the current state of an organization. When combined with organizational charts and organizational network analysis, descriptives can provide a clear picture of how an organization functions and how information flows within it. However, traditional analytics often rely on visible, structured data—what is readily available and openly shared. But what if something crucial is hidden in your organization? What if there are behaviors, relationships, or patterns that are not immediately observable? This is where forensic people analytics shifts the focus from what is known to what is *concealed*.

Forensic people analytics applies investigative techniques to analyze organizational anomalies, hidden connections, and potential risks. It is less about simple measurement and more about detection, pattern recognition, and even anomaly detection. It functions like organizational detective work, uncovering unknown or unacknowledged activities that may be crucial to understanding the workforce and its operations and potential risks to the company.

Practical Applications: The Case of Dual Employment in Remote Work

One of the most common concerns among executives in the remote work era is whether employees are holding multiple full-time jobs simultaneously. While remote work offers flexibility and increased productivity for many, it also raises questions about accountability and if a person is actually doing what they say they are doing. How could forensic people analytics address this issue? Some examples could be: Analyzing system logins, response times, project outputs, and cross-referencing employment records with external data sources to provide insight into potential cases of dual employment. However, such an investigation must be carefully designed to balance corporate interests with employee privacy. Forensic people analytics must navigate ethical boundaries to ensure fairness and avoid creating an invasive surveillance culture.

Investigating Financial Misconduct

Consider a more serious case: Uncovering a network of embezzlement within an organization. Standard financial audits may detect discrepancies, but forensic people analytics could enhance detection by analyzing patterns of collaboration, transaction histories, budget allocations, and employee communication data. Organizational network analysis could reveal clusters of individuals interacting outside expected workflows, potentially highlighting collusion or irregular activity. The challenge here is ensuring that investigations are conducted with precision and integrity, maintaining trust within the organization while rooting out unethical behavior.

The Most Intriguing Use Case: Unveiling Secret Programs

Perhaps the most fascinating application of forensic people analytics would be within the defense and defense contractor sectors. Recent congressional hearings on Unidentified Aerial Phenomena (UAPs) have sparked interest in long-standing claims that secret aerospace and defense programs have existed for decades, often hidden within layers of organizational bureaucracy, such as UFO crash retrieval programs, advanced scientific findings that come from alien craft (e.g., zero-point energy, electrogravitics, etc.), and most provocatively, "biologics" that come from alien beings. If you were working at a defense contractor and suspected the existence of a classified, unacknowledged program, how might forensic people analytics help uncover its existence?

Potential investigative approaches could include:

- **Workforce Planning and Headcount Analysis:** Identifying unexplained hiring spikes in niche technical fields that align with rumored activities.
- **Org Charts and Organizational Network Analysis:** Mapping interactions between employees to detect closed-off or high-security clusters.
- **Budget and Resource Allocation:** Analyzing funding shifts that don't align with publicly acknowledged projects.
- **Talent Intelligence and Skill Trends:** Tracking employee skills and training patterns that suggest involvement in specialized, classified work.
- **Real Estate and Facility Analysis:** Identifying obscure locations that may house secretive operations.

Would such forensic analytics uncover long-hidden programs? Perhaps. But the real lesson here is that people analytics has the potential to evolve into an investigative discipline, shedding light on hidden organizational structures and dynamics in ways previously unimagined.

The Role of Gen AI in Forensic People Analytics

With the rise of generative AI, forensic people analytics becomes even more powerful. Gen AI can rapidly process and synthesize vast amounts of unstructured data, automate pattern detection, and generate investigative insights at scale. What once required months of manual analysis can now be done in days or even hours. This acceleration raises both possibilities and ethical dilemmas. The ability to investigate workforce behaviors, relationships, and potential misconduct with AI-powered tools presents a fine line between organizational intelligence and corporate overreach.

As forensic people analytics advances, it inevitably raises the question: How far is too far? Transparency, trust, and ethical considerations must guide the evolution of this discipline. If misused, forensic analytics could create a dystopian workplace where privacy is nonexistent. The goal should not be to turn organizations into surveillance states but to enhance integrity, security, and fairness. Perhaps the future of people analytics is weirder than we think. But one thing is certain: As we develop these powerful capabilities, we must also take responsibility for creating a future that we would want to live and work in.

The Future is in Your Hands

Thank you for reading this chapter and this book. I hope it has expanded your perspective on how people analytics can add value, how Gen AI can be used effectively in your organization, and how we can disrupt HR operations for the better using people analytics. The future of our function isn't about merely analyzing HR data—it's about making people analytics the decision-making engine for HR itself. If we embrace this shift, we can transform HR into a strategic powerhouse—a value-added function that is no longer seen as an overhead or a "luxury," but as a driver of better business outcomes and a more positive work environment. I appreciate you taking this journey with me—now, let's go build the future.

Summary

The future of HR and business is no longer just about managing people—it's about harnessing data, AI, and analytics to drive strategic decision-making. Historically, HR has been constrained by limited resources, manual processes, and organizational inertia. However, with the rise of generative AI (Gen AI) and advanced analytics, these barriers are disappearing. The cost of running sophisticated analytics is plummeting, allowing HR leaders to shift from reactive problem-solving to proactive, data-driven strategies.

This chapter explores how the analytical transformation of HR will redefine workforce planning, decision-making, and business competitiveness in the years to come.

Key Takeaways

1 **HR Must Shift from Reactive to Proactive Decision-Making**

   o Traditionally, HR has focused on solving immediate business needs, often sidelining complex, strategic problems due to time and resource constraints. With AI and automation, HR can now address deeper issues like workforce planning, leadership impact, and compensation equity.

2 **People Analytics is Moving Beyond Basic Reporting to Predictive and Prescriptive Insights**

   o The field of people analytics has evolved from basic metrics to AI-powered decision-making engines. Organizations leveraging predictive and prescriptive analytics will gain a competitive edge by anticipating workforce trends rather than just reacting to them.

3 **Generative AI is Driving an Unprecedented Productivity Boom in HR**

   o The integration of AI-powered analytics is making HR faster, smarter, and more scalable. Tasks that once took weeks—like job analysis, workforce forecasting, and hiring predictions—can now be completed in real-time, allowing HR to focus on high-value, strategic work.

4 **The Future of Work is Evolving Beyond Traditional Job Structures**

   o Work is shifting away from rigid job roles toward a model focused on skills, tasks, and automation. AI will augment employees rather than replace them, making human–AI collaboration a critical competency for the future workforce.

5 **HR's Competitive Advantage Lies in Workforce Intelligence and Talent Strategy**

   o Organizations that master workforce planning, talent intelligence, and labor market analytics will outperform competitors. HR must become an intelligence-driven function, leveraging real-time labor market data to optimize hiring, retention, and skills development.

6 **AI-Driven Workforce Planning Will Eliminate Costly Hiring and Layoff Cycles**

   o The traditional boom-and-bust cycle of over-hiring followed by mass layoffs can be avoided with AI-powered workforce planning. By continuously analyzing talent supply, demand, and business needs, organizations can make better long-term staffing decisions.

7 HR Must Navigate the Ethical Risks of AI and Algorithmic Management

o AI is introducing new complexities in workforce management, from algorithmic decision-making to potential biases in hiring and compensation. HR leaders must ensure that AI-driven insights remain transparent, fair, and aligned with ethical business practices.

8 The Future of Pay Transparency and Compensation Will be Data-Driven

o AI will enable HR to analyze pay equity, compensation structures, and wage trends with greater precision. However, as pay transparency increases, organizations must balance fairness with competitive salary strategies to attract and retain top talent.

9 Forensic People Analytics is the Next Frontier for Workforce Insights

o HR analytics is expanding into investigative areas, using data to uncover hidden organizational trends, financial misconduct, or even dual employment fraud. This shift positions HR as a critical function for corporate risk management and organizational integrity.

10 HR Must Lead the Charge in Shaping the Future of Work, Not Just Responding to It

o The transformation of HR is not just about adopting new technology— it's about fundamentally redefining how work is structured, how employees are managed, and how business value is created. Those who embrace this analytical future will set the standard for the next era of HR.

HR and business leaders must shift their mindset from merely adapting to constraints to actively shaping the future with data. The analytical revolution in HR is here, and organizations that fail to embrace it will fall behind. The future belongs to those who use AI, automation, and advanced analytics to drive strategic, high-impact decisions. Now is the time to build the future of HR as a powerhouse of business intelligence and competitive advantage.

References

Adrian, L. (2019, September 19). Conjoint Analysis: What, Why, and How. Cleverism. cleverism.com/conjoint-analysis-what-why-how/ (archived at https://perma.cc/SS7C-GBEJ).

DC News (2023). Workforce Planning and Tech Layoffs. Substack. directionallycorrectnews.substack.com/p/workforce-planning-and-tech-layoffs (archived at https://perma.cc/U7A7-XMRH).

Hawkins, F. (2025). A Clear-Eyed Look at Salary Transparency Laws. Frank Hawkins Kenan Institute of Private Enterprise. kenaninstitute.unc.edu/kenan-insight/a-clear-eyed-look-at-salary-transparency-laws/?%3E (archived at https://perma.cc/LF4F-AZ9H).

Jesuthasan, R. and Boudreau, J. W. (2023). *Work Without Jobs: How to Reboot Your Organization's Operating System*. MIT Press.

Napper, C., Hines, S. and Denton, J. (2023). Labor Economics and Does Everyone Get Paid the Same? Directionally Correct. www.podbean.com/eas/pb-mg79i-151f6ee (archived at https://perma.cc/NPT6-3J3K) Ep. 32.

Napper, C., Hines, S. and Handler, C. (2023). Gen AI for Talent Assessment vs Traditional Methods. Directionally Correct. www.podbean.com/eas/pb-ej6cc-151f6cc (archived at https://perma.cc/LJU3-TVJ8) Ep. 65.

Napper, C., Hines, S. and Oswald, F. (2023). Gen AI and The Future of Selection with I-O Psychology. Directionally Correct. www.podbean.com/eas/pb-guemu-151f6d8 (archived at https://perma.cc/79XG-SANP) Ep. 53.

Shaw, G. B. (1903). *Man and Superman*. "Maxims for Revolutionists: Reason."

SIOP (2024). Deciphering the Employee Value Proposition (EVP): A Conjoint Analysis Approach to Strategic EVP Development. Society for Industrial and Organizational Psychology. www.siop.org/tip-article/deciphering-the-employee-value-proposition-evp-a-conjoint-analysis-approach-to-strategic-evp-development/ (archived at https://perma.cc/9GMQ-ZPL2).

Society for Industrial and Organizational Psychology. (2025). SIOP Releases Recommendations for AI-Based Assessments. www.siop.org/Research-Publications/Items-of-Interest/ArtMID/19366/ArticleID/7327/SIOP (archived at https://perma.cc/HDE5-W22V).

Truglia, R. (2022). Ricardo Perez-Truglia. ricardotruglia.bol.ucla.edu/research.html (archived at https://perma.cc/8HH6-F8QT).

Uniform Guidelines (2025). Uniform Employee Selection Guidelines on Employee Selection Procedures. www.uniformguidelines.com/ (archived at https://perma.cc/9C2M-DNAH).

INDEX

NB: page numbers in *italic* indicate figures or tables

Looking for another book?

Explore our award-winning
books from global business
experts in Human Resources,
Learning and Development

Scan the code to browse

www.koganpage.com/hr-learning-
development

More From Kogan Page

ISBN: 9781398614567

ISBN: 9781398615656

www.koganpage.com

EU Representative (GPSR)

Authorised Rep Compliance Ltd, Ground Floor, 71 Lower Baggot Street, Dublin, D02 P593, Ireland

www.arccompliance.com